BLACK CAT

ALL DRESSED UP

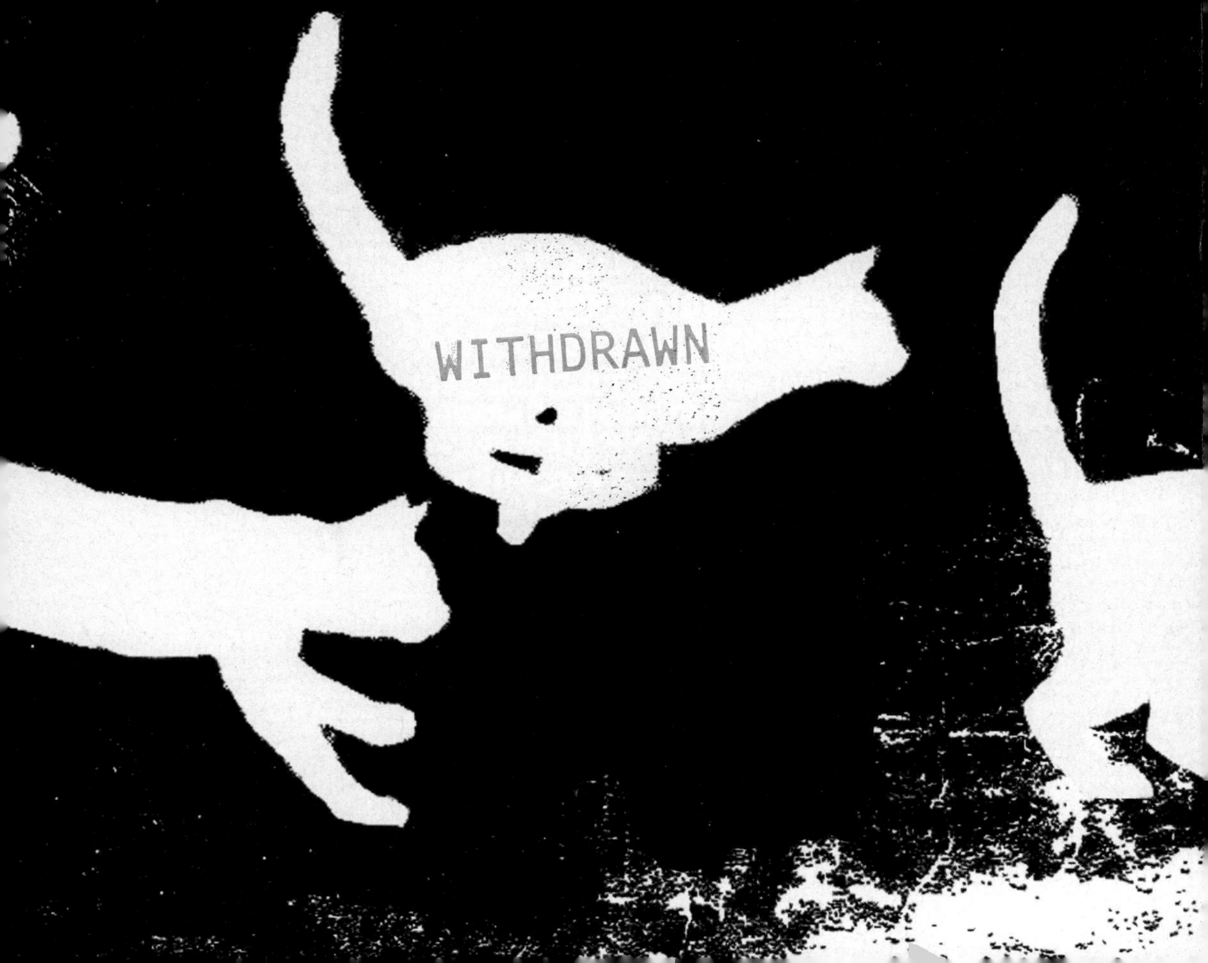

writer **JED MACKAY**

BLACK CAT #11-12

artist **C.F. VILLA**
color artist **BRIAN REBER**
letterer **FERRAN DELGADO**
cover art **J. SCOTT CAMPBELL** with **PETER STEIGERWALD** (#11) & **SABINE RICH** (#12)
assistant editor **LINDSEY COHICK**
editor **NICK LOWE**

collection editor **JENNIFER GRÜNWALD** ♦ assistant managing editor **MAIA LOY**
assistant managing editor **LISA MONTALBANO** ♦ vp production & special projects **JEFF YOUNGQUIST**
book designer **STACIE ZUCKER** with **JAY BOWEN**
svp print, sales & marketing **DAVID GABRIEL** ♦ editor in chief **C.B. CEBULSKI**

BLACK CAT VOL. 3: ALL DRESSED UP. Contains material originally published in magazine form as BLACK CAT (2019) #11-12, BLACK CAT ANNUAL (2019) #1 and FREE COMIC BOOK DAY 2020 (SPIDER-MAN/VENOM) #1. First printing 2020. ISBN 978-1-302-92292-4. Published by MARVEL WORLDWIDE, INC., a subsidiary of MARVEL ENTERTAINMENT, LLC. OFFICE OF PUBLICATION: 1290 Avenue of the Americas, New York, NY 10104. **Printed in Canada.** KEVIN FEIGE, Chief Creative Officer; DAN BUCKLEY, President, Marvel Entertainment; JOE QUESADA, EVP & Creative Director; DAVID BOGART, Associate Publisher & SVP of Talent Affairs; TOM BREVOORT, VP, Executive Editor; NICK LOWE, Executive Editor, VP of Content, Digital Publishing; DAVID GABRIEL, VP of Print & Digital Publishing; JEFF YOUNGQUIST, VP of Production & Special Projects; ALEX MORALES, Director of Publishing Operations; DAN EDINGTON, Managing Editor; RICKEY PURDIN, Director of Talent Relations; JENNIFER GRÜNWALD, Senior Editor, Special Projects; SUSAN CRESPI, Production Manager; STAN LEE, Chairman Emeritus. For information regarding advertising in Marvel Comics or on Marvel.com, please contact Vit DeBellis, Custom Solutions & Integrated Advertising Manager, at vdebellis@marvel.com. For Marvel subscription inquiries, please call 888-511-5480. **Manufactured between 11/20/2020 and 12/22/2020 by SOLISCO PRINTERS, SCOTT, QC, CANADA.**

10 9 8 7 6 5 4 3 2 1

KCAT
ALL DRESSED UP

Black Cat Annual #1

artists	**JOEY VAZQUEZ, NATACHA BUSTOS** & **JUAN GEDEON**
color artist	**BRIAN REBER**
letterer	**FERRAN DELGADO**
cover art	**J. SCOTT CAMPBELL** & **SABINE RICH**
assistant editor	**KATHLEEN WISNESKI**
editor	**NICK LOWE**

Free Comic Book Day 2020

artist	**PATRICK GLEASON**
color artist	**DAVID CURIEL**
letterer	**VC's CLAYTON COWLES**
cover art	**J. SCOTT CAMPBELL** & **SABINE RICH**
assistant editor	**KATHLEEN WISNESKI**
editor	**NICK LOWE**

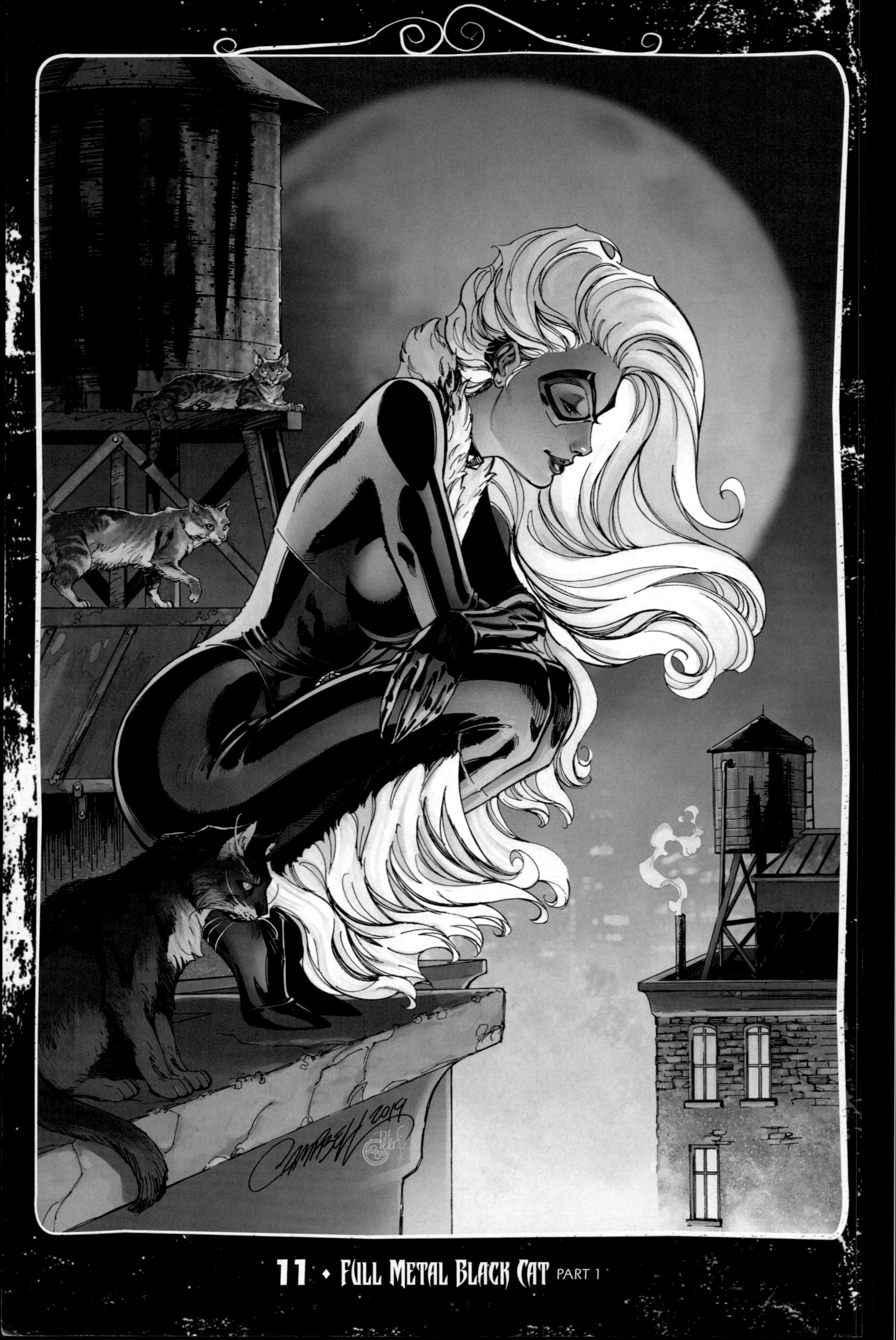

11 • FULL METAL BLACK CAT PART 1

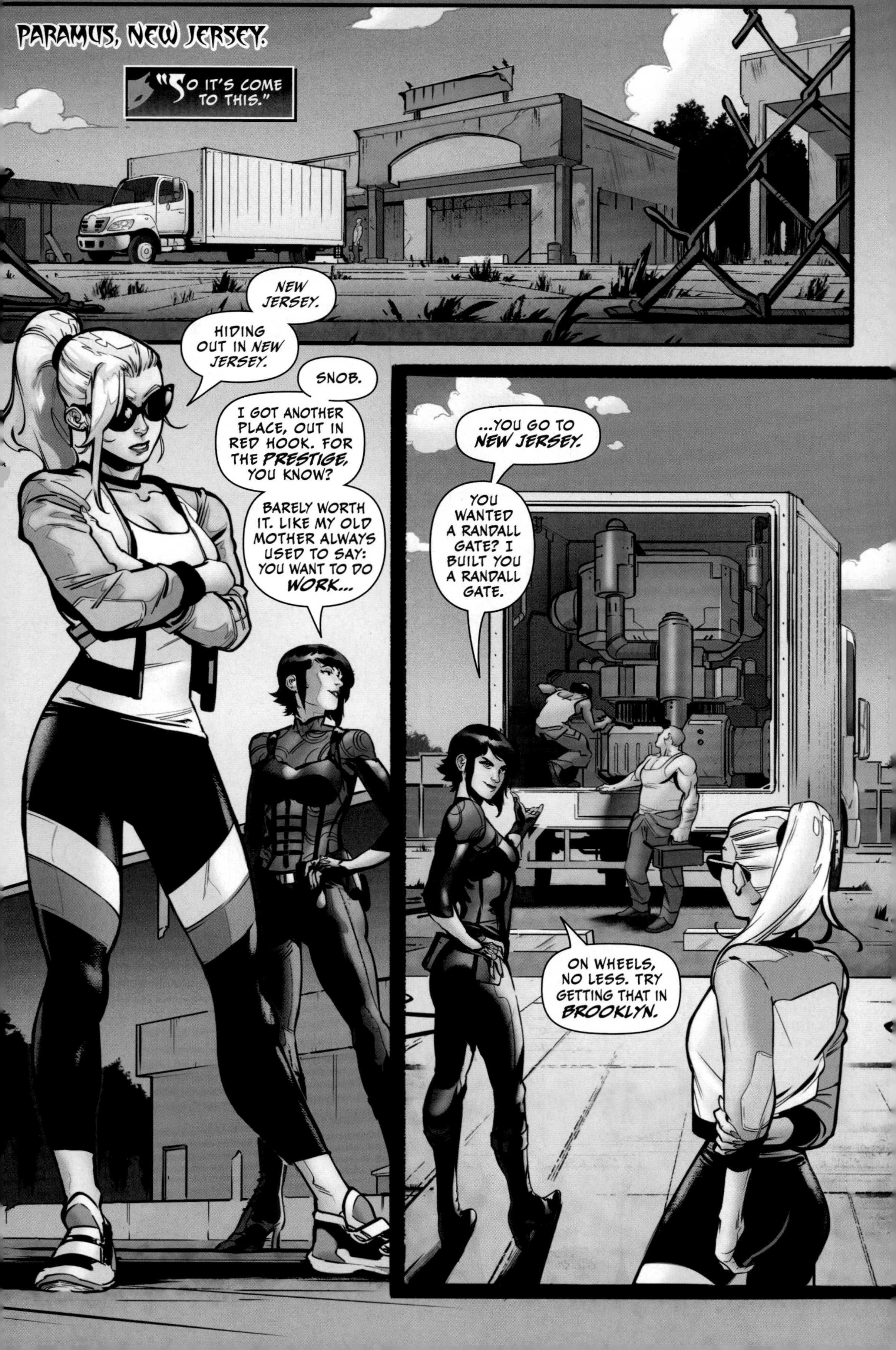
PARAMUS, NEW JERSEY.
"SO IT'S COME TO THIS."
NEW JERSEY.
HIDING OUT IN NEW JERSEY.
SNOB.
I GOT ANOTHER PLACE, OUT IN RED HOOK. FOR THE PRESTIGE, YOU KNOW?
BARELY WORTH IT. LIKE MY OLD MOTHER ALWAYS USED TO SAY: YOU WANT TO DO WORK...
...YOU GO TO NEW JERSEY.
YOU WANTED A RANDALL GATE? I BUILT YOU A RANDALL GATE.
ON WHEELS, NO LESS. TRY GETTING THAT IN BROOKLYN.

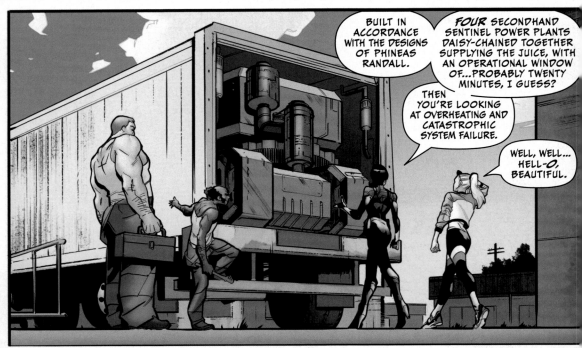

BUILT IN ACCORDANCE WITH THE DESIGNS OF PHINEAS RANDALL.

FOUR SECONDHAND SENTINEL POWER PLANTS DAISY-CHAINED TOGETHER SUPPLYING THE JUICE, WITH AN OPERATIONAL WINDOW OF...PROBABLY TWENTY MINUTES, I GUESS?

THEN YOU'RE LOOKING AT OVERHEATING AND CATASTROPHIC SYSTEM FAILURE.

WELL, WELL... HELL-*O*, BEAUTIFUL.

SPLENDID, ISN'T IT?

IT IS. THIS IS IT, ISN'T IT?

IT IS.

OR RATHER, IT *ALMOST* IS.

OF COURSE.

WE HAVE THE DOOR, AND THE COORDINATES TO WHICH WE WISH OUR DOOR TO OPEN.

WE REQUIRE BUT *ONE* MORE PIECE BEFORE WE CRACK THE DIMENSIONAL BARRIER AND GO DOWN IN HISTORY.

LET ME GUESS. A *KEY.*

PRECISELY.

PROBLEM IS, THIS IS SPECIAL STUFF, THIS KEY.

OR DIMENSIONAL RESONATOR, WHATEVER YOU LIKE. I CAN'T BUILD IT.

I DON'T HAVE THE TOOLS.

SO WHO DOES?

SHE ASKED, TERRIFIED OF THE ANSWER...

Oh...

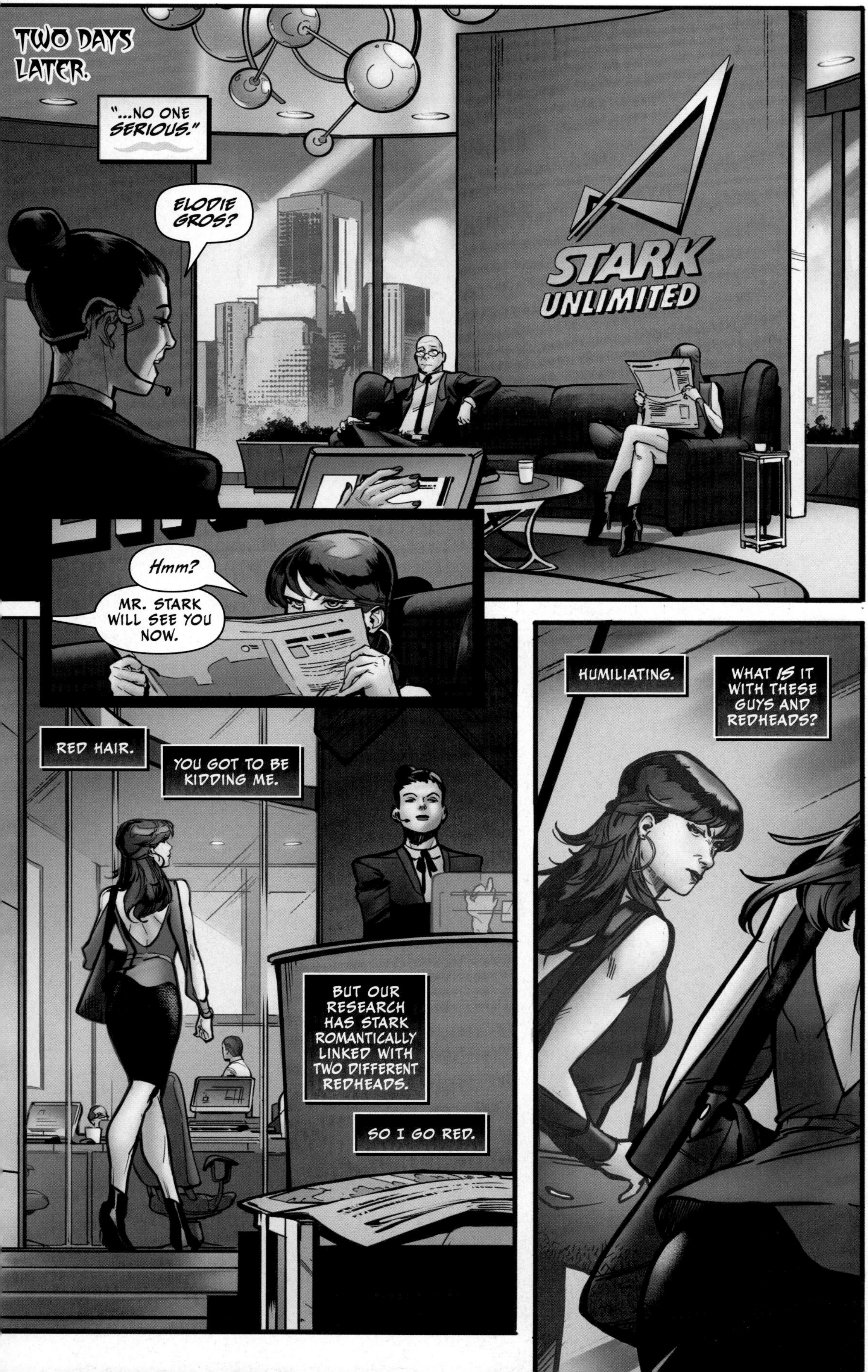
TWO DAYS LATER.
"...NO ONE SERIOUS."
ELODIE GROS?
STARK UNLIMITED
Hmm?
MR. STARK WILL SEE YOU NOW.
RED HAIR.
YOU GOT TO BE KIDDING ME.
BUT OUR RESEARCH HAS STARK ROMANTICALLY LINKED WITH TWO DIFFERENT REDHEADS.
SO I GO RED.
HUMILIATING.
WHAT *IS* IT WITH THESE GUYS AND REDHEADS?

SO WHAT'S OUR *IN*?

THIS IS *STARK* SECURITY. THE CAT BURGLAR GAG IS NOT AN OPTION HERE.

EVERY MAN HAS WEAKNESSES. WHAT ARE STARK'S?

HE'S A DRUNK, SO...THE *WAGERING VICAR*?

THUMP!

ISN'T HE FAMOUSLY OFF THE SAUCE? I SAW IT IN THAT HENRY HELLRUNG MOVIE.

BESIDES, WE'D NEED A BADGER FOR THE WAGERING VICAR AND I'M *NOT* BREAKING INTO THE ZOO *AGAIN.*

WOMEN! HE'S A NOTORIOUS WOMANIZER!

THE *SEVENTEEN STEPBROTHERS* IS THE ONLY PLAY.

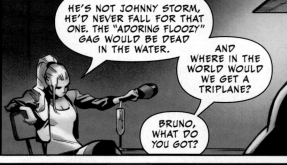

HE'S NOT JOHNNY STORM, HE'D NEVER FALL FOR THAT ONE. THE "ADORING FLOOZY" GAG WOULD BE DEAD IN THE WATER.

AND WHERE IN THE WORLD WOULD WE GET A TRIPLANE?

BRUNO, WHAT DO YOU GOT?

STARK'S A SMART GUY.

AND YOU KNOW WHAT'S LIKE CATNIP FOR SMART GUYS, SOMETHING THEY CAN'T RESIST?

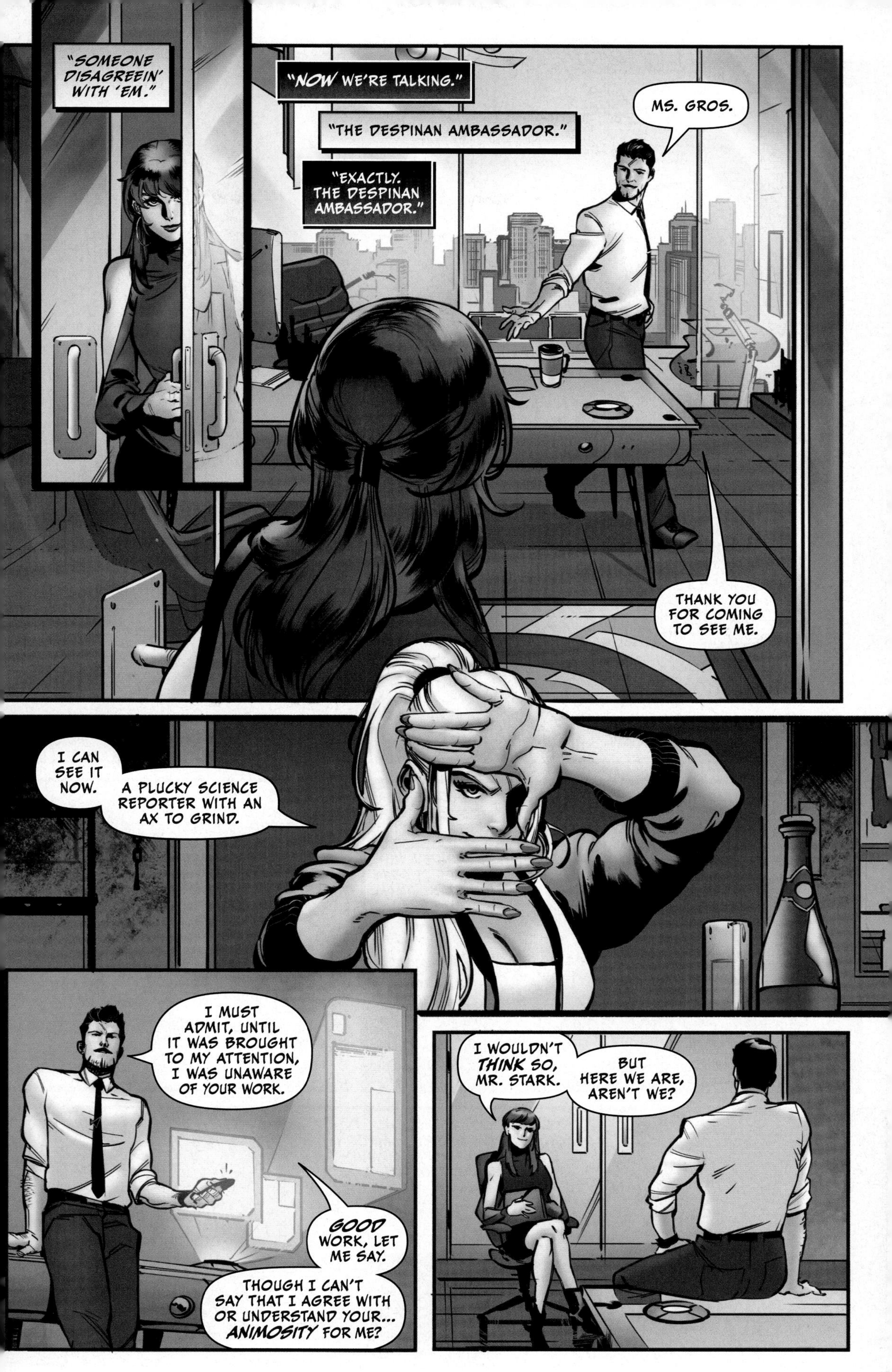
"SOMEONE DISAGREEIN' WITH 'EM."
"NOW WE'RE TALKING."
"THE DESPINAN AMBASSADOR."
"EXACTLY. THE DESPINAN AMBASSADOR."
MS. GROS.
THANK YOU FOR COMING TO SEE ME.
I CAN SEE IT NOW.
A PLUCKY SCIENCE REPORTER WITH AN AX TO GRIND.
I MUST ADMIT, UNTIL IT WAS BROUGHT TO MY ATTENTION, I WAS UNAWARE OF YOUR WORK.
GOOD WORK, LET ME SAY.
THOUGH I CAN'T SAY THAT I AGREE WITH OR UNDERSTAND YOUR... ANIMOSITY FOR ME?
I WOULDN'T THINK SO, MR. STARK.
BUT HERE WE ARE, AREN'T WE?

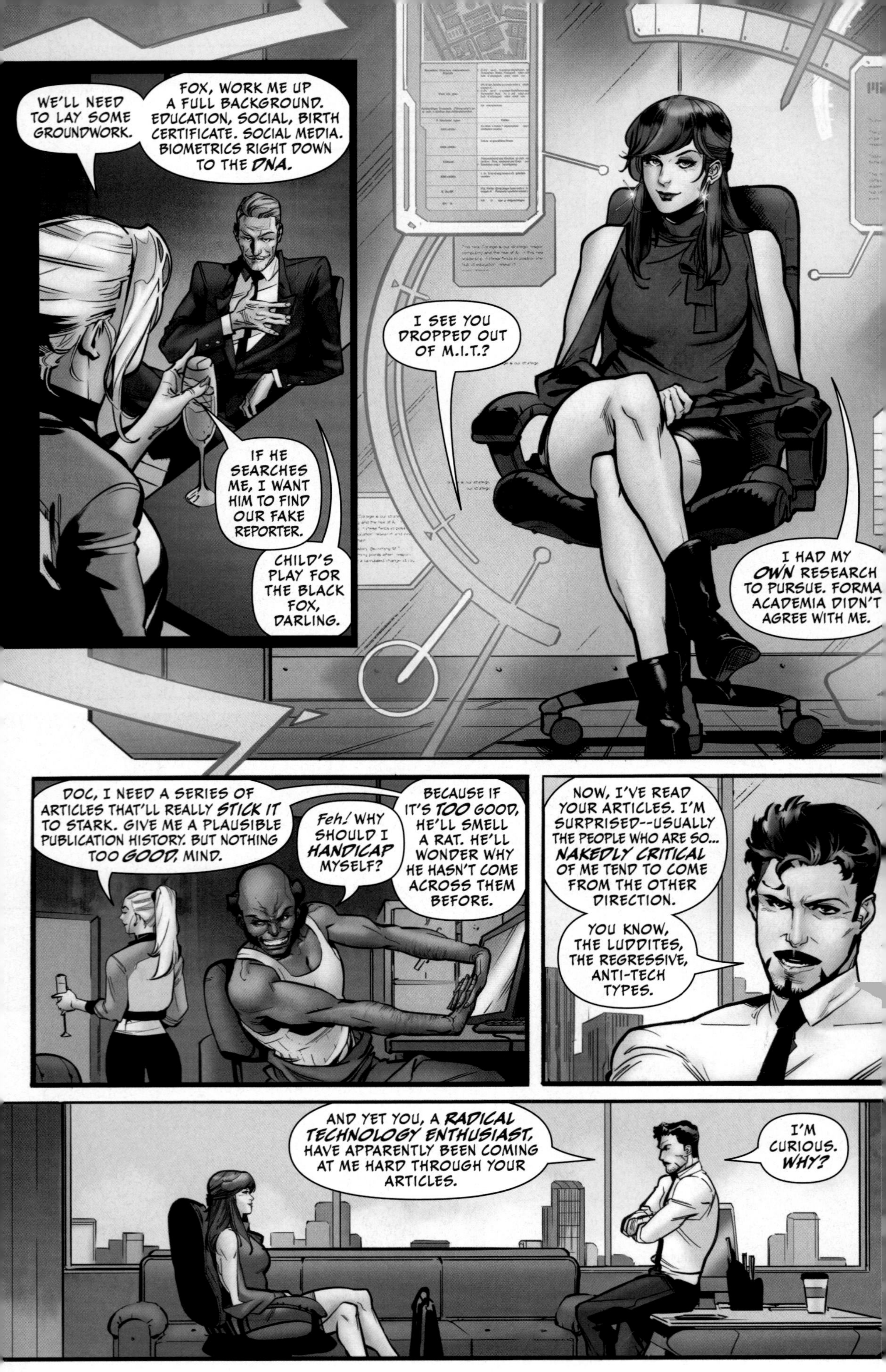
WE'LL NEED TO LAY SOME GROUNDWORK.
FOX, WORK ME UP A FULL BACKGROUND. EDUCATION, SOCIAL, BIRTH CERTIFICATE. SOCIAL MEDIA. BIOMETRICS RIGHT DOWN TO THE DNA.
IF HE SEARCHES ME, I WANT HIM TO FIND OUR FAKE REPORTER.
CHILD'S PLAY FOR THE BLACK FOX, DARLING.
I SEE YOU DROPPED OUT OF M.I.T.?
I HAD MY OWN RESEARCH TO PURSUE. FORMA ACADEMIA DIDN'T AGREE WITH ME.
DOC, I NEED A SERIES OF ARTICLES THAT'LL REALLY STICK IT TO STARK. GIVE ME A PLAUSIBLE PUBLICATION HISTORY. BUT NOTHING TOO GOOD, MIND.
Feh! WHY SHOULD I HANDICAP MYSELF?
BECAUSE IF IT'S TOO GOOD, HE'LL SMELL A RAT. HE'LL WONDER WHY HE HASN'T COME ACROSS THEM BEFORE.
NOW, I'VE READ YOUR ARTICLES. I'M SURPRISED--USUALLY THE PEOPLE WHO ARE SO... NAKEDLY CRITICAL OF ME TEND TO COME FROM THE OTHER DIRECTION.
YOU KNOW, THE LUDDITES, THE REGRESSIVE, ANTI-TECH TYPES.
AND YET YOU, A RADICAL TECHNOLOGY ENTHUSIAST, HAVE APPARENTLY BEEN COMING AT ME HARD THROUGH YOUR ARTICLES.
I'M CURIOUS. WHY?

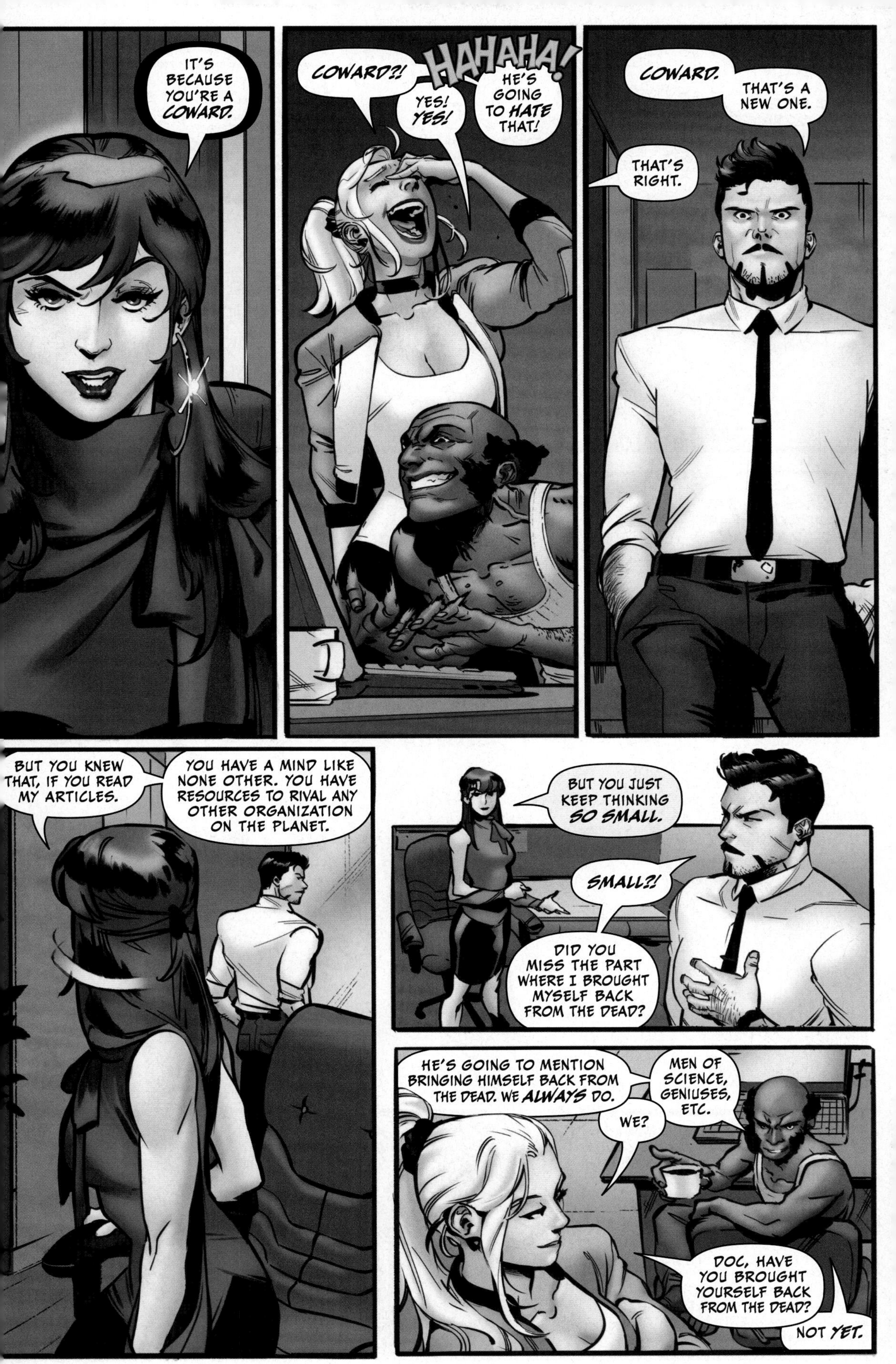
IT'S BECAUSE YOU'RE A COWARD.
COWARD?!
HAHAHA!
YES! YES!
HE'S GOING TO HATE THAT!
COWARD.
THAT'S A NEW ONE.
THAT'S RIGHT.
BUT YOU KNEW THAT, IF YOU READ MY ARTICLES.
YOU HAVE A MIND LIKE NONE OTHER. YOU HAVE RESOURCES TO RIVAL ANY OTHER ORGANIZATION ON THE PLANET.
BUT YOU JUST KEEP THINKING SO SMALL.
SMALL?!
DID YOU MISS THE PART WHERE I BROUGHT MYSELF BACK FROM THE DEAD?
HE'S GOING TO MENTION BRINGING HIMSELF BACK FROM THE DEAD. WE ALWAYS DO.
MEN OF SCIENCE, GENIUSES, ETC.
WE?
DOC, HAVE YOU BROUGHT YOURSELF BACK FROM THE DEAD?
NOT YET.

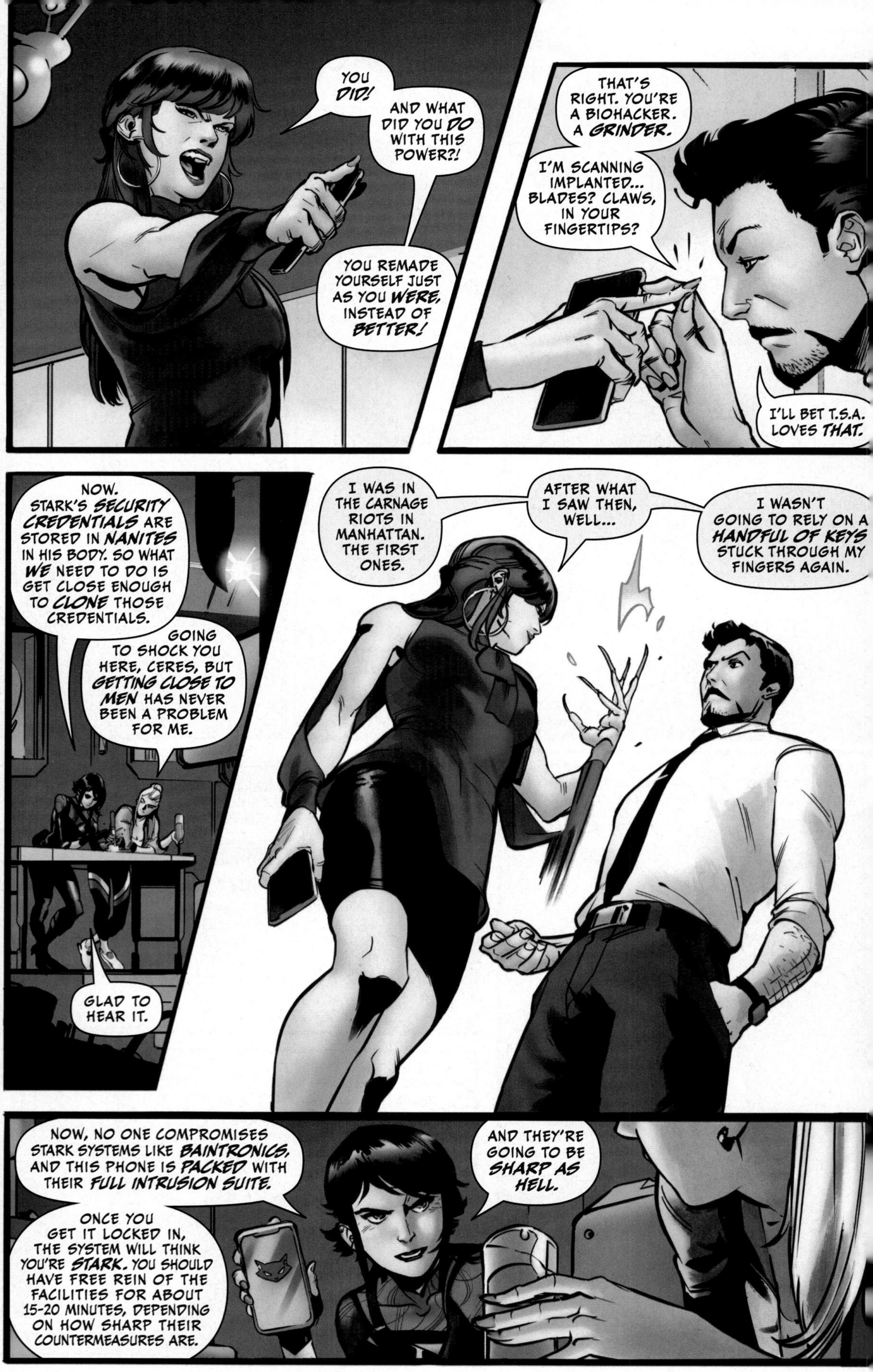

YOU DID!
AND WHAT DID YOU DO WITH THIS POWER?!
YOU REMADE YOURSELF JUST AS YOU WERE, INSTEAD OF BETTER!
THAT'S RIGHT. YOU'RE A BIOHACKER. A GRINDER.
I'M SCANNING IMPLANTED... BLADES? CLAWS, IN YOUR FINGERTIPS?
I'LL BET T.S.A. LOVES THAT.
NOW. STARK'S SECURITY CREDENTIALS ARE STORED IN NANITES IN HIS BODY. SO WHAT WE NEED TO DO IS GET CLOSE ENOUGH TO CLONE THOSE CREDENTIALS.
GOING TO SHOCK YOU HERE, CERES, BUT GETTING CLOSE TO MEN HAS NEVER BEEN A PROBLEM FOR ME.
GLAD TO HEAR IT.
I WAS IN THE CARNAGE RIOTS IN MANHATTAN. THE FIRST ONES.
AFTER WHAT I SAW THEN, WELL...
I WASN'T GOING TO RELY ON A HANDFUL OF KEYS STUCK THROUGH MY FINGERS AGAIN.
NOW, NO ONE COMPROMISES STARK SYSTEMS LIKE BAINTRONICS, AND THIS PHONE IS PACKED WITH THEIR FULL INTRUSION SUITE.
ONCE YOU GET IT LOCKED IN, THE SYSTEM WILL THINK YOU'RE STARK. YOU SHOULD HAVE FREE REIN OF THE FACILITIES FOR ABOUT 15-20 MINUTES, DEPENDING ON HOW SHARP THEIR COUNTERMEASURES ARE.
AND THEY'RE GOING TO BE SHARP AS HELL.

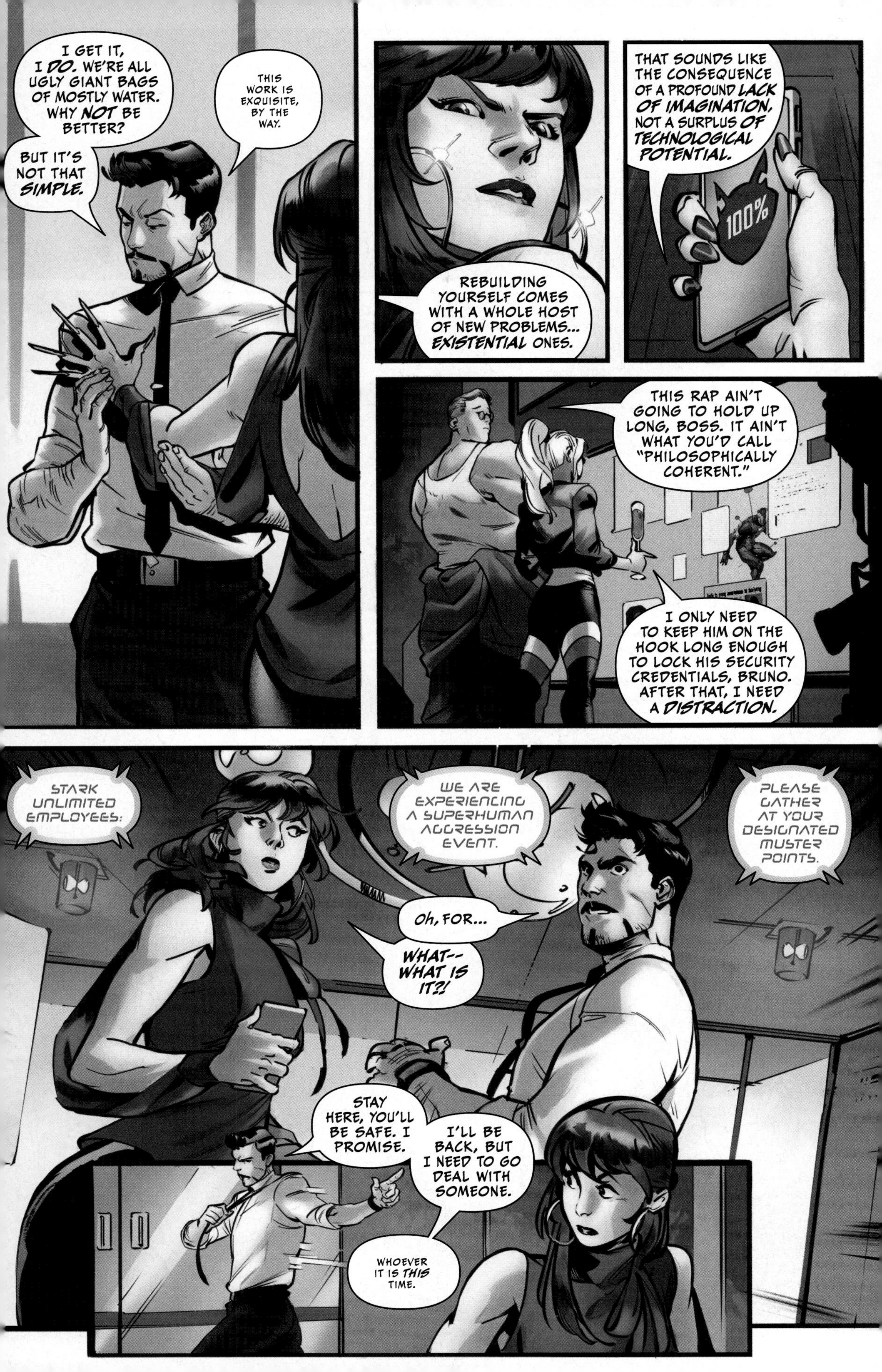
I GET IT, I DO. WE'RE ALL UGLY GIANT BAGS OF MOSTLY WATER. WHY NOT BE BETTER?
BUT IT'S NOT THAT SIMPLE.
THIS WORK IS EXQUISITE, BY THE WAY.
REBUILDING YOURSELF COMES WITH A WHOLE HOST OF NEW PROBLEMS... EXISTENTIAL ONES.
THAT SOUNDS LIKE THE CONSEQUENCE OF A PROFOUND LACK OF IMAGINATION, NOT A SURPLUS OF TECHNOLOGICAL POTENTIAL.
100%
THIS RAP AIN'T GOING TO HOLD UP LONG, BOSS. IT AIN'T WHAT YOU'D CALL "PHILOSOPHICALLY COHERENT."
I ONLY NEED TO KEEP HIM ON THE HOOK LONG ENOUGH TO LOCK HIS SECURITY CREDENTIALS, BRUNO. AFTER THAT, I NEED A DISTRACTION.
STARK UNLIMITED EMPLOYEES:
WE ARE EXPERIENCING A SUPERHUMAN AGGRESSION EVENT.
PLEASE GATHER AT YOUR DESIGNATED MUSTER POINTS.
Oh, FOR...
WHAT-- WHAT IS IT?!
STAY HERE, YOU'LL BE SAFE. I PROMISE.
I'LL BE BACK, BUT I NEED TO GO DEAL WITH SOMEONE.
WHOEVER IT IS THIS TIME.

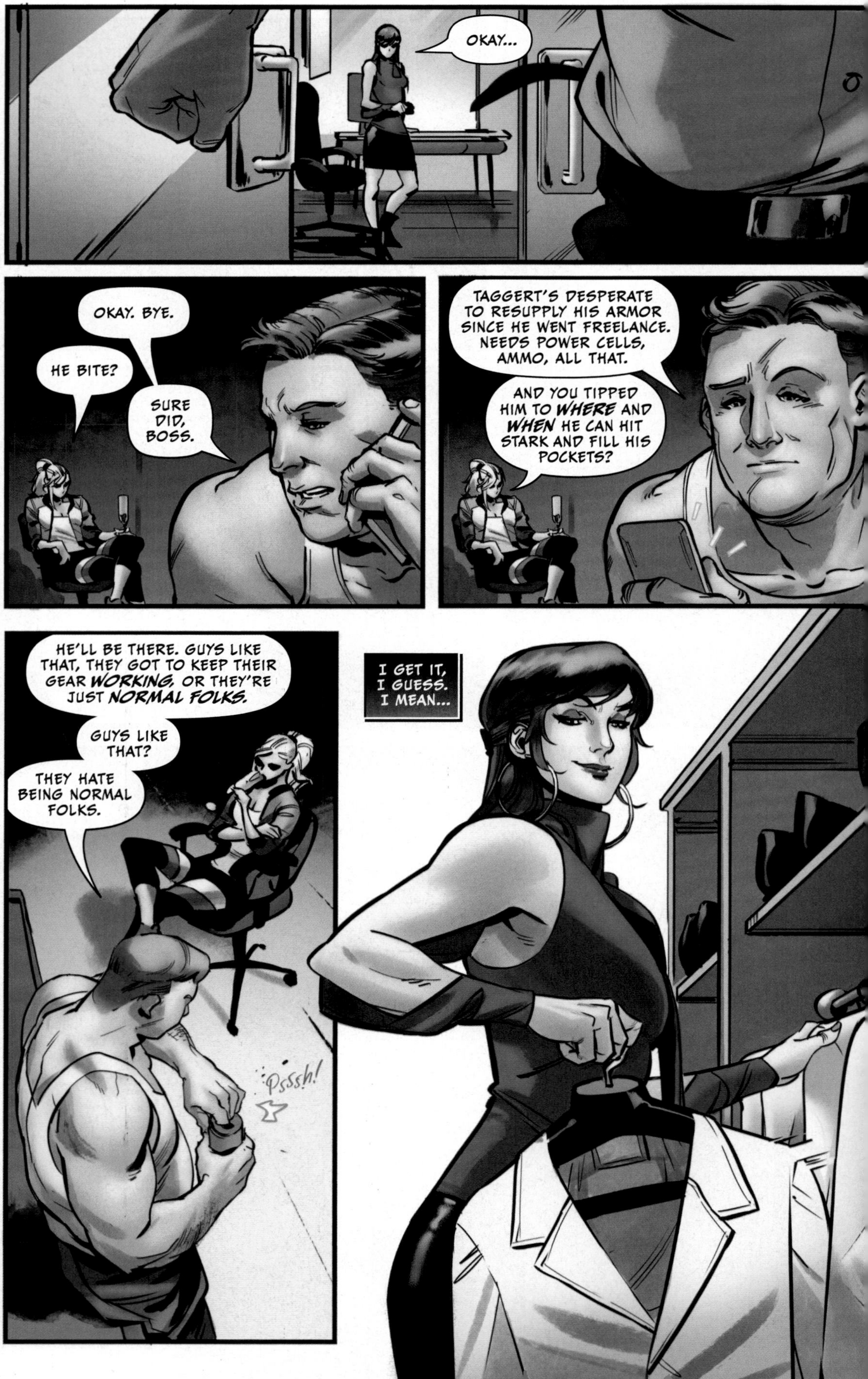

OKAY...
OKAY. BYE.
HE BITE?
SURE DID, BOSS.
TAGGERT'S DESPERATE TO RESUPPLY HIS ARMOR SINCE HE WENT FREELANCE. NEEDS POWER CELLS, AMMO, ALL THAT.
AND YOU TIPPED HIM TO WHERE AND WHEN HE CAN HIT STARK AND FILL HIS POCKETS?
HE'LL BE THERE. GUYS LIKE THAT, THEY GOT TO KEEP THEIR GEAR WORKING, OR THEY'RE JUST NORMAL FOLKS.
GUYS LIKE THAT?
THEY HATE BEING NORMAL FOLKS.
Psssh!
I GET IT, I GUESS. I MEAN...

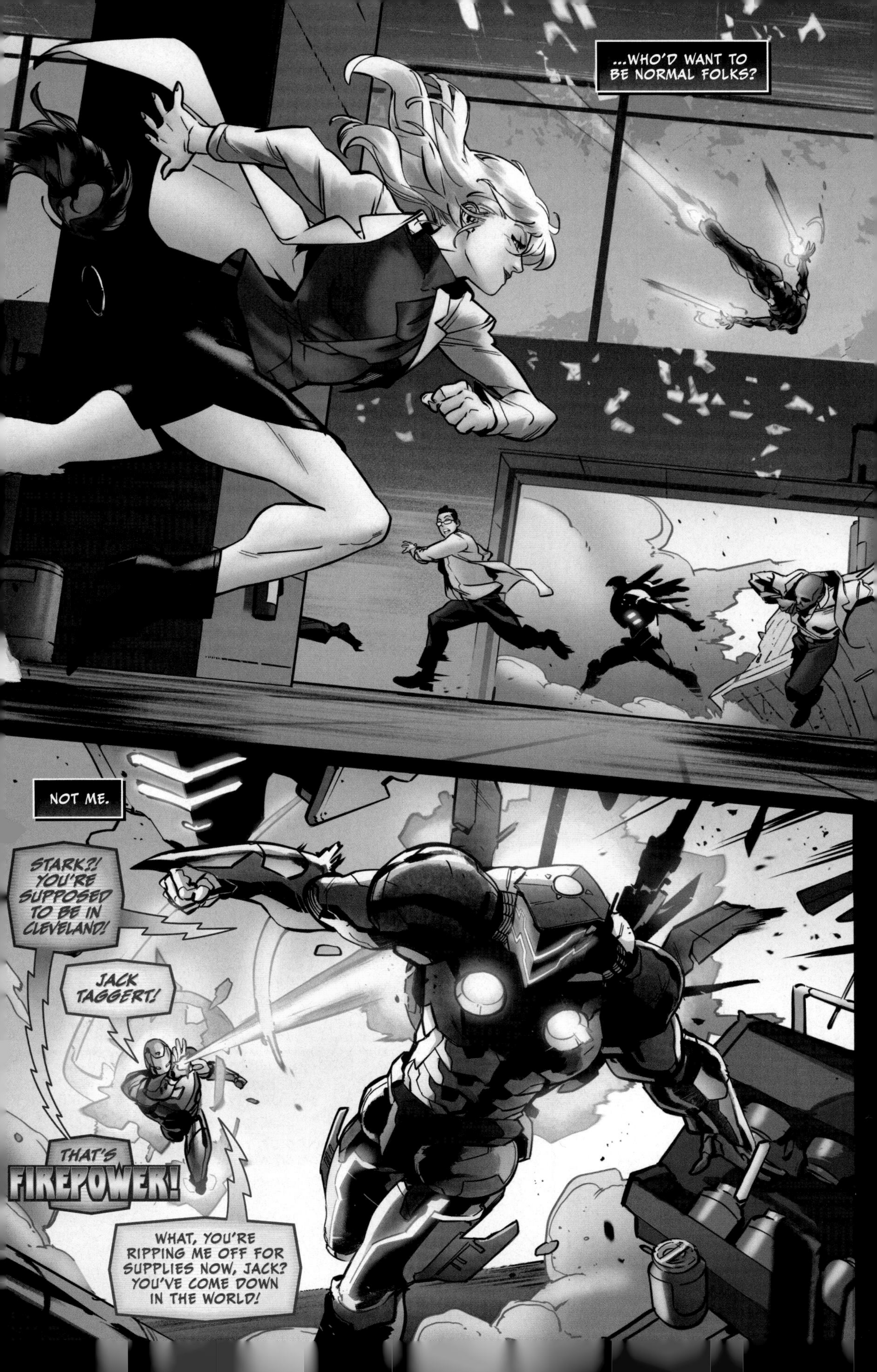
...WHO'D WANT TO BE NORMAL FOLKS?
NOT ME.
STARK?! YOU'RE SUPPOSED TO BE IN CLEVELAND!
JACK TAGGERT!
THAT'S FIREPOWER!
WHAT, YOU'RE RIPPING ME OFF FOR SUPPLIES NOW, JACK? YOU'VE COME DOWN IN THE WORLD!

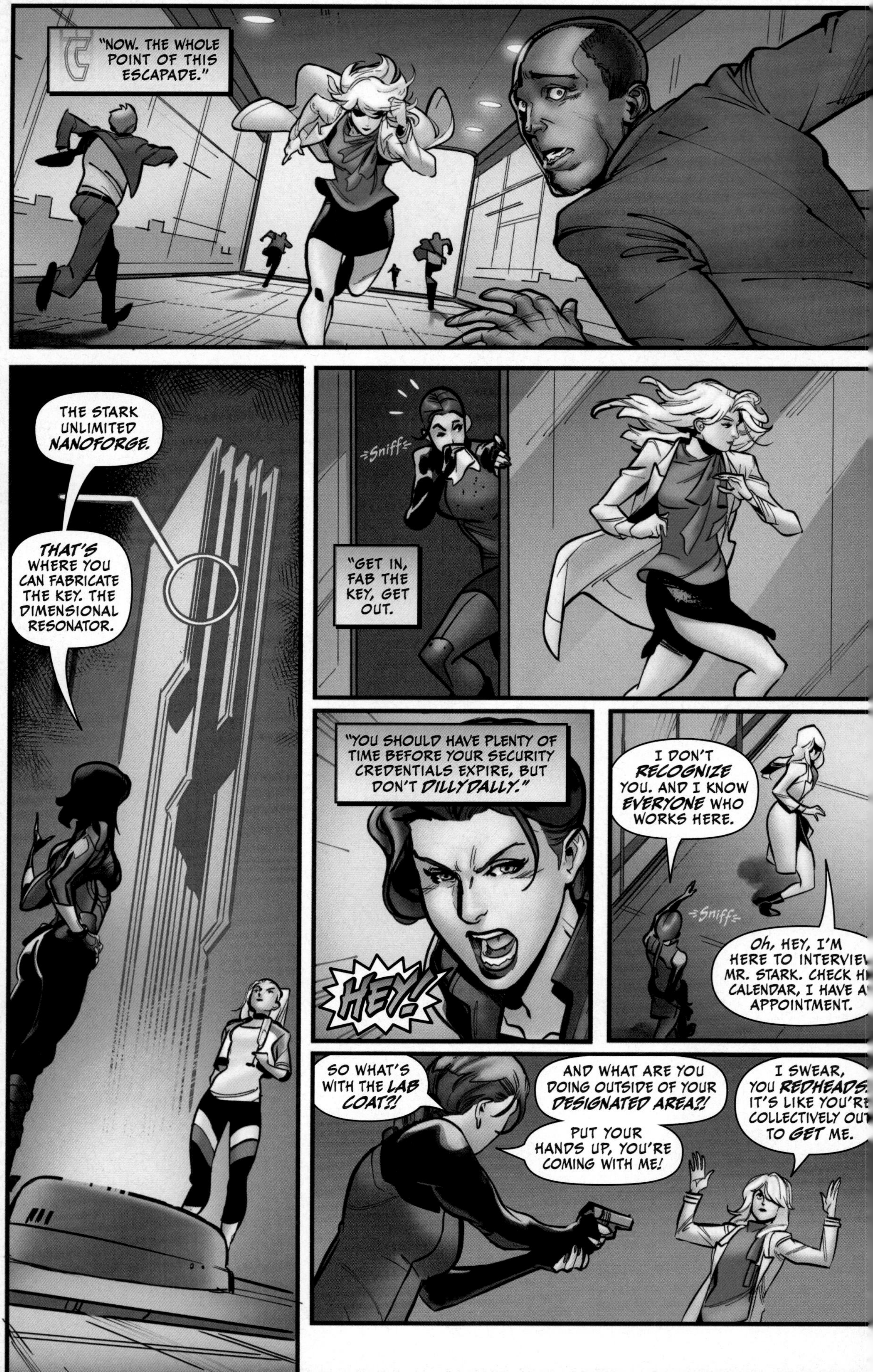
"NOW. THE WHOLE POINT OF THIS ESCAPADE."
THE STARK UNLIMITED NANOFORGE.
THAT'S WHERE YOU CAN FABRICATE THE KEY. THE DIMENSIONAL RESONATOR.
SNIFF
"GET IN, FAB THE KEY, GET OUT.
"YOU SHOULD HAVE PLENTY OF TIME BEFORE YOUR SECURITY CREDENTIALS EXPIRE, BUT DON'T DILLYDALLY."
HEY!
I DON'T RECOGNIZE YOU. AND I KNOW EVERYONE WHO WORKS HERE.
SNIFF
OH, HEY, I'M HERE TO INTERVIEW MR. STARK. CHECK HIS CALENDAR, I HAVE AN APPOINTMENT.
SO WHAT'S WITH THE LAB COAT?!
AND WHAT ARE YOU DOING OUTSIDE OF YOUR DESIGNATED AREA?!
PUT YOUR HANDS UP, YOU'RE COMING WITH ME!
I SWEAR, YOU REDHEADS. IT'S LIKE YOU'RE COLLECTIVELY OUT TO GET ME.

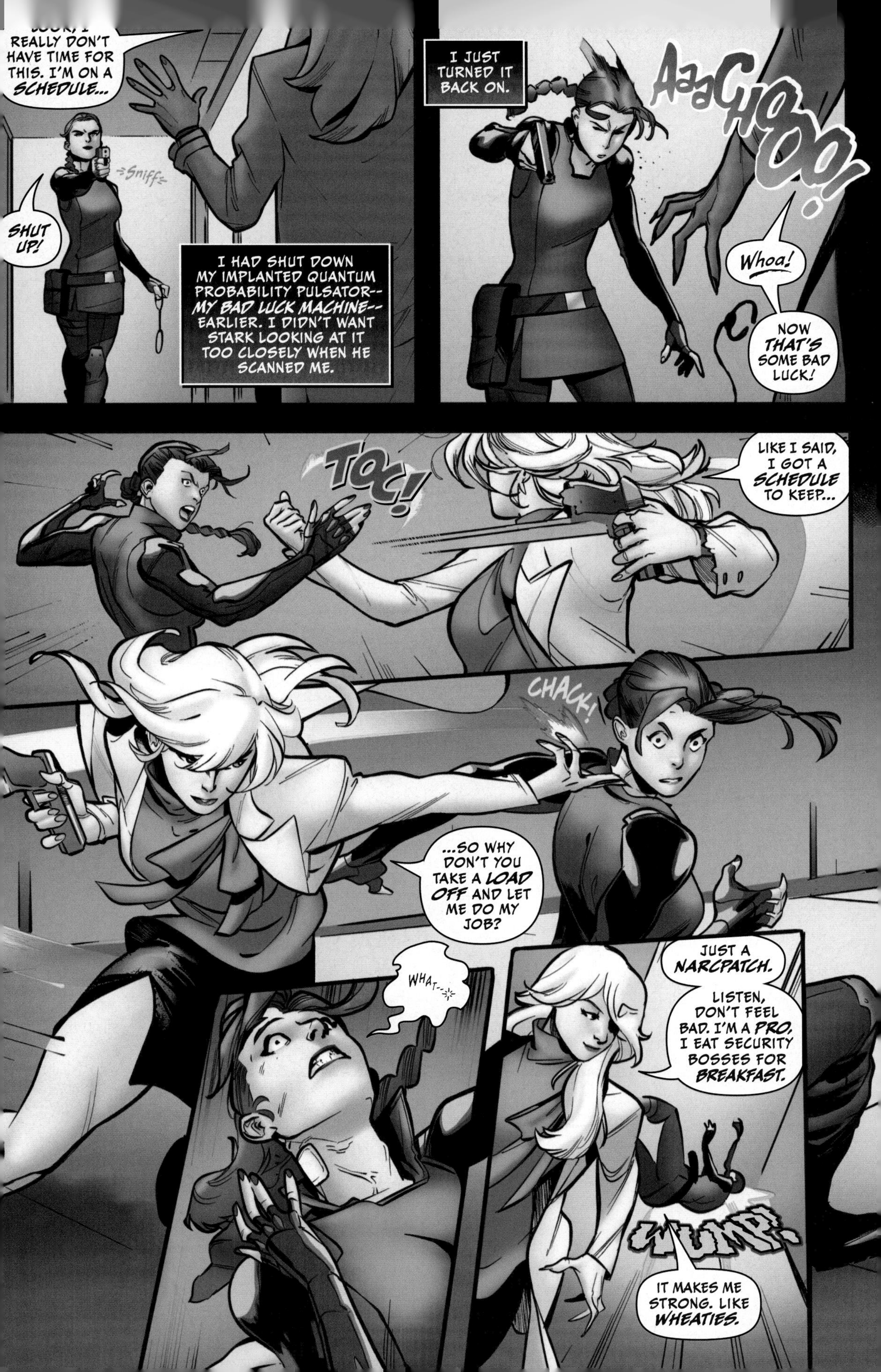

LOOK, I REALLY DON'T HAVE TIME FOR THIS. I'M ON A SCHEDULE...
SNIFF
SHUT UP!
I HAD SHUT DOWN MY IMPLANTED QUANTUM PROBABILITY PULSATOR-- MY BAD LUCK MACHINE-- EARLIER. I DIDN'T WANT STARK LOOKING AT IT TOO CLOSELY WHEN HE SCANNED ME.
I JUST TURNED IT BACK ON.
AAACHOOOO!
Whoa!
NOW THAT'S SOME BAD LUCK!
TOC!
LIKE I SAID, I GOT A SCHEDULE TO KEEP...
CHACK!
...SO WHY DON'T YOU TAKE A LOAD OFF AND LET ME DO MY JOB?
WHAT--
JUST A NARCPATCH.
LISTEN, DON'T FEEL BAD. I'M A PRO, I EAT SECURITY BOSSES FOR BREAKFAST.
WUMP!
IT MAKES ME STRONG. LIKE WHEATIES.

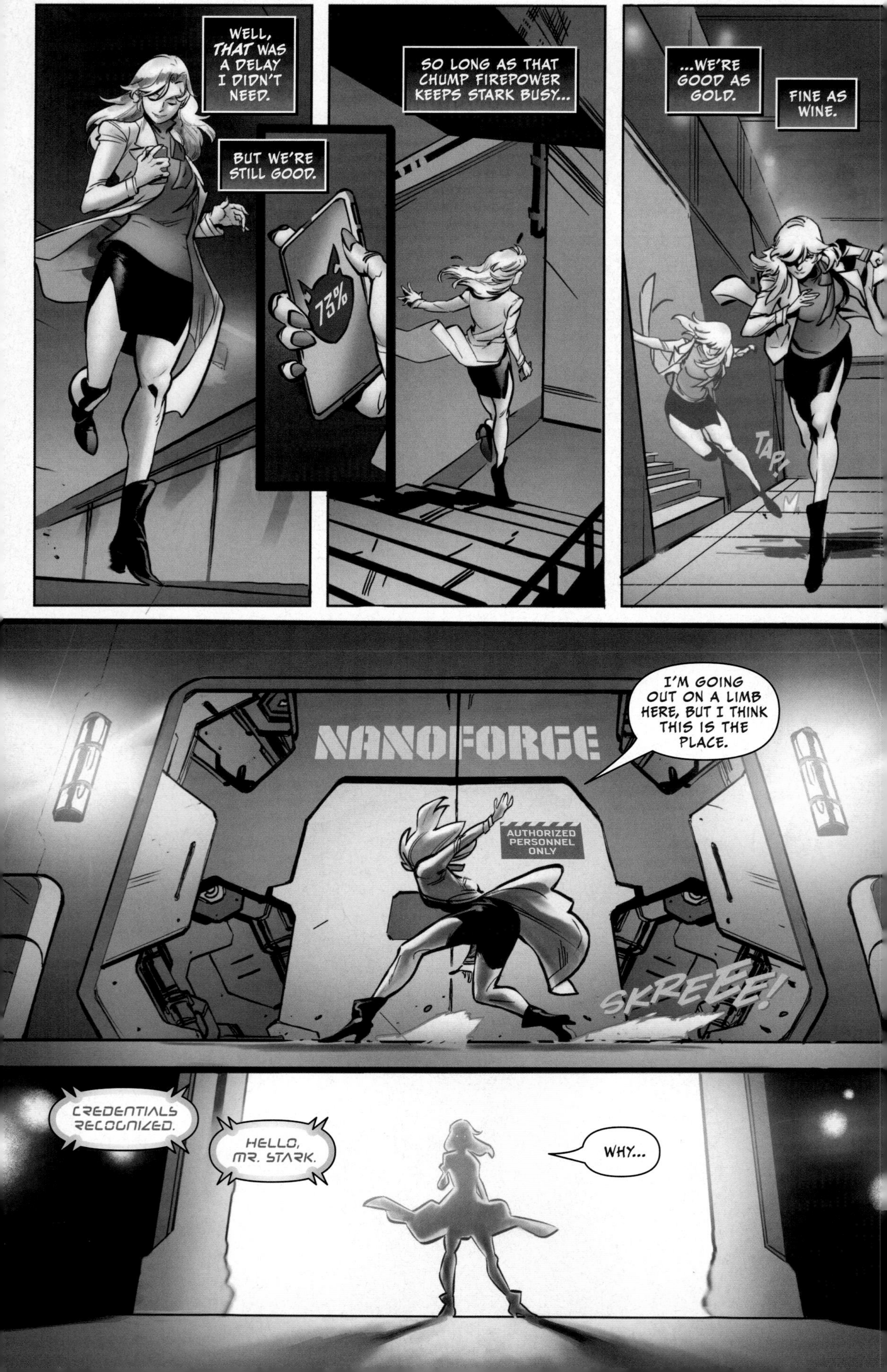
WELL, THAT WAS A DELAY I DIDN'T NEED.
BUT WE'RE STILL GOOD.
73%
SO LONG AS THAT CHUMP FIREPOWER KEEPS STARK BUSY...
...WE'RE GOOD AS GOLD.
FINE AS WINE.
TAP!
NANOFORGE
I'M GOING OUT ON A LIMB HERE, BUT I THINK THIS IS THE PLACE.
AUTHORIZED PERSONNEL ONLY
SKREEEE!
CREDENTIALS RECOGNIZED.
HELLO, MR. STARK.
WHY...

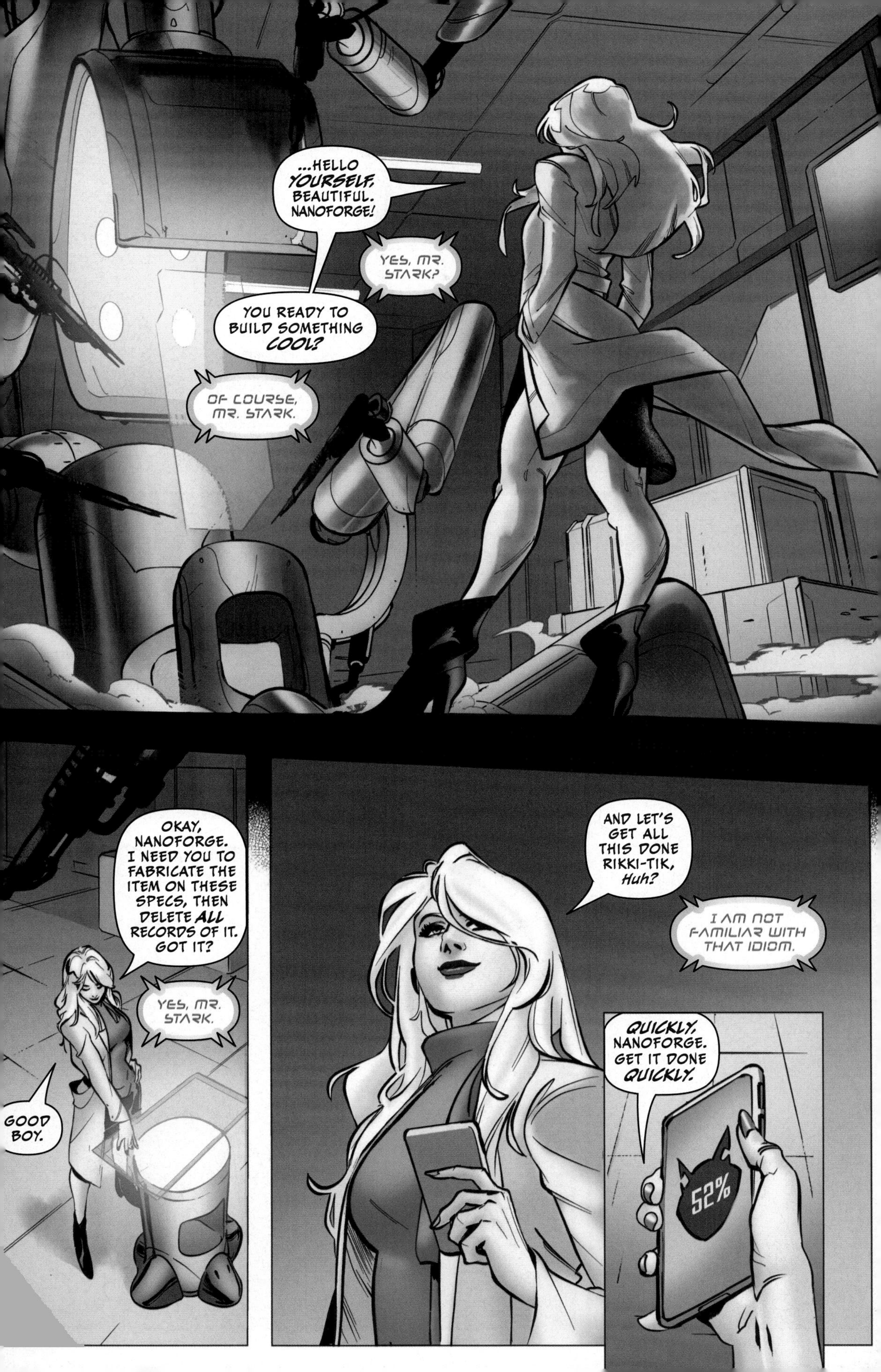
...HELLO YOURSELF, BEAUTIFUL. NANOFORGE!
YES, MR. STARK?
YOU READY TO BUILD SOMETHING COOL?
OF COURSE, MR. STARK.
OKAY, NANOFORGE. I NEED YOU TO FABRICATE THE ITEM ON THESE SPECS, THEN DELETE ALL RECORDS OF IT. GOT IT?
YES, MR. STARK.
GOOD BOY.
AND LET'S GET ALL THIS DONE RIKKI-TIK, Huh?
I AM NOT FAMILIAR WITH THAT IDIOM.
QUICKLY, NANOFORGE. GET IT DONE QUICKLY.
52%

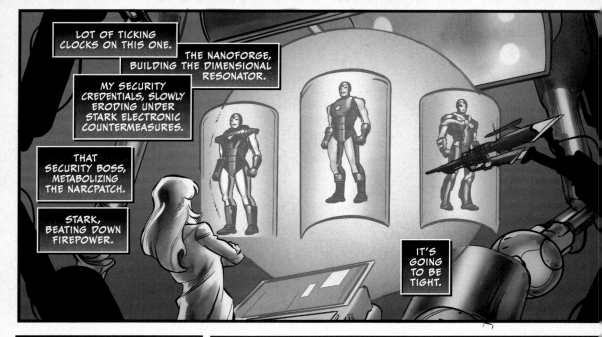

LOT OF TICKING CLOCKS ON THIS ONE.

THE NANOFORGE, BUILDING THE DIMENSIONAL RESONATOR.

MY SECURITY CREDENTIALS, SLOWLY ERODING UNDER STARK ELECTRONIC COUNTERMEASURES.

THAT SECURITY BOSS, METABOLIZING THE NARCPATCH.

STARK, BEATING DOWN FIREPOWER.

IT'S GOING TO BE TIGHT.

BUT THERE'S PLENTY TO PLAY WITH WHILE I'M WAITING.

WHEN I WAS A KID, I LOVED PAPER DOLLS.

CUT 'EM OUT, PUT DIFFERENT OUTFITS ON. DIFFERENT ACCESSORIES.

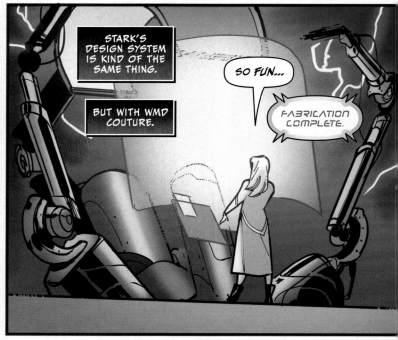

STARK'S DESIGN SYSTEM IS KIND OF THE SAME THING.

BUT WITH WMD COUTURE.

SO FUN...

FABRICATION COMPLETE.

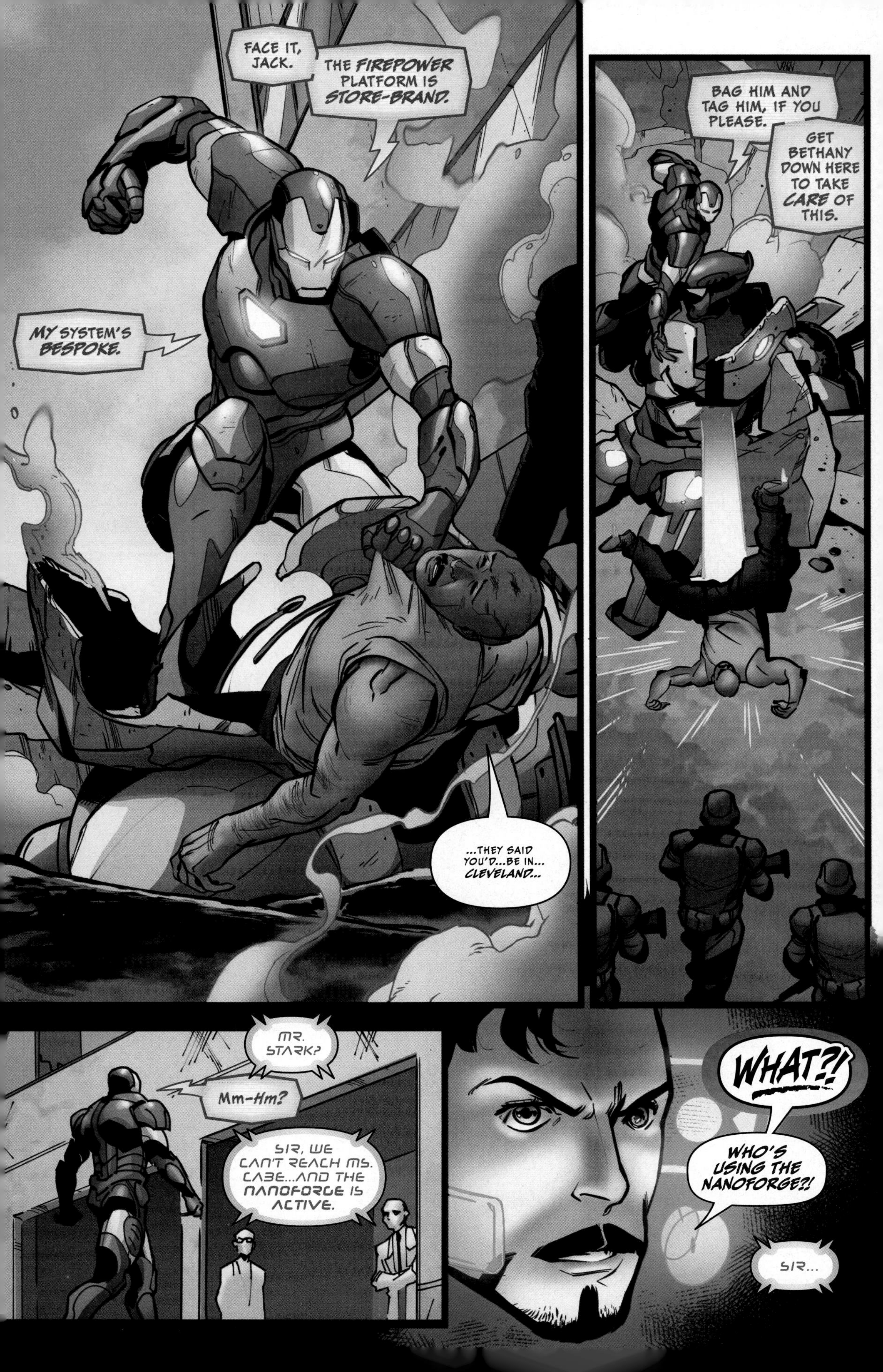

FACE IT, JACK.
THE FIREPOWER PLATFORM IS STORE-BRAND.
MY SYSTEM'S BESPOKE.
...THEY SAID YOU'D...BE IN... CLEVELAND...
BAG HIM AND TAG HIM, IF YOU PLEASE.
GET BETHANY DOWN HERE TO TAKE CARE OF THIS.
MR. STARK?
Mm-Hm?
SIR, WE CAN'T REACH MS. CABE...AND THE NANOFORGE IS ACTIVE.
WHAT?!
WHO'S USING THE NANOFORGE?!
SIR...

"...YOU ARE."

Oooh... WELL DONE, NANOFORGE!

THANK YOU, MR. STARK.

AAH!

I THINK MAYBE YOU'D BETTER OPEN THESE DOORS AND EXIT MY NANOFORGE.

AND TELL ME WHAT HAPPENED TO MY HEAD OF SECURITY.

FIREPOWER, YOU PUNK!

YOU MUST'V' GONE DOWN LIKE GLASS JOE!

SHE'S JUST SLEEPING IT OFF, DON'T WORRY ABOUT IT.

WHAT IS THIS? WHO ARE YOU WORKING FOR?

LET ME GUESS, THERE'S NO ELODIE GROS, IS THERE?

NOPE. INSULT TO INJURY, I KNOW, BUT I'M NOT A REAL REDHEAD EITHER.

HAD YOU GOING THOUGH, DIDN'T I?

OKAY, NANOFORGE. GOT ANOTHER JOB FOR YOU.

YES, MR. STARK?

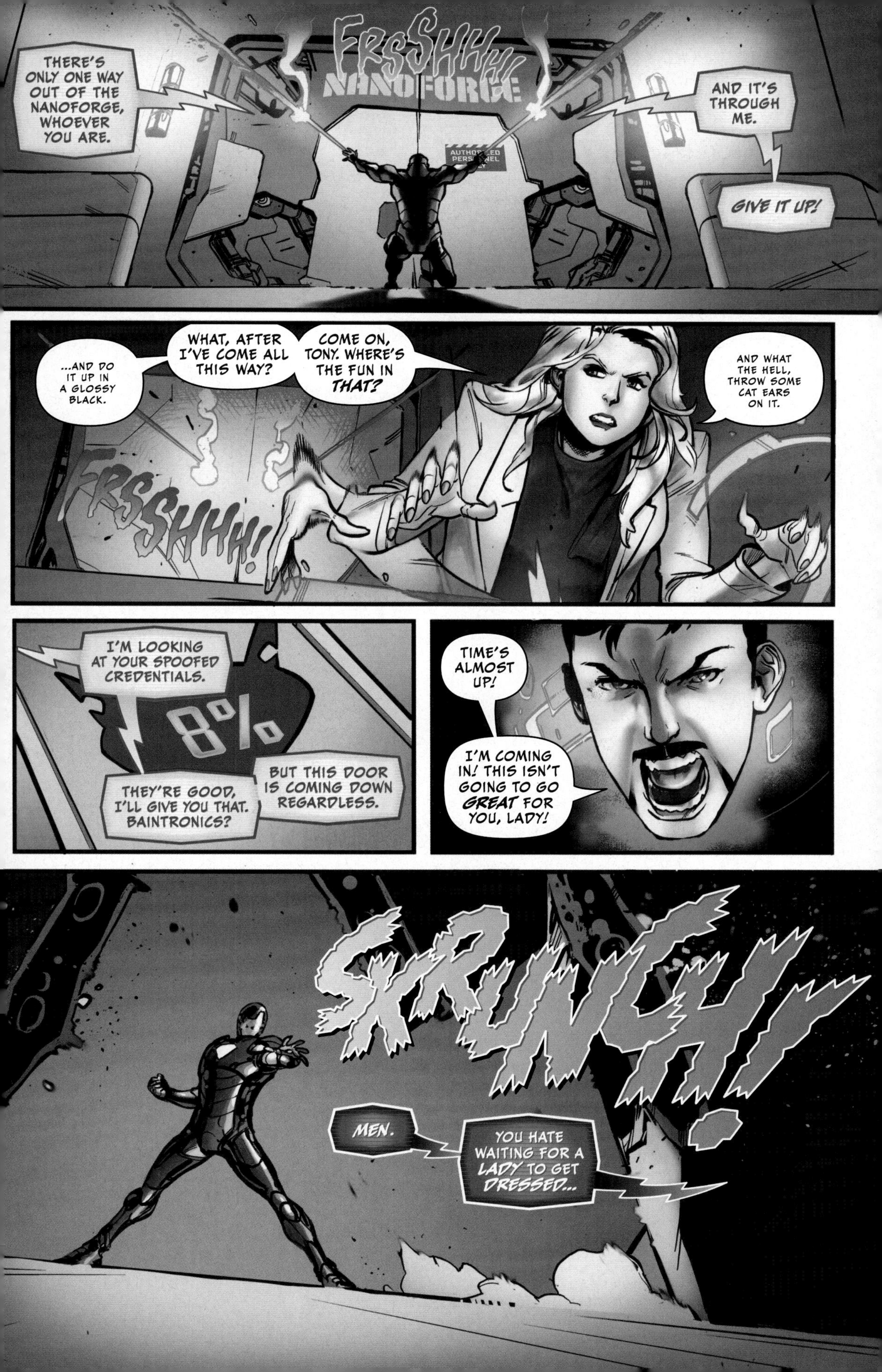
FRSSHHH!
NANOFORGE
THERE'S ONLY ONE WAY OUT OF THE NANOFORGE, WHOEVER YOU ARE.
AND IT'S THROUGH ME.
GIVE IT UP!
...AND DO IT UP IN A GLOSSY BLACK.
WHAT, AFTER I'VE COME ALL THIS WAY?
COME ON, TONY. WHERE'S THE FUN IN THAT?
AND WHAT THE HELL, THROW SOME CAT EARS ON IT.
FRSSHHH!
I'M LOOKING AT YOUR SPOOFED CREDENTIALS.
8%
THEY'RE GOOD, I'LL GIVE YOU THAT. BAINTRONICS?
BUT THIS DOOR IS COMING DOWN REGARDLESS.
TIME'S ALMOST UP!
I'M COMING IN! THIS ISN'T GOING TO GO GREAT FOR YOU, LADY!
SKRUNCH!
MEN.
YOU HATE WAITING FOR A LADY TO GET DRESSED...

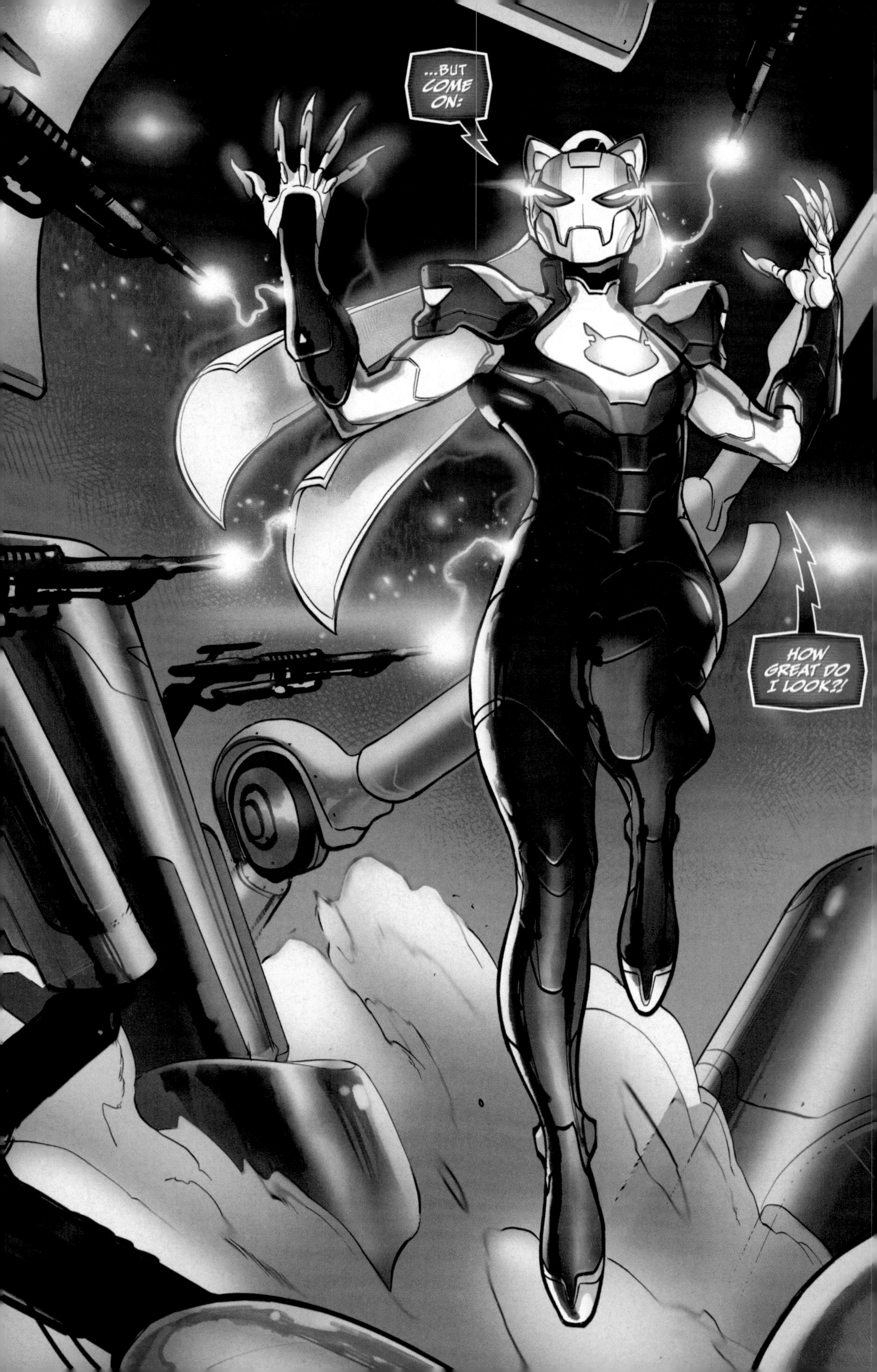
...BUT COME ON:
HOW GREAT DO I LOOK?!

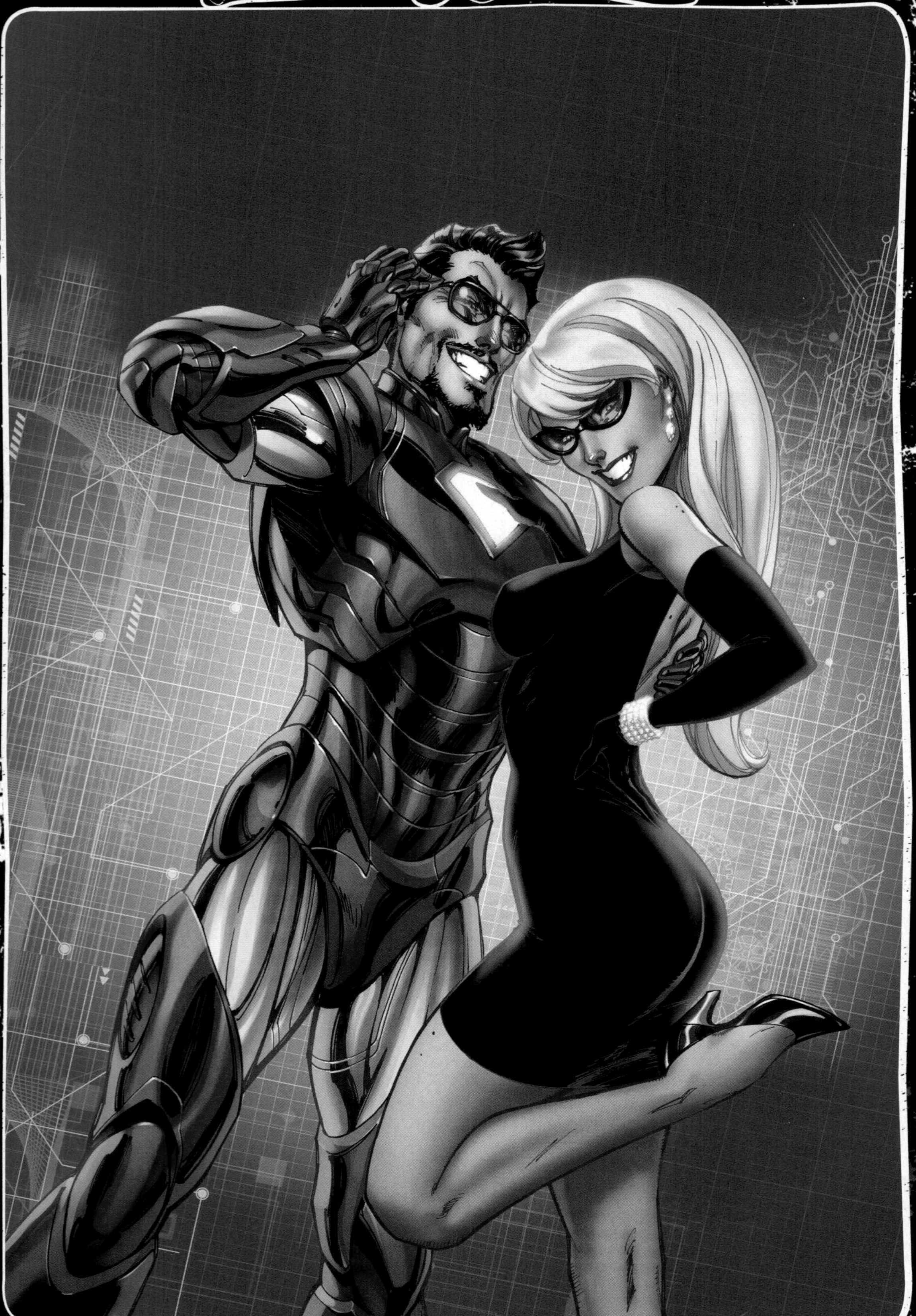

12 • Full Metal Black Cat PART 2

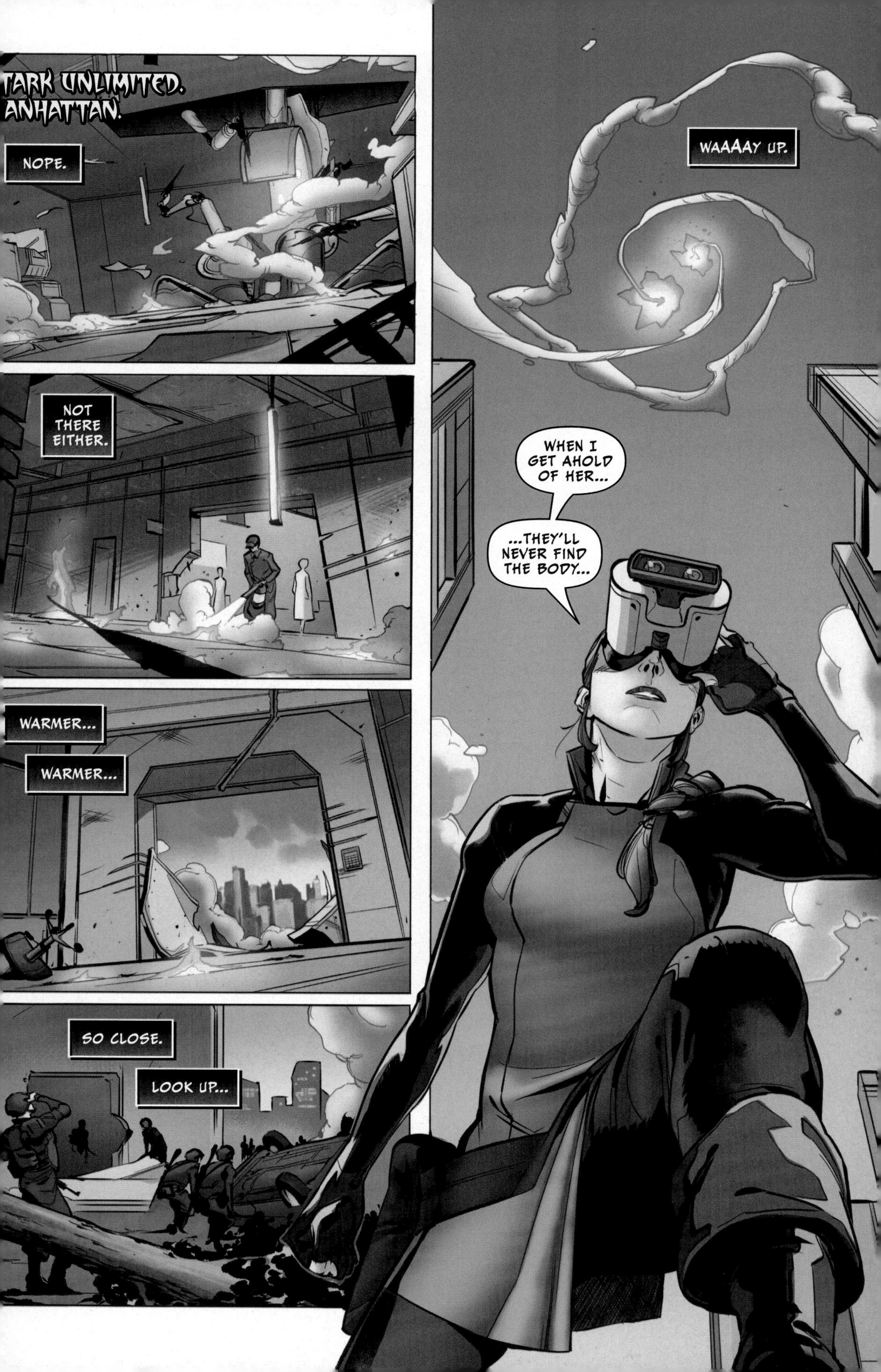
TARK UNLIMITED.
ANHATTAN.
NOPE.
NOT THERE EITHER.
WARMER...
WARMER...
SO CLOSE.
LOOK UP...
WAAAAY UP.
WHEN I GET AHOLD OF HER...
...THEY'LL NEVER FIND THE BODY...

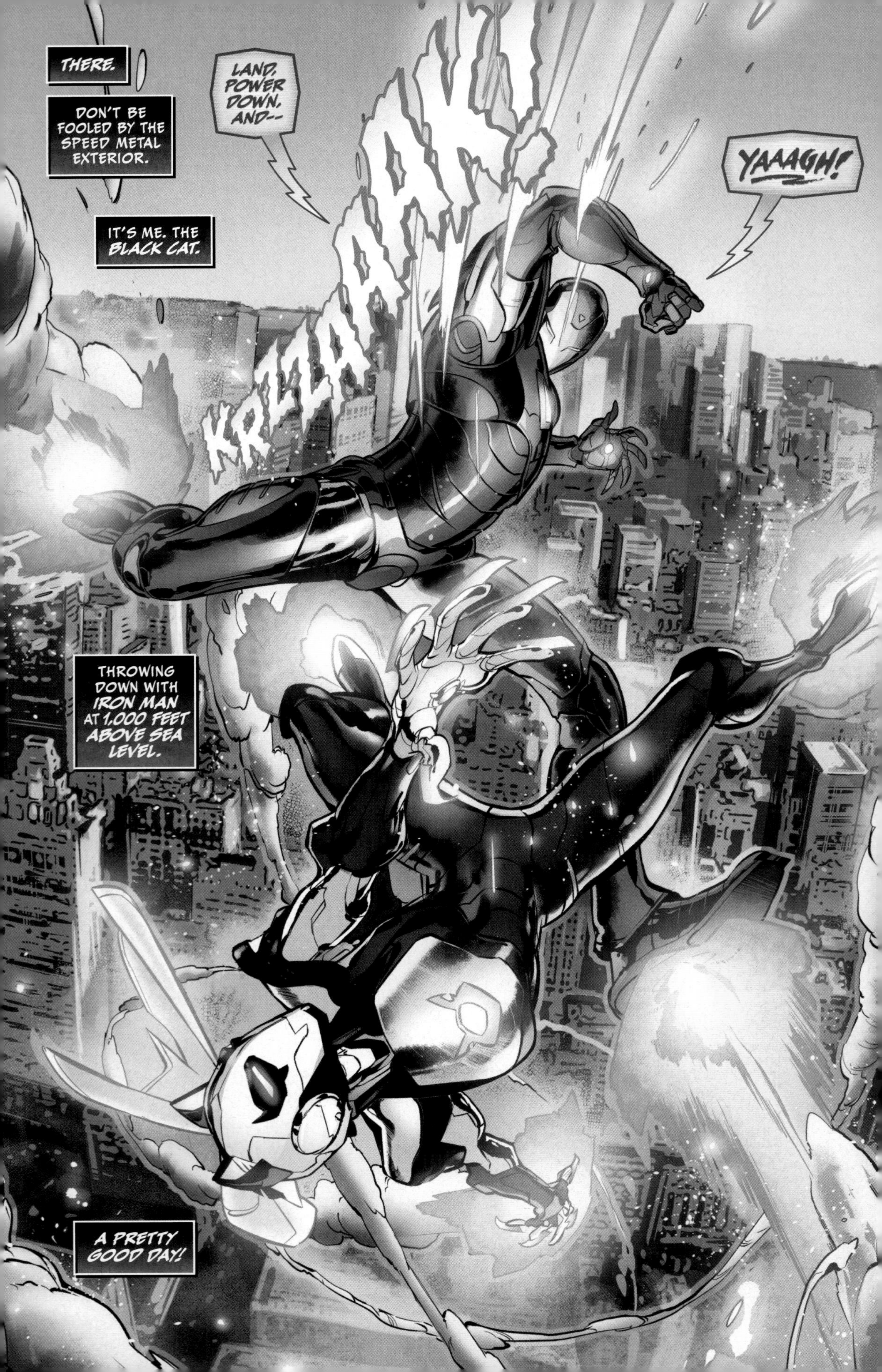
THERE.
DON'T BE FOOLED BY THE SPEED METAL EXTERIOR.
IT'S ME. THE BLACK CAT.
LAND, POWER DOWN, AND--
YAAAGH!
THROWING DOWN WITH IRON MAN AT 1,000 FEET ABOVE SEA LEVEL.
A PRETTY GOOD DAY!

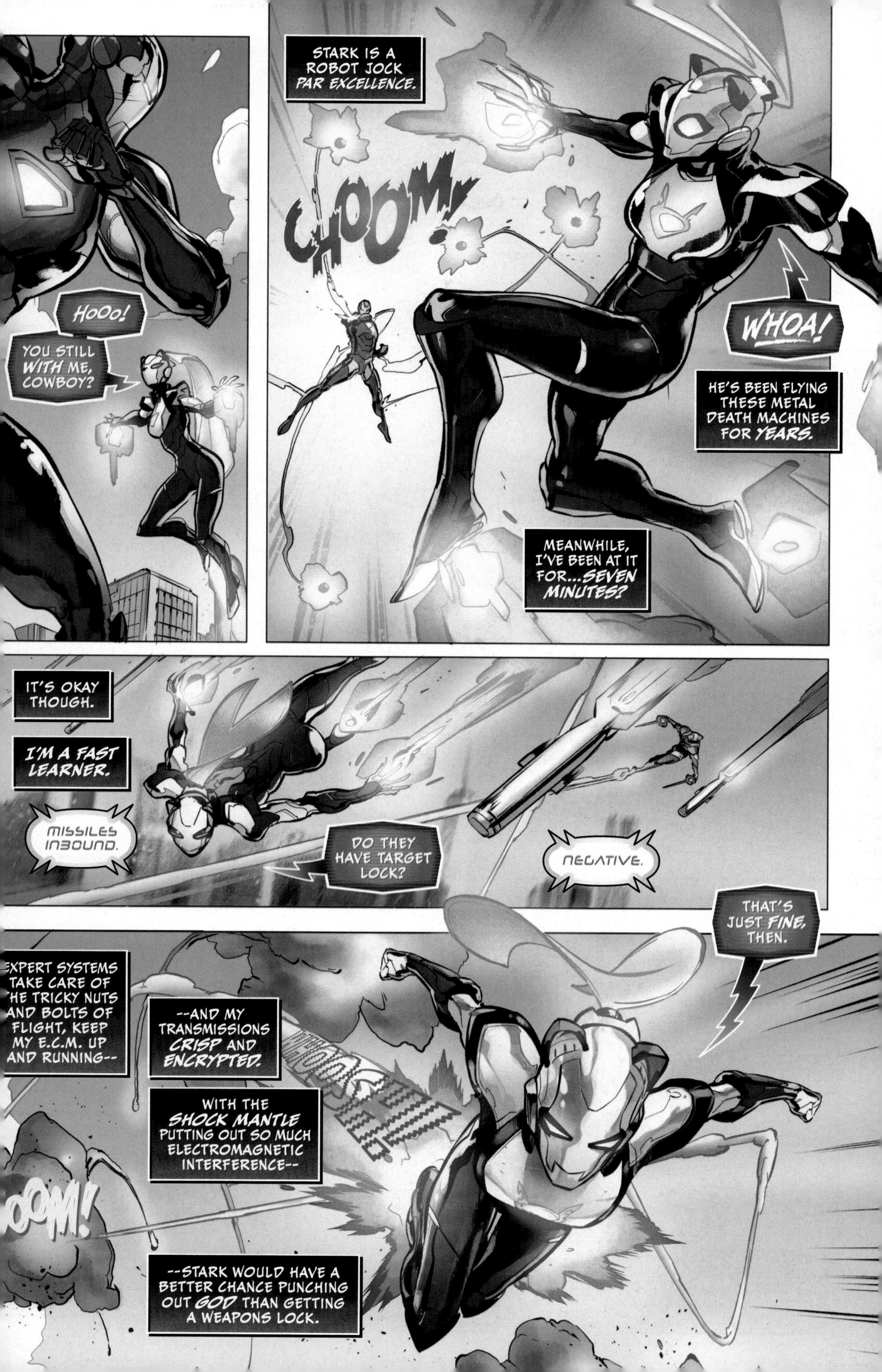

HoOo!
YOU STILL WITH ME, COWBOY?
STARK IS A ROBOT JOCK PAR EXCELLENCE.
CHOOM!
WHOA!
HE'S BEEN FLYING THESE METAL DEATH MACHINES FOR YEARS.
MEANWHILE, I'VE BEEN AT IT FOR...SEVEN MINUTES?
IT'S OKAY THOUGH.
I'M A FAST LEARNER.
MISSILES INBOUND.
DO THEY HAVE TARGET LOCK?
NEGATIVE.
THAT'S JUST FINE, THEN.
EXPERT SYSTEMS TAKE CARE OF THE TRICKY NUTS AND BOLTS OF FLIGHT, KEEP MY E.C.M. UP AND RUNNING--
--AND MY TRANSMISSIONS CRISP AND ENCRYPTED.
WITH THE SHOCK MANTLE PUTTING OUT SO MUCH ELECTROMAGNETIC INTERFERENCE--
OOM!
--STARK WOULD HAVE A BETTER CHANCE PUNCHING OUT GOD THAN GETTING A WEAPONS LOCK.

PLUS, MY LITTLE BLACK DRESS HERE HAS A *SECRET WEAPON.*

I CAN'T FLY LIKE STARK...

...BUT I CAN *OUTMANEUVER* HIM.

THIS CAT IS *NOTHING* IF NOT *NIMBLE.*

SHRRzZZZ!

URGHHH--

HOW IS SHE PULLING THESE Gs?

SEE, *TURN TOO HARD* IN FLIGHT, PUT *TOO HEAVY* A FOOT ON THE *PEDAL,* AND THE G-FORCES HIT YOU LIKE A *TRUCK.*

THE MORE Gs YOU PULL, THE MORE STRAIN YOU PUT ON YOUR SOFT BLOOD-AND-BONE BODY.

BOOM!!

TOO MAN~~Y~~ AND THE~~N~~ BLOOD I~~N~~ YOUR BOD~~Y~~ POOLS. DRAINING AWAY FRO~~M~~ YOUR BRA~~IN~~

FIRST YOU *LOSE VISION,* THEN YOU BLACK OUT ENTIRELY.

UNLESS *YOU'RE ME.*

WHICH IS WHY THIS IS STILL A *CHASE.*

INCOMING TRANSMISSION FROM IRON MAN.

SCAN FOR VIRUSES.

NEGATIVE.

OPEN COMMS, THEN, BABY.

SO YOU'RE THE BLACK CAT.

FELICIA HARDY.

JEEPERS, COLUMBO, WHAT GAVE ME AWAY?

I'M ONLY WEARING 200 POUNDS OF CAT-THEMED W.M.D.

YOU'VE GOT A LOT OF NERVE.

PLEASE. I HEARD SQUIRREL GIRL BUSTED INTO YOUR PLACE AND STOLE A SUIT OF ARMOR.

BUT WHEN I DO IT, YOU PITCH AN ABSOLUTE HISSY FIT...

YOU KNOW SQUIRREL GIRL?!

SHE WANTED ME TO TALK TO A CAT OR SOMETHING ONE TIME. WEIRD KID.

HOW--

HOW ARE YOU DOING THAT WITHOUT BLACKING OUT?!

WHSH!

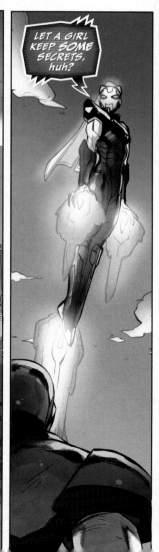

LET A GIRL KEEP SOME SECRETS, HUH?

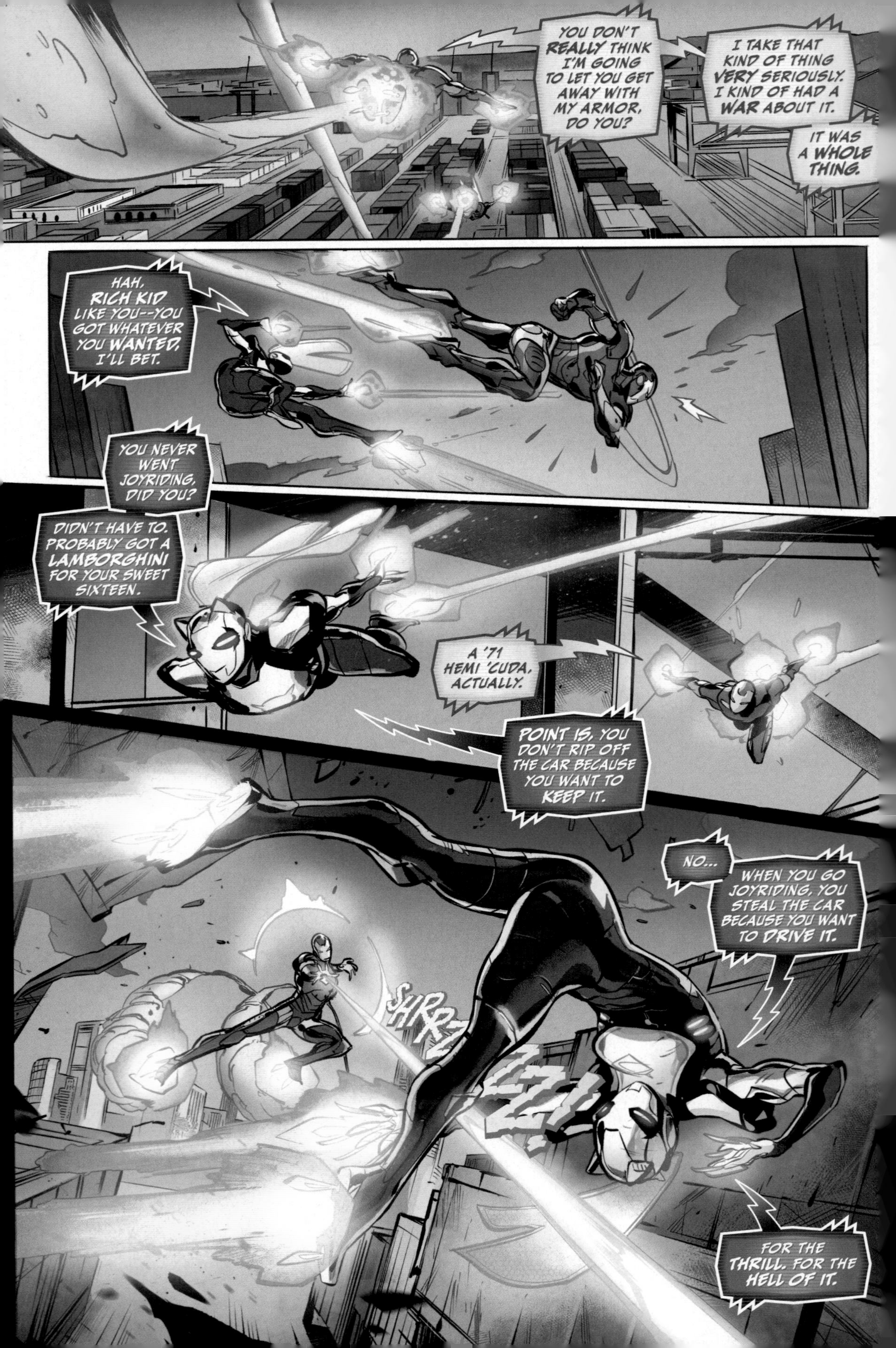
YOU DON'T REALLY THINK I'M GOING TO LET YOU GET AWAY WITH MY ARMOR, DO YOU?
I TAKE THAT KIND OF THING VERY SERIOUSLY. I KIND OF HAD A WAR ABOUT IT.
IT WAS A WHOLE THING.
HAH, RICH KID LIKE YOU--YOU GOT WHATEVER YOU WANTED, I'LL BET.
YOU NEVER WENT JOYRIDING, DID YOU?
DIDN'T HAVE TO. PROBABLY GOT A LAMBORGHINI FOR YOUR SWEET SIXTEEN.
A '71 HEMI 'CUDA, ACTUALLY.
POINT IS, YOU DON'T RIP OFF THE CAR BECAUSE YOU WANT TO KEEP IT.
NO...
WHEN YOU GO JOYRIDING, YOU STEAL THE CAR BECAUSE YOU WANT TO DRIVE IT.
SHRRZZZZ!
FOR THE THRILL. FOR THE HELL OF IT.

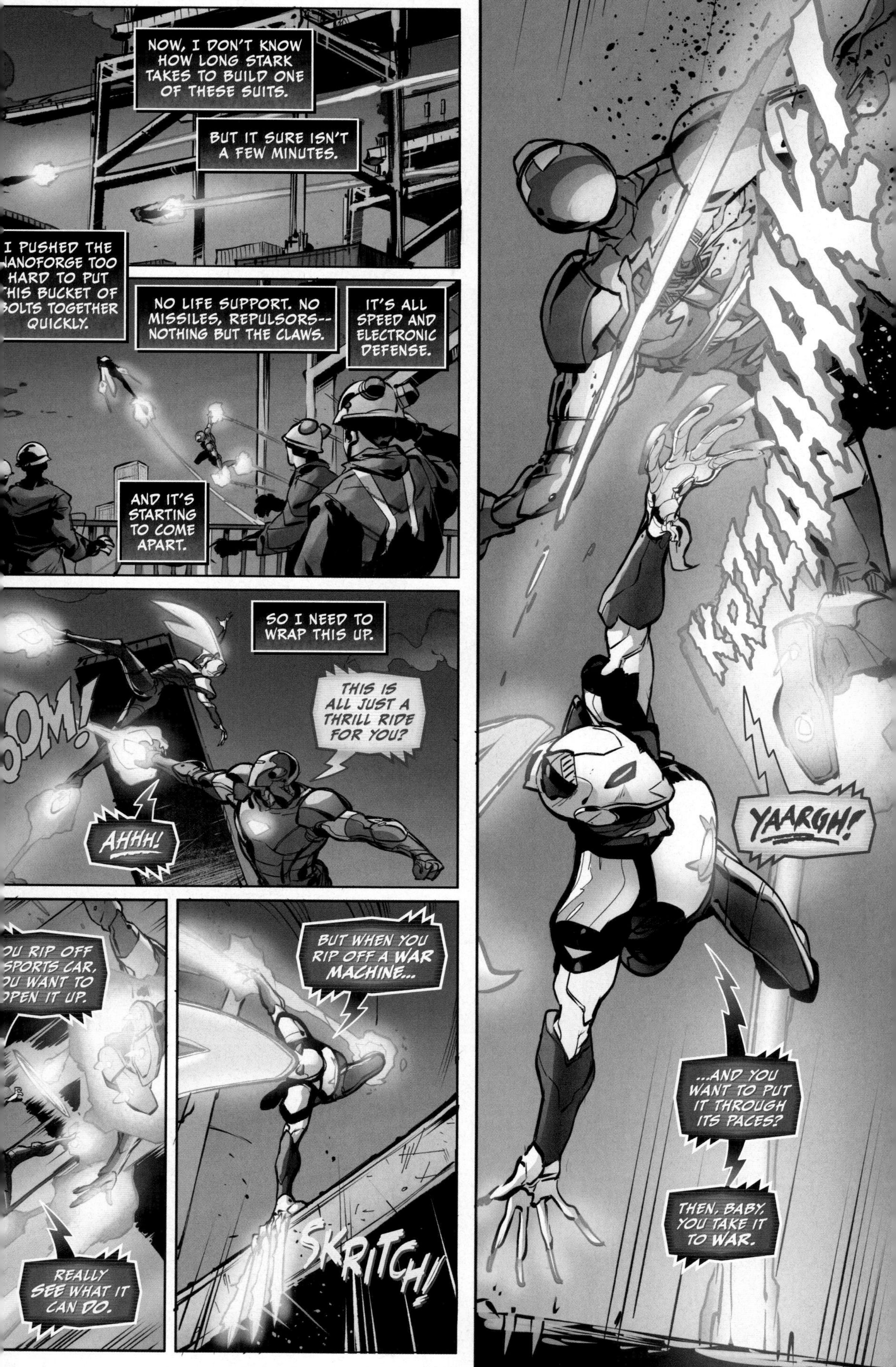
NOW, I DON'T KNOW HOW LONG STARK TAKES TO BUILD ONE OF THESE SUITS.
BUT IT SURE ISN'T A FEW MINUTES.
I PUSHED THE NANOFORGE TOO HARD TO PUT THIS BUCKET OF BOLTS TOGETHER QUICKLY.
NO LIFE SUPPORT. NO MISSILES, REPULSORS-- NOTHING BUT THE CLAWS.
IT'S ALL SPEED AND ELECTRONIC DEFENSE.
AND IT'S STARTING TO COME APART.
SO I NEED TO WRAP THIS UP.
THIS IS ALL JUST A THRILL RIDE FOR YOU?
AHHH!
YOU RIP OFF SPORTS CAR, YOU WANT TO OPEN IT UP.
REALLY SEE WHAT IT CAN DO.
BUT WHEN YOU RIP OFF A WAR MACHINE...
SKRITCH!
YAARGH!
...AND YOU WANT TO PUT IT THROUGH ITS PACES?
THEN, BABY, YOU TAKE IT TO WAR.

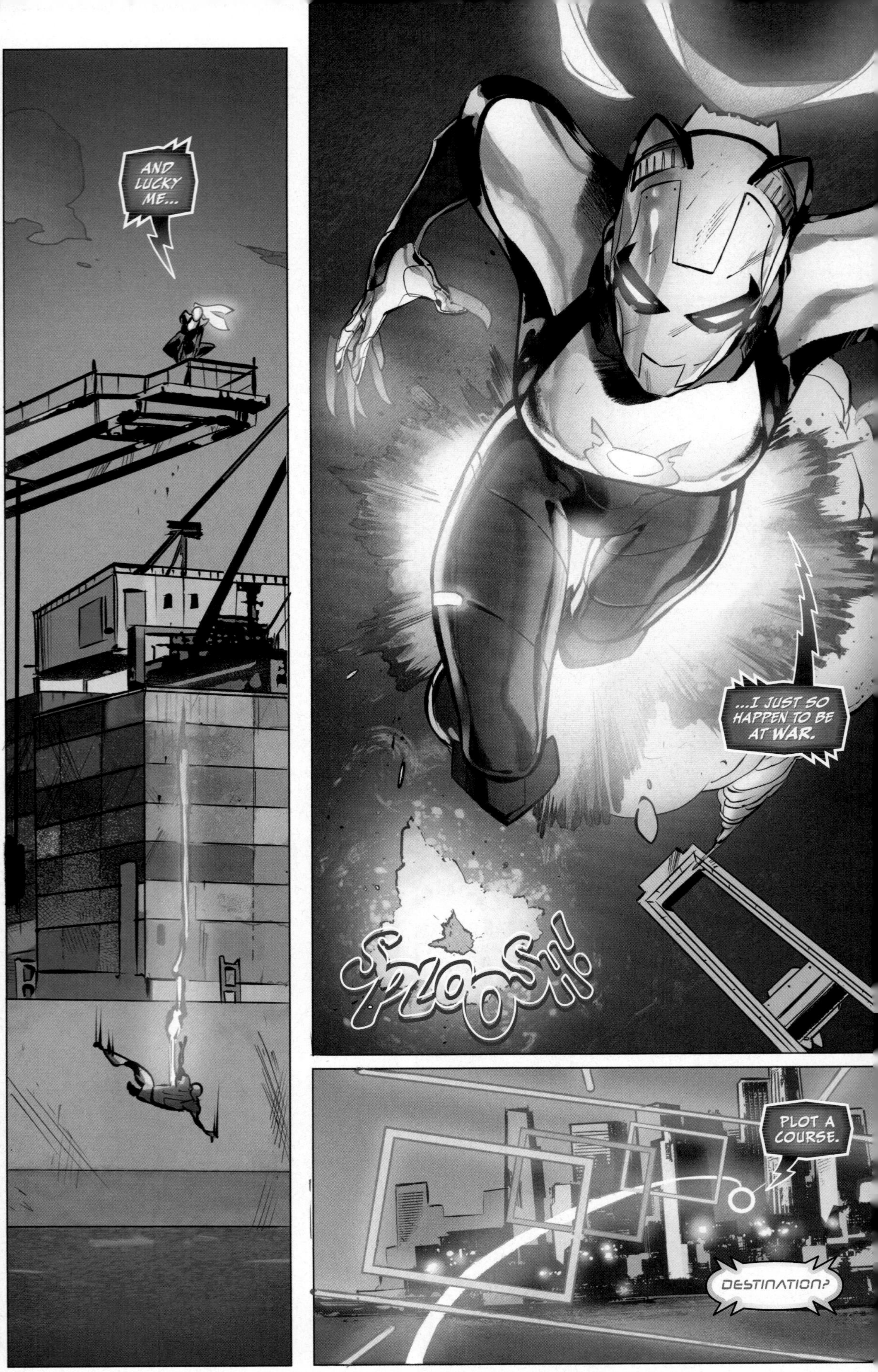
AND LUCKY ME...
...I JUST SO HAPPEN TO BE AT WAR.
SPLOOSH!!
PLOT A COURSE.
DESTINATION?

THE UPPER EAST SIDE.

RATTLERATTLERATTLERATTLE

WHAT--

Oh.

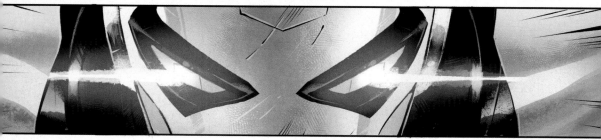

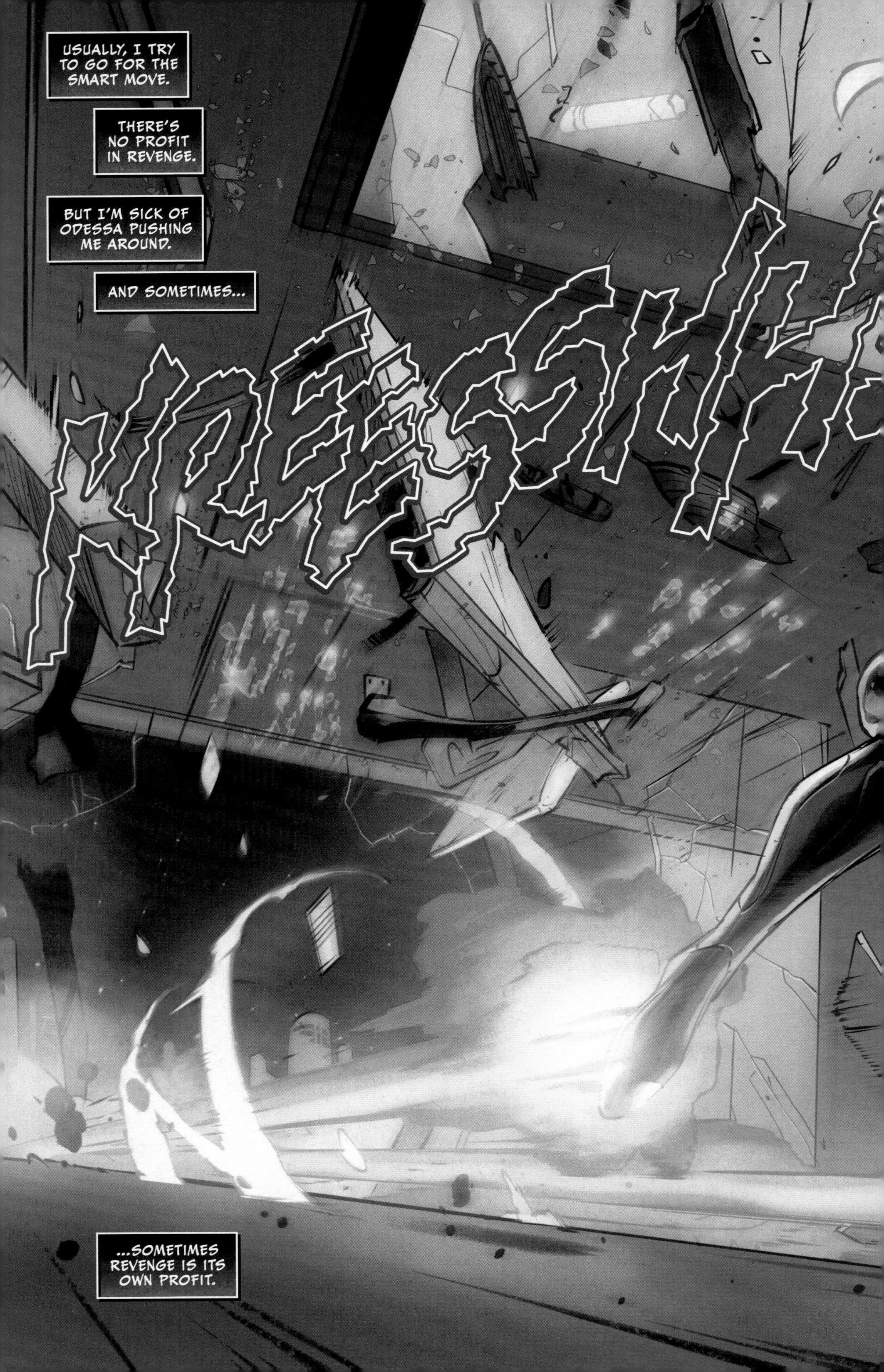
USUALLY, I TRY TO GO FOR THE SMART MOVE.
THERE'S NO PROFIT IN REVENGE.
BUT I'M SICK OF ODESSA PUSHING ME AROUND.
AND SOMETIMES...
...SOMETIMES REVENGE IS ITS OWN PROFIT.

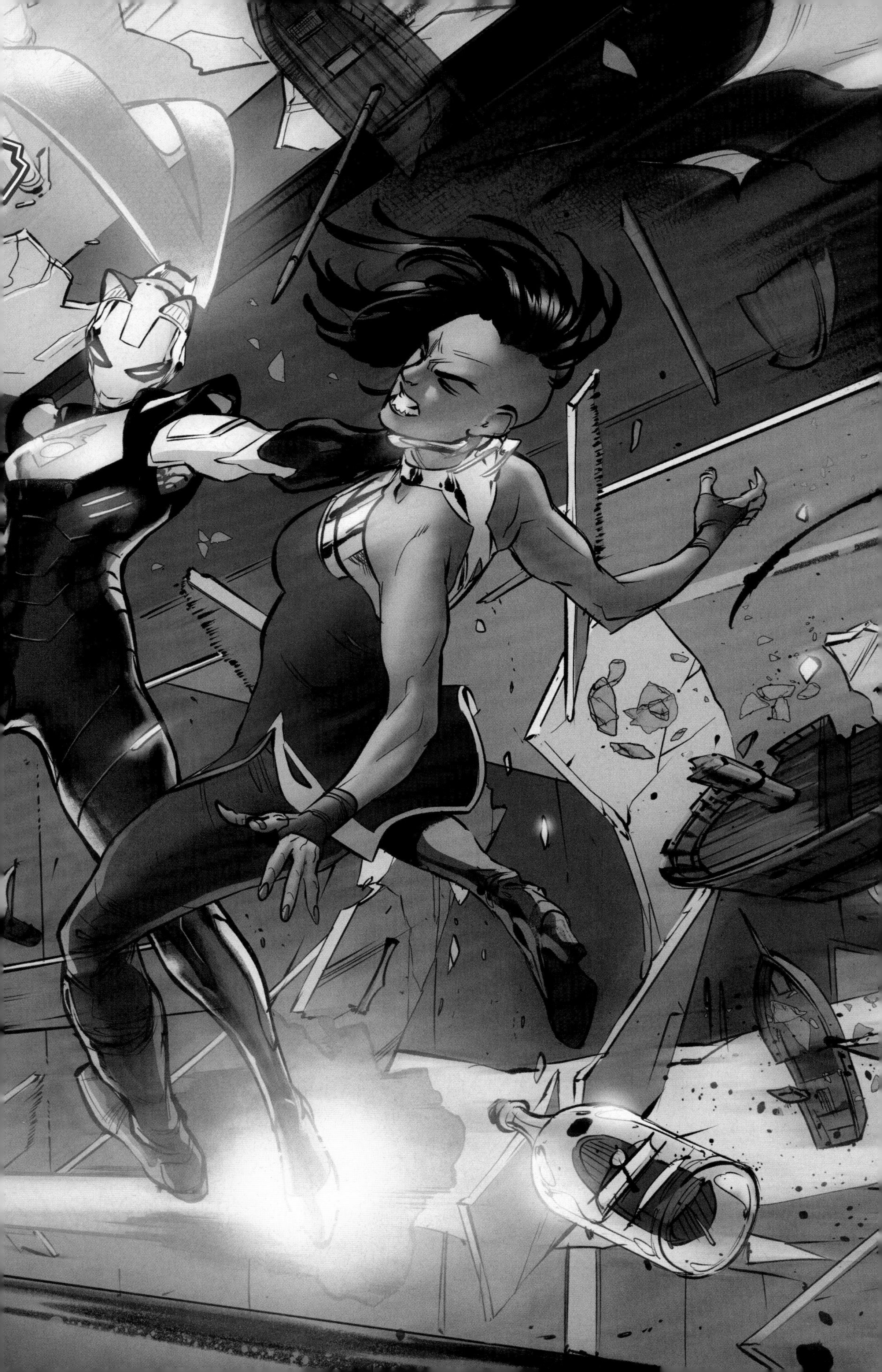

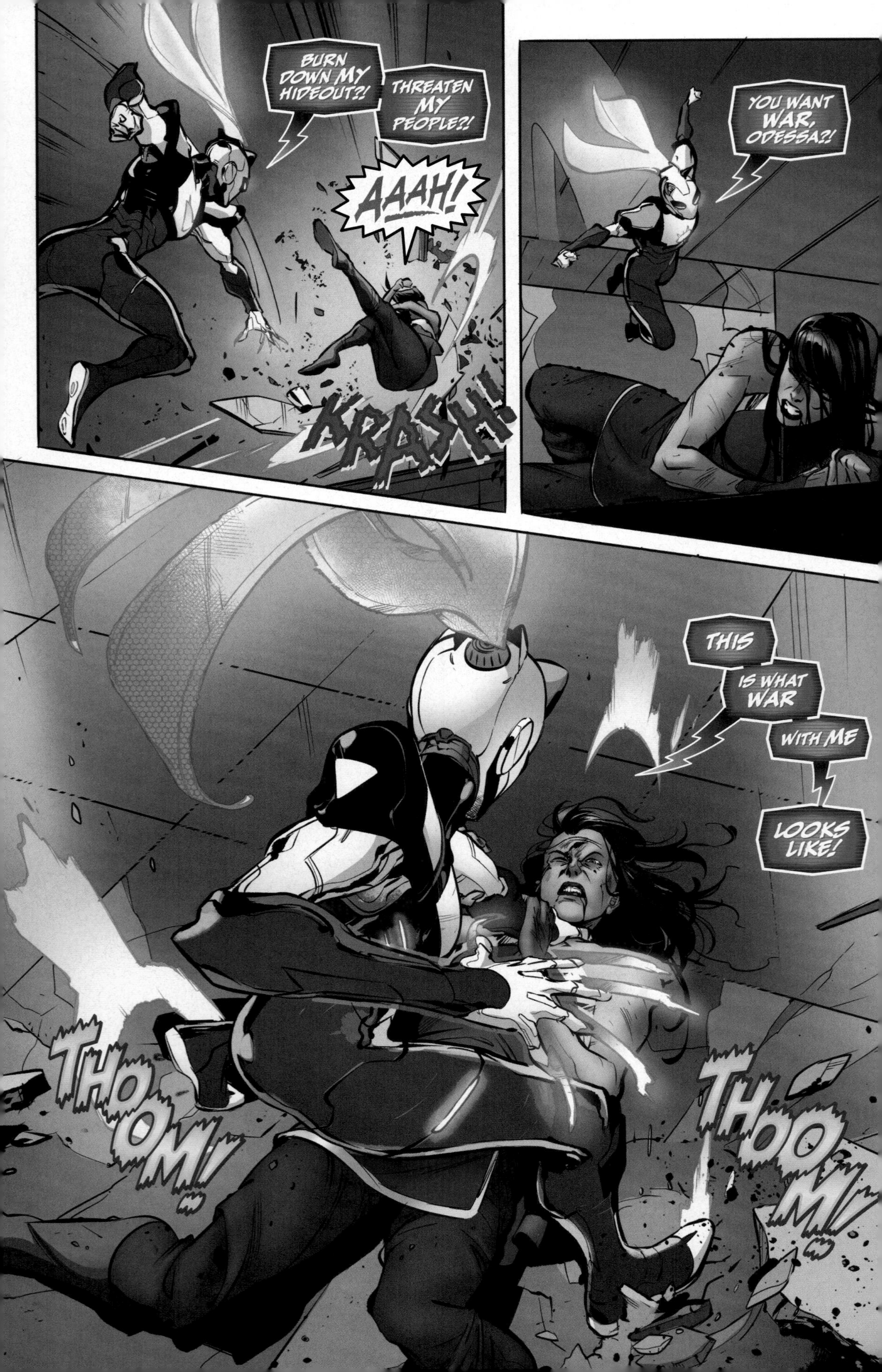
BURN DOWN MY HIDEOUT?!
THREATEN MY PEOPLE?!
AAAH!
KRASH!
YOU WANT WAR, ODESSA?!
THIS
IS WHAT WAR
WITH ME
LOOKS LIKE!
THOOM!
THOOM!

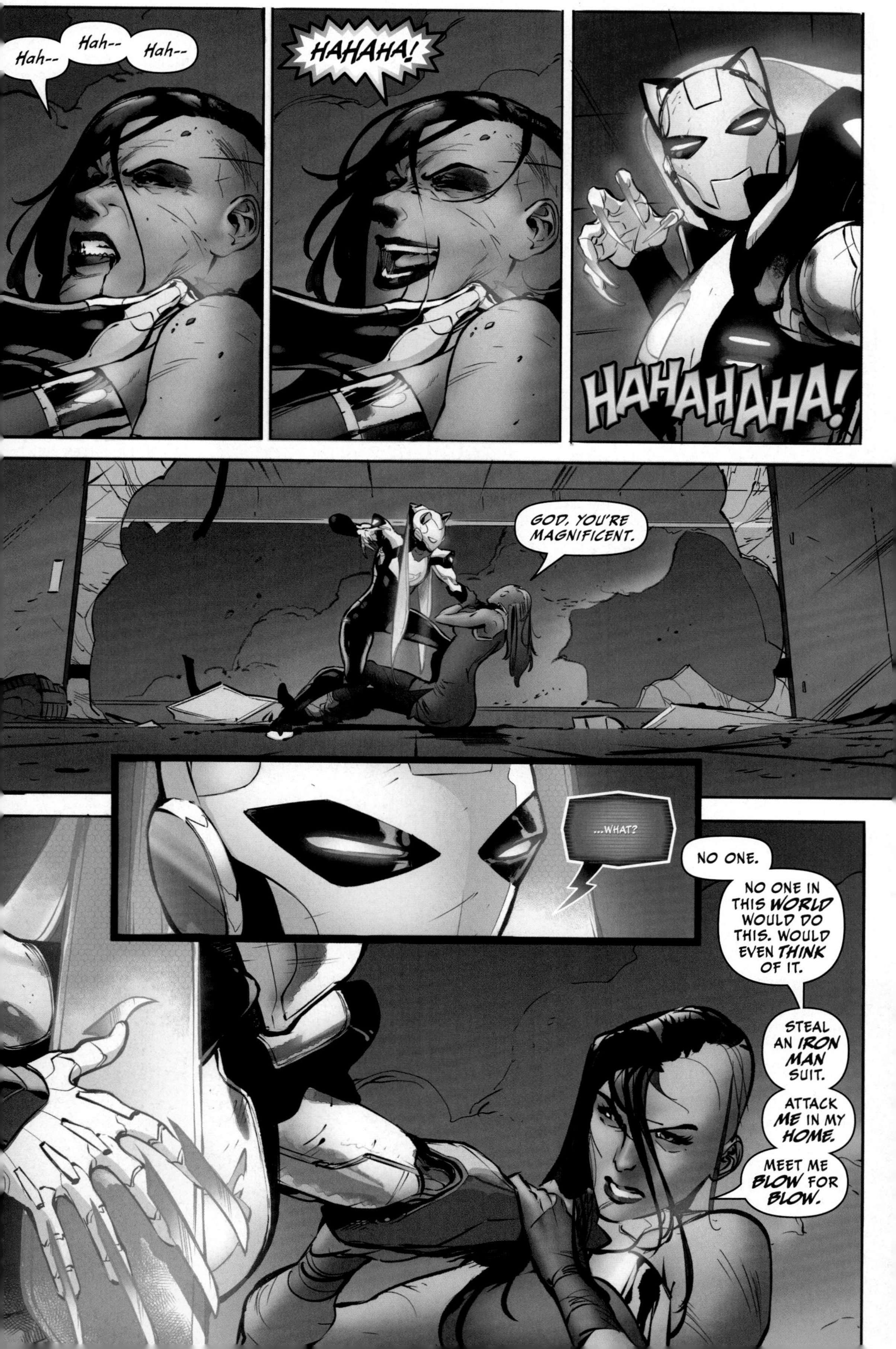

Hah--
Hah--
Hah--
HAHAHA!
HAHAHAHA!
GOD, YOU'RE MAGNIFICENT.
...WHAT?
NO ONE.
NO ONE IN THIS WORLD WOULD DO THIS. WOULD EVEN THINK OF IT.
STEAL AN IRON MAN SUIT.
ATTACK ME IN MY HOME.
MEET ME BLOW FOR BLOW.

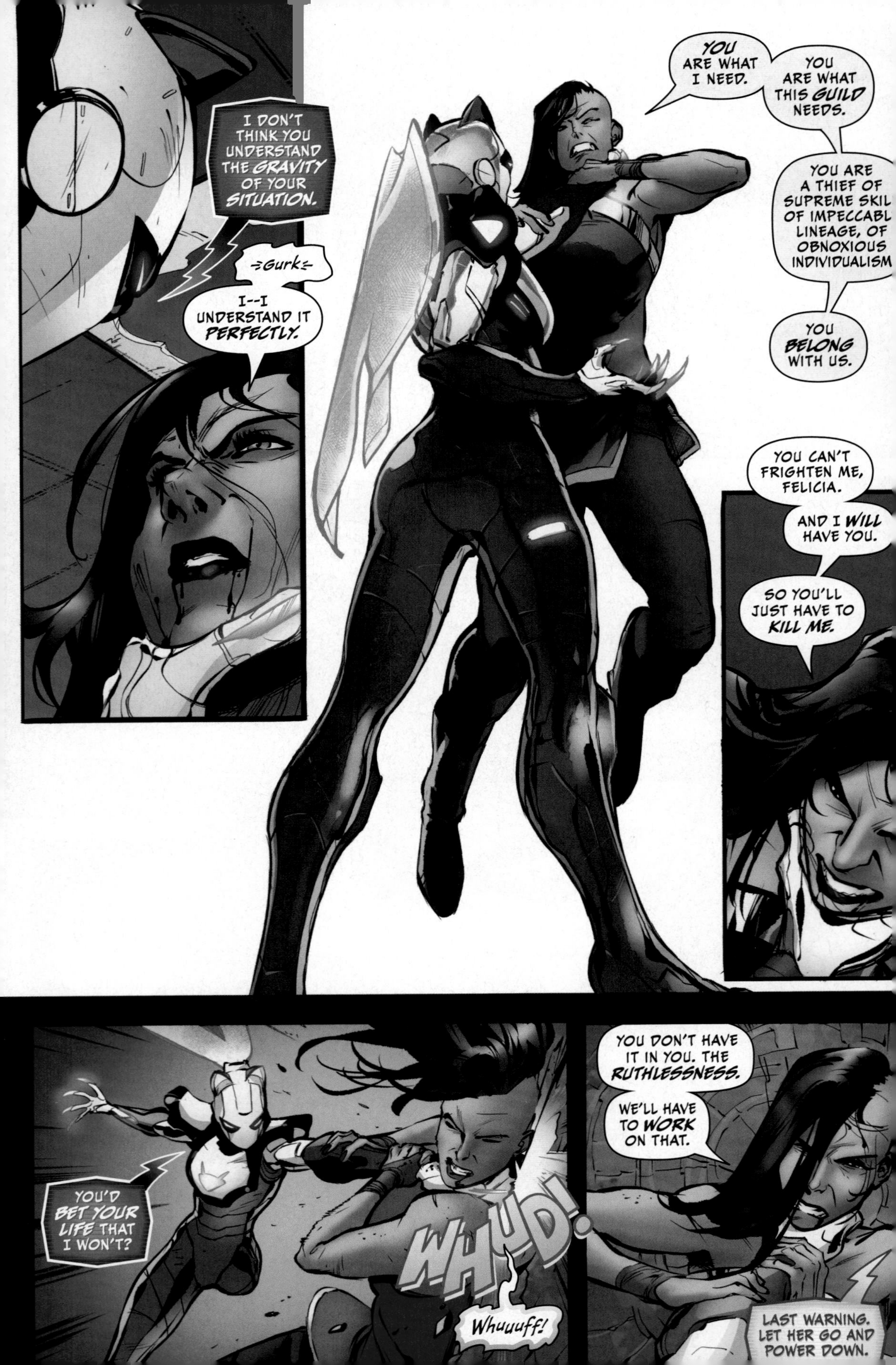
I DON'T THINK YOU UNDERSTAND THE GRAVITY OF YOUR SITUATION.
=Gurk=
I--I UNDERSTAND IT PERFECTLY.
YOU ARE WHAT I NEED.
YOU ARE WHAT THIS GUILD NEEDS.
YOU ARE A THIEF OF SUPREME SKIL OF IMPECCABL LINEAGE, OF OBNOXIOUS INDIVIDUALISM
YOU BELONG WITH US.
YOU CAN'T FRIGHTEN ME, FELICIA.
AND I WILL HAVE YOU.
SO YOU'LL JUST HAVE TO KILL ME.
YOU'D BET YOUR LIFE THAT I WON'T?
WHUD!
Whuuuff!
YOU DON'T HAVE IT IN YOU. THE RUTHLESSNESS.
WE'LL HAVE TO WORK ON THAT.
LAST WARNING. LET HER GO AND POWER DOWN.

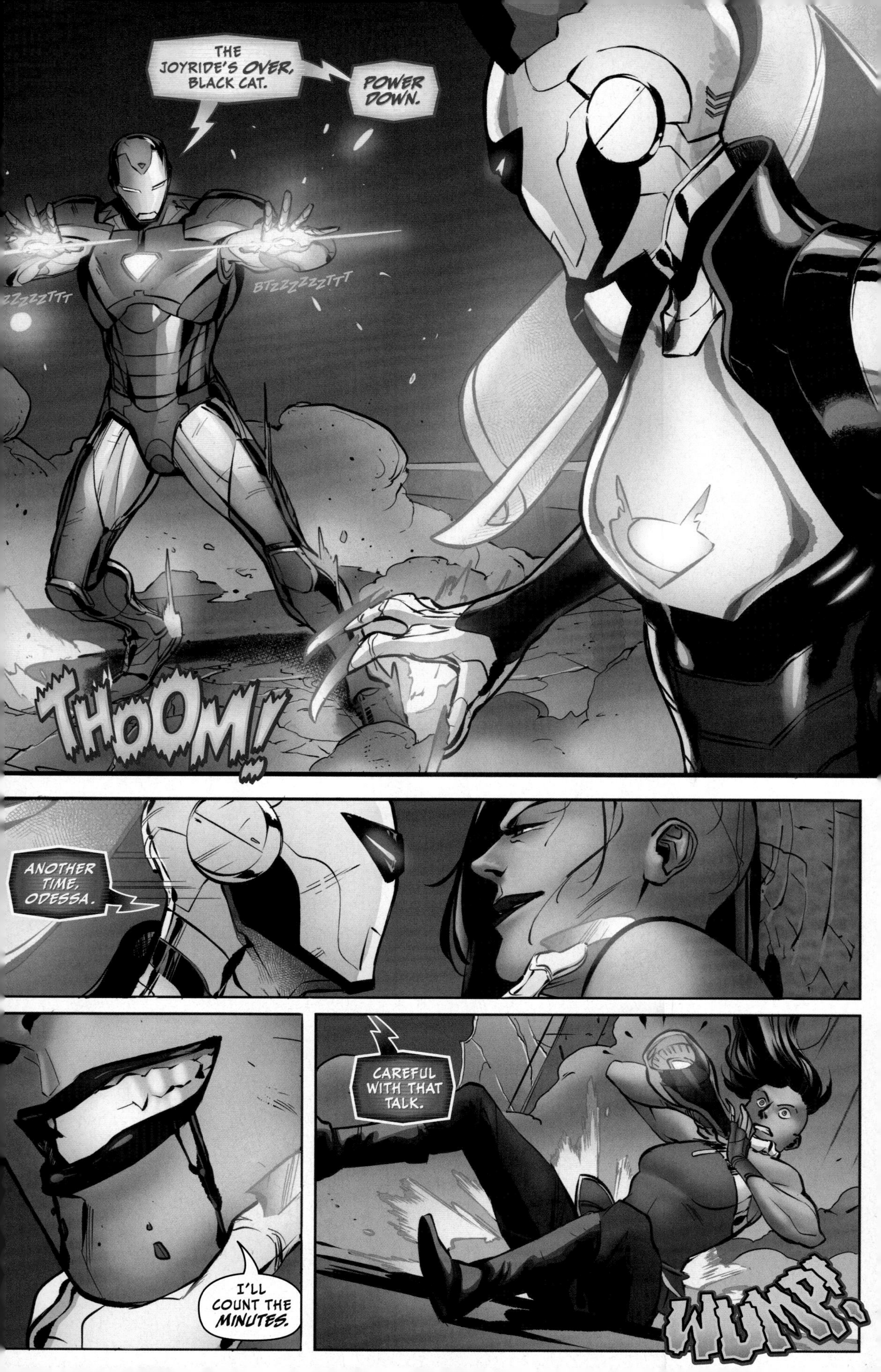
THE JOYRIDE'S OVER, BLACK CAT.
POWER DOWN.
ZZZZZTTTT
BTZZZZZZTTT
THOOM!
ANOTHER TIME, ODESSA.
I'LL COUNT THE MINUTES.
CAREFUL WITH THAT TALK.
WUMP!

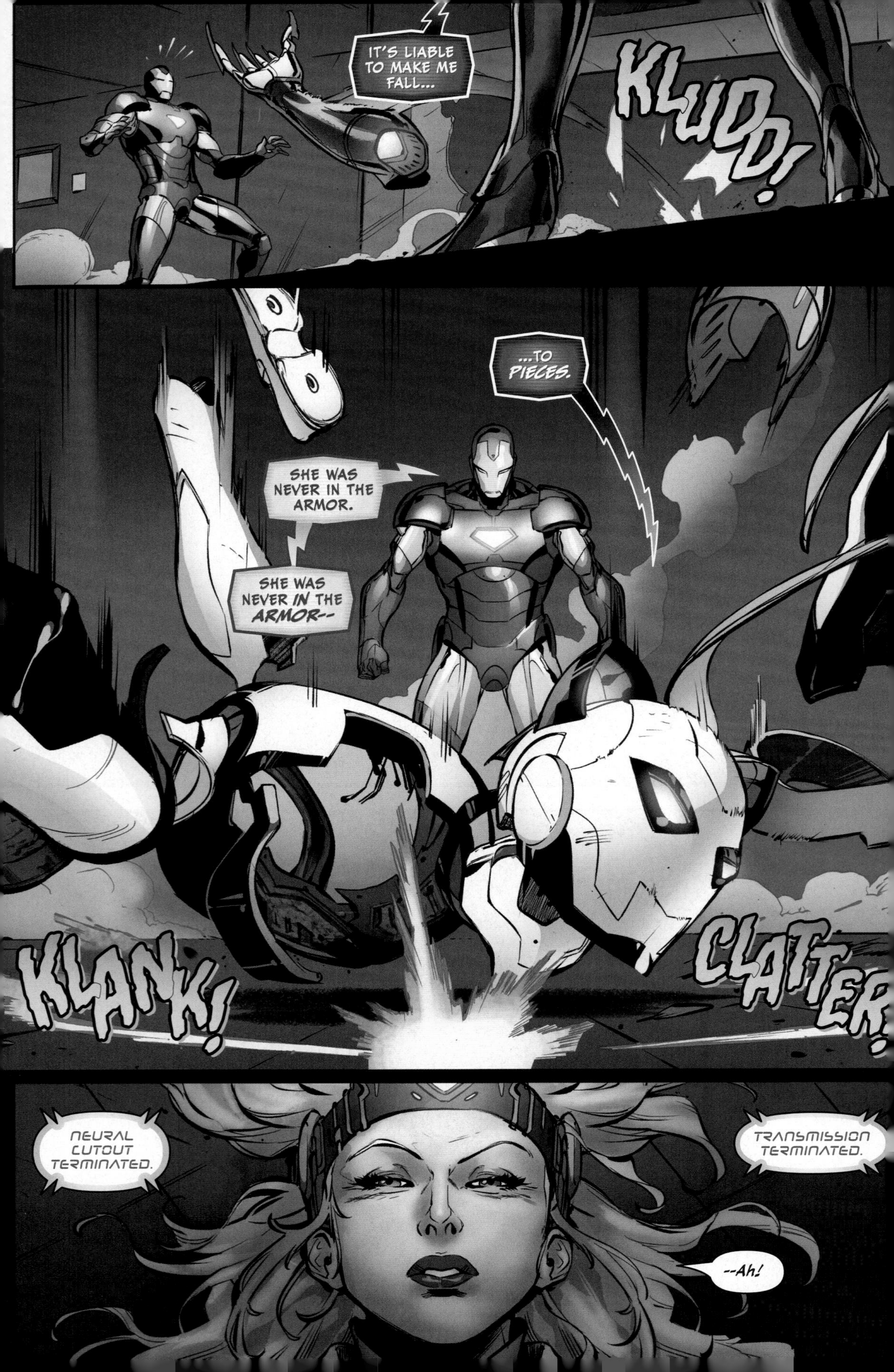
IT'S LIABLE TO MAKE ME FALL...
KLUDD!
...TO PIECES.
SHE WAS NEVER IN THE ARMOR.
SHE WAS NEVER IN THE ARMOR--
KLANK!
CLATTER!
NEURAL CUTOUT TERMINATED.
TRANSMISSION TERMINATED.
--Ah!

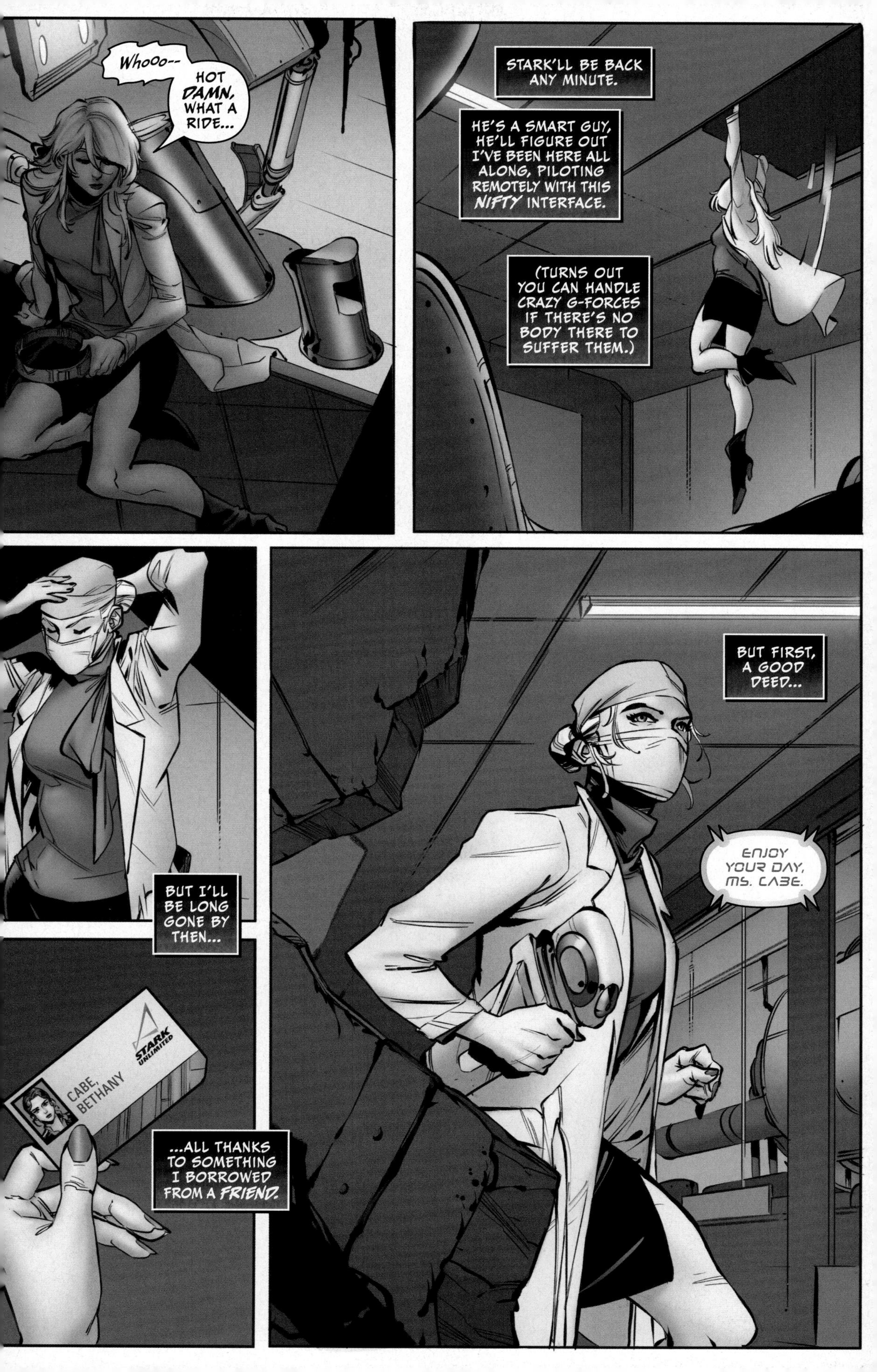
Whooo--
HOT DAMN, WHAT A RIDE...
STARK'LL BE BACK ANY MINUTE.
HE'S A SMART GUY, HE'LL FIGURE OUT I'VE BEEN HERE ALL ALONG, PILOTING REMOTELY WITH THIS NIFTY INTERFACE.
(TURNS OUT YOU CAN HANDLE CRAZY G-FORCES IF THERE'S NO BODY THERE TO SUFFER THEM.)
BUT I'LL BE LONG GONE BY THEN...
STARK UNLIMITED
CABE, BETHANY
...ALL THANKS TO SOMETHING I BORROWED FROM A FRIEND.
BUT FIRST, A GOOD DEED...
ENJOY YOUR DAY, MS. CABE.

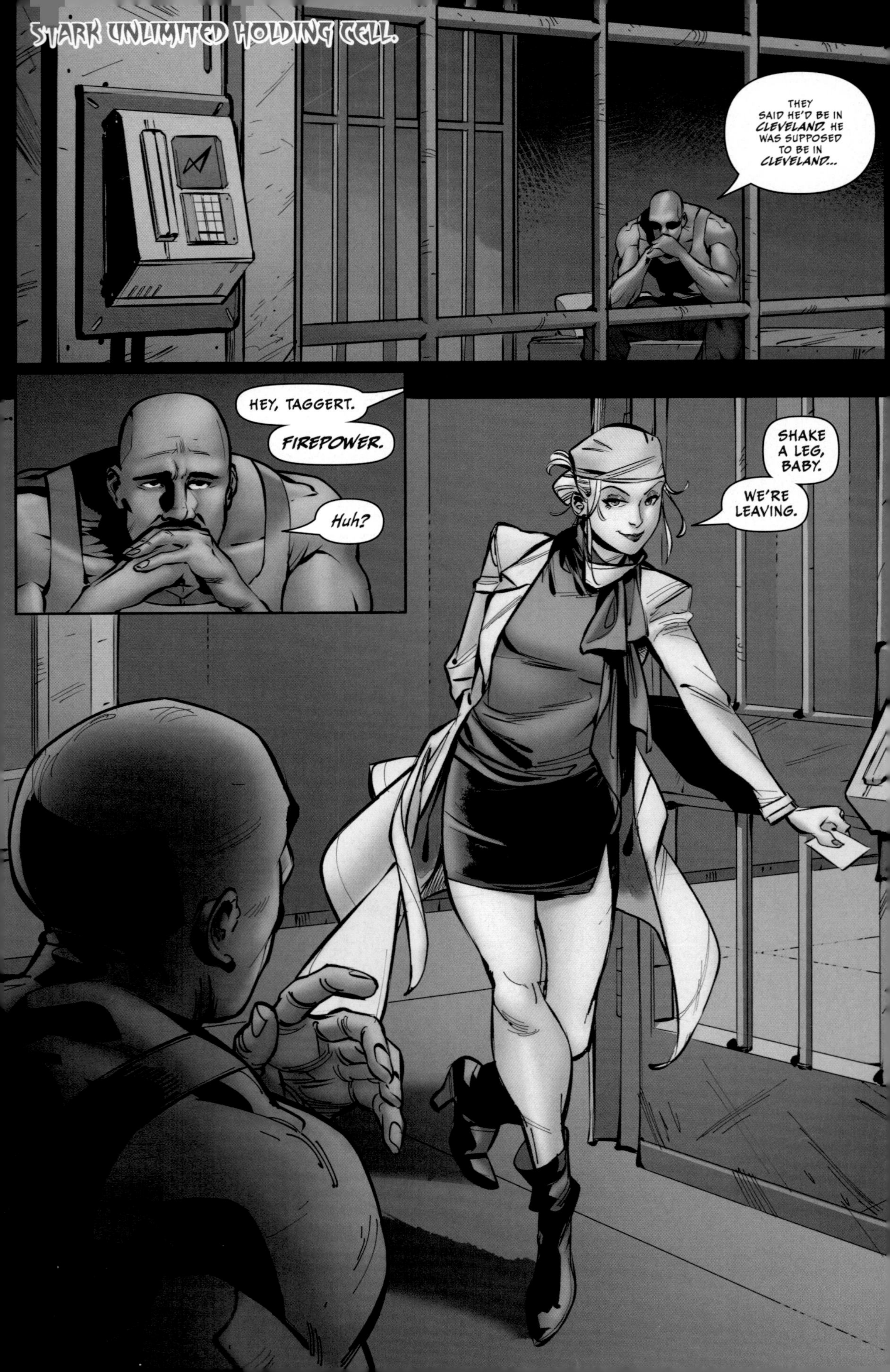
STARK UNLIMITED HOLDING CELL.
THEY SAID HE'D BE IN CLEVELAND. HE WAS SUPPOSED TO BE IN CLEVELAND...
HEY, TAGGERT.
FIREPOWER.
Huh?
SHAKE A LEG, BABY.
WE'RE LEAVING.

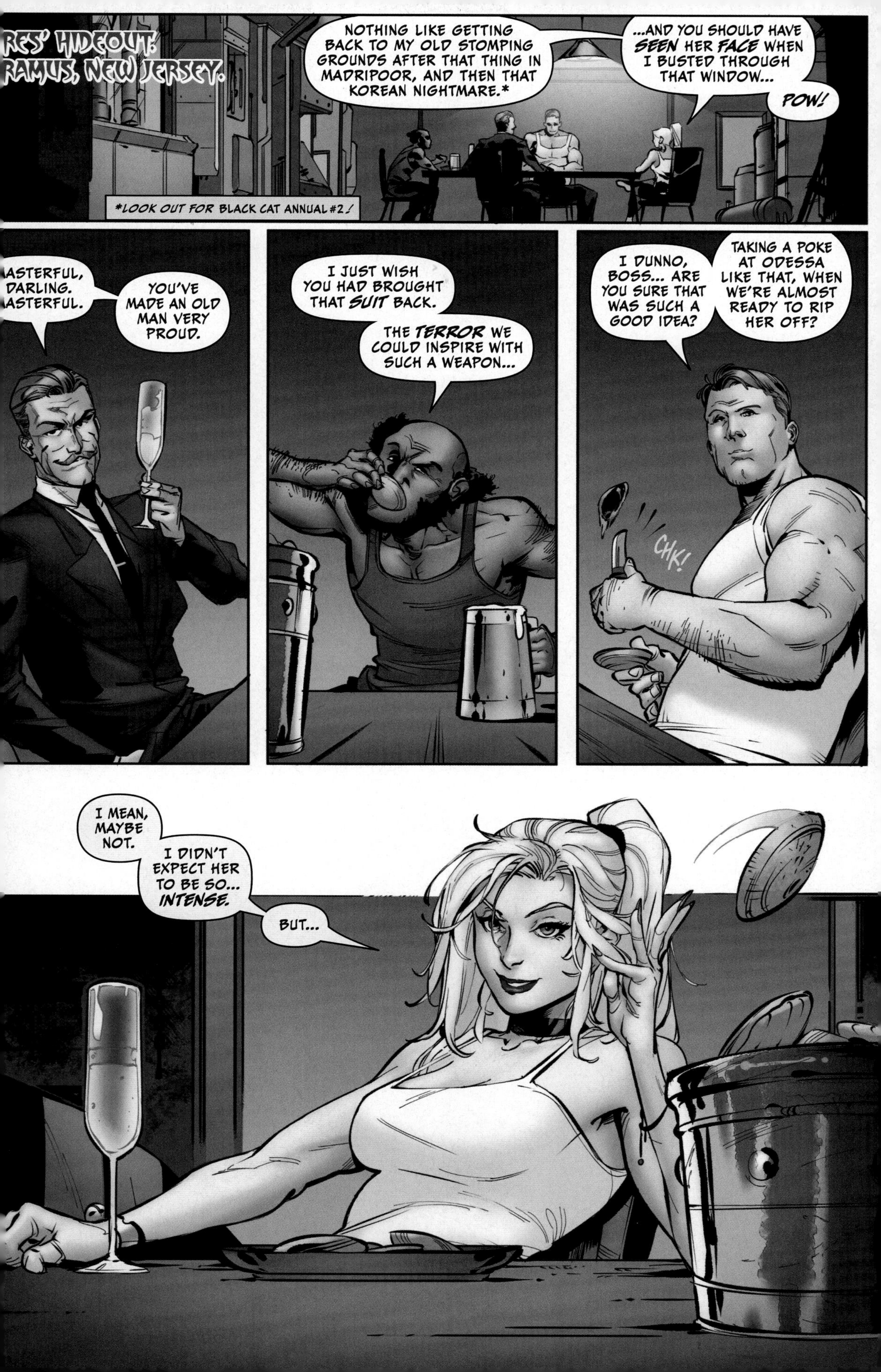
RES' HIDEOUT: RAMUS, NEW JERSEY.
NOTHING LIKE GETTING BACK TO MY OLD STOMPING GROUNDS AFTER THAT THING IN MADRIPOOR, AND THEN THAT KOREAN NIGHTMARE.*
...AND YOU SHOULD HAVE SEEN HER FACE WHEN I BUSTED THROUGH THAT WINDOW...
POW!
*LOOK OUT FOR BLACK CAT ANNUAL #2!
MASTERFUL, DARLING. MASTERFUL.
YOU'VE MADE AN OLD MAN VERY PROUD.
I JUST WISH YOU HAD BROUGHT THAT SUIT BACK.
THE TERROR WE COULD INSPIRE WITH SUCH A WEAPON...
I DUNNO, BOSS... ARE YOU SURE THAT WAS SUCH A GOOD IDEA?
TAKING A POKE AT ODESSA LIKE THAT, WHEN WE'RE ALMOST READY TO RIP HER OFF?
CHK!
I MEAN, MAYBE NOT.
I DIDN'T EXPECT HER TO BE SO... INTENSE.
BUT...

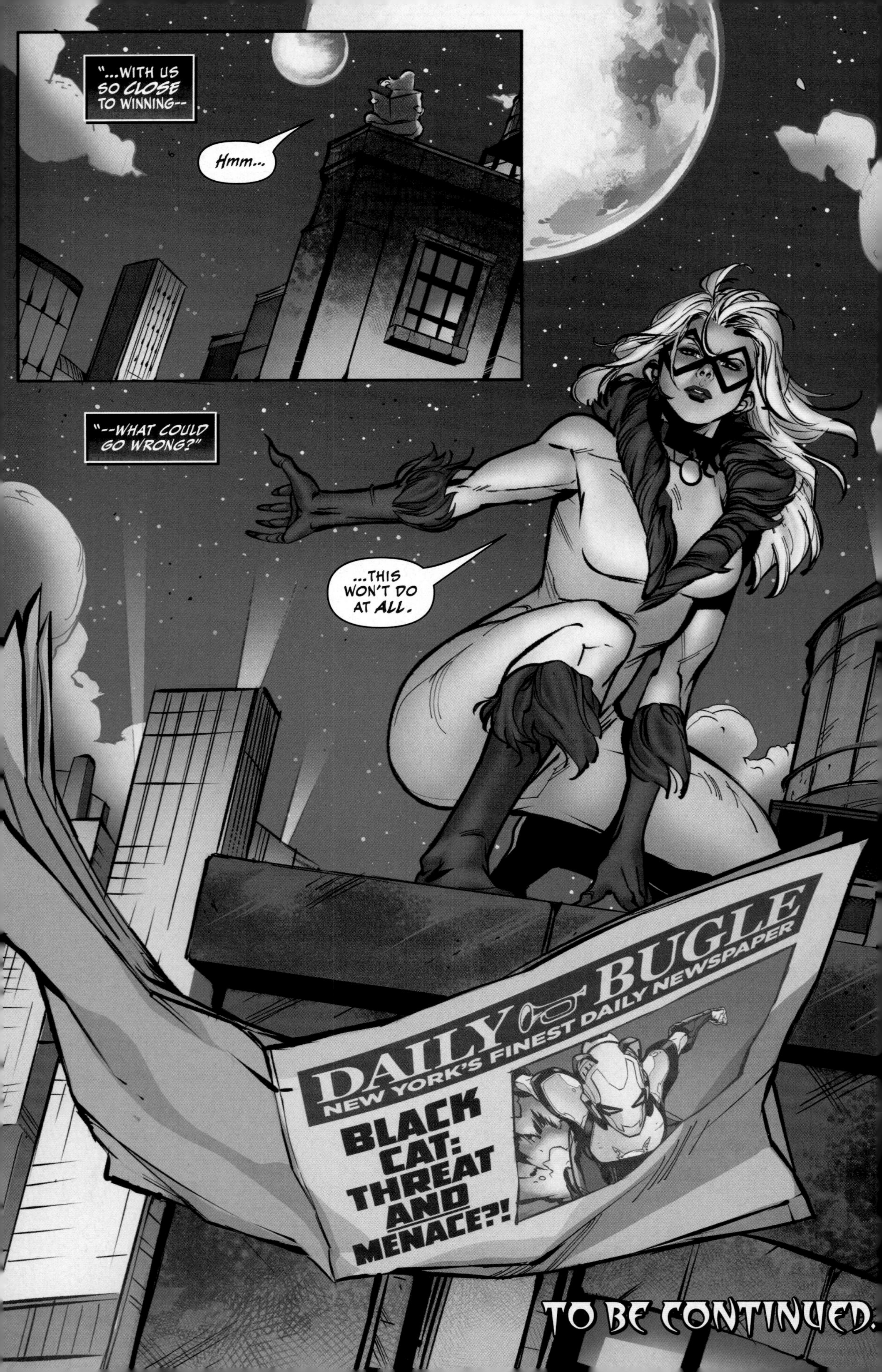
"...WITH US SO CLOSE TO WINNING--
Hmm...
"--WHAT COULD GO WRONG?"
...THIS WON'T DO AT ALL.
DAILY BUGLE
NEW YORK'S FINEST DAILY NEWSPAPER
BLACK CAT: THREAT AND MENACE?!
TO BE CONTINUED.

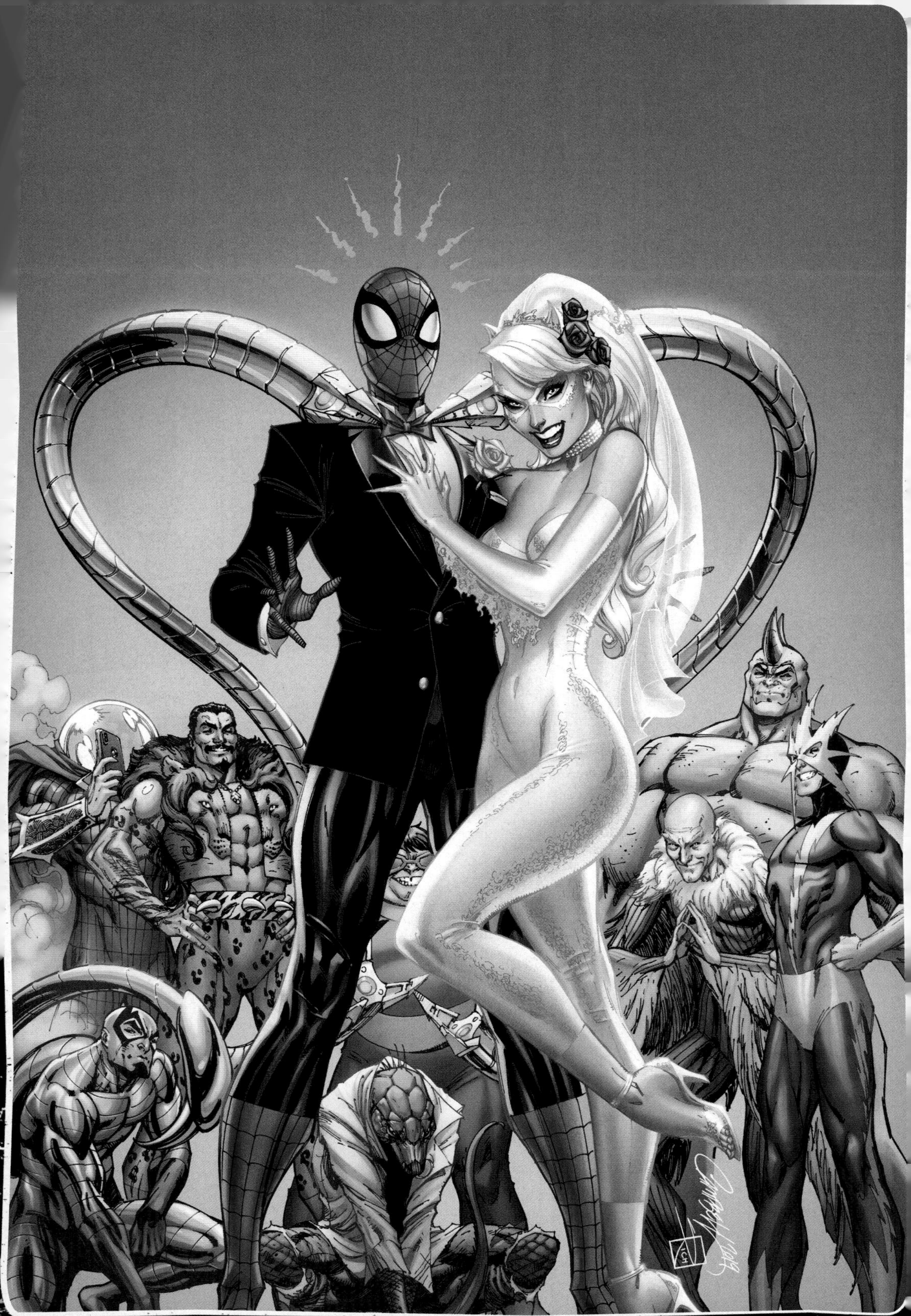

BLACK CAT ANNUAL 1

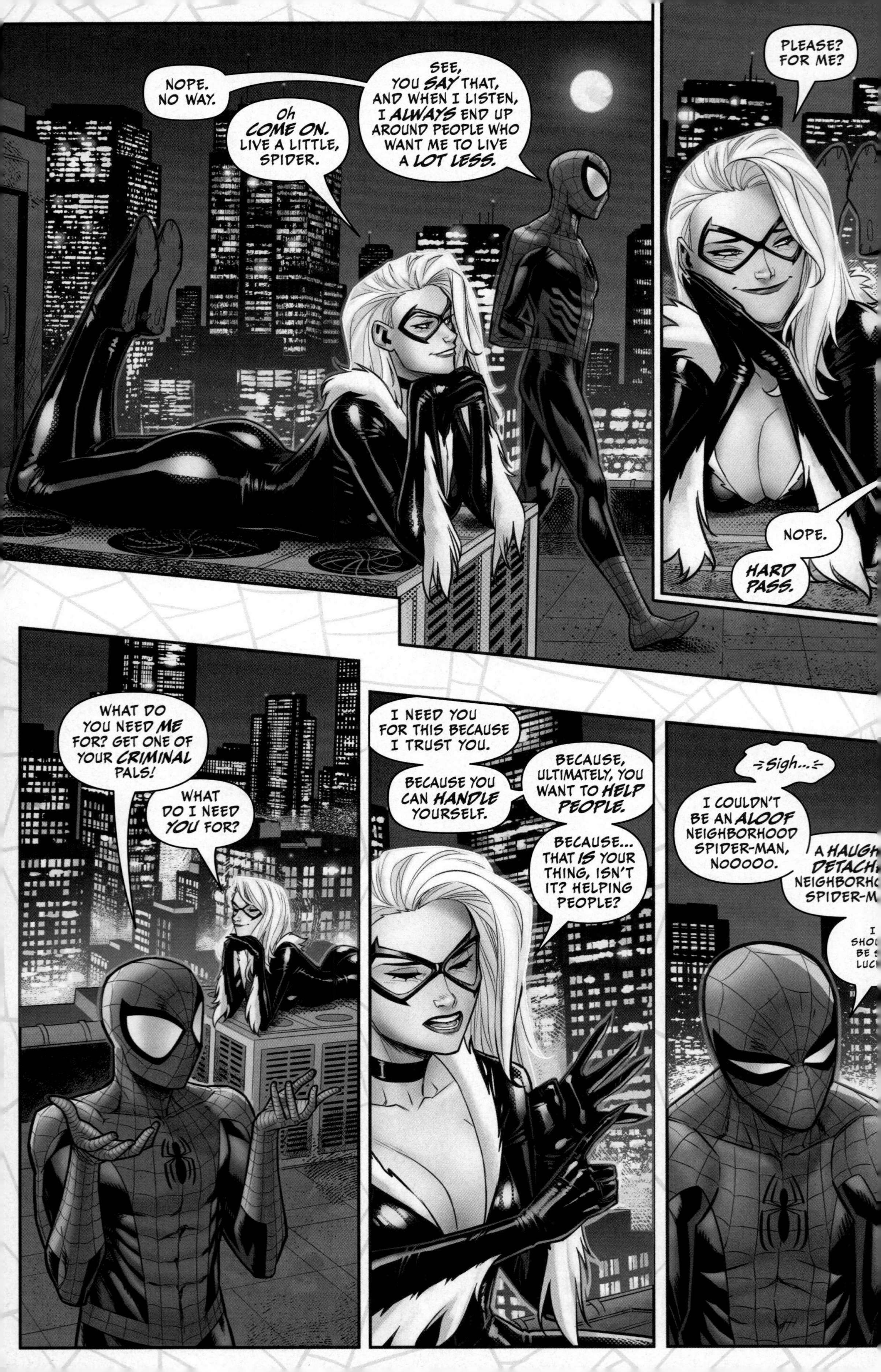
NOPE. NO WAY.
Oh *COME ON.* LIVE A LITTLE, SPIDER.
SEE, YOU *SAY* THAT, AND WHEN I LISTEN, I *ALWAYS* END UP AROUND PEOPLE WHO WANT ME TO LIVE A *LOT LESS.*
PLEASE? FOR ME?
NOPE.
HARD PASS.
WHAT DO YOU NEED *ME* FOR? GET ONE OF YOUR *CRIMINAL* PALS!
WHAT DO I NEED *YOU* FOR?
I NEED YOU FOR THIS BECAUSE I TRUST YOU.
BECAUSE YOU CAN *HANDLE* YOURSELF.
BECAUSE, ULTIMATELY, YOU WANT TO *HELP PEOPLE.*
BECAUSE... THAT *IS* YOUR THING, ISN'T IT? HELPING PEOPLE?
Sigh...
I COULDN'T BE AN *ALOOF* NEIGHBORHOOD SPIDER-MAN, NOOOOO.
A *HAUGH* *DETACH* NEIGHBORHO SPIDER-M
I SHOU BE S LUCK

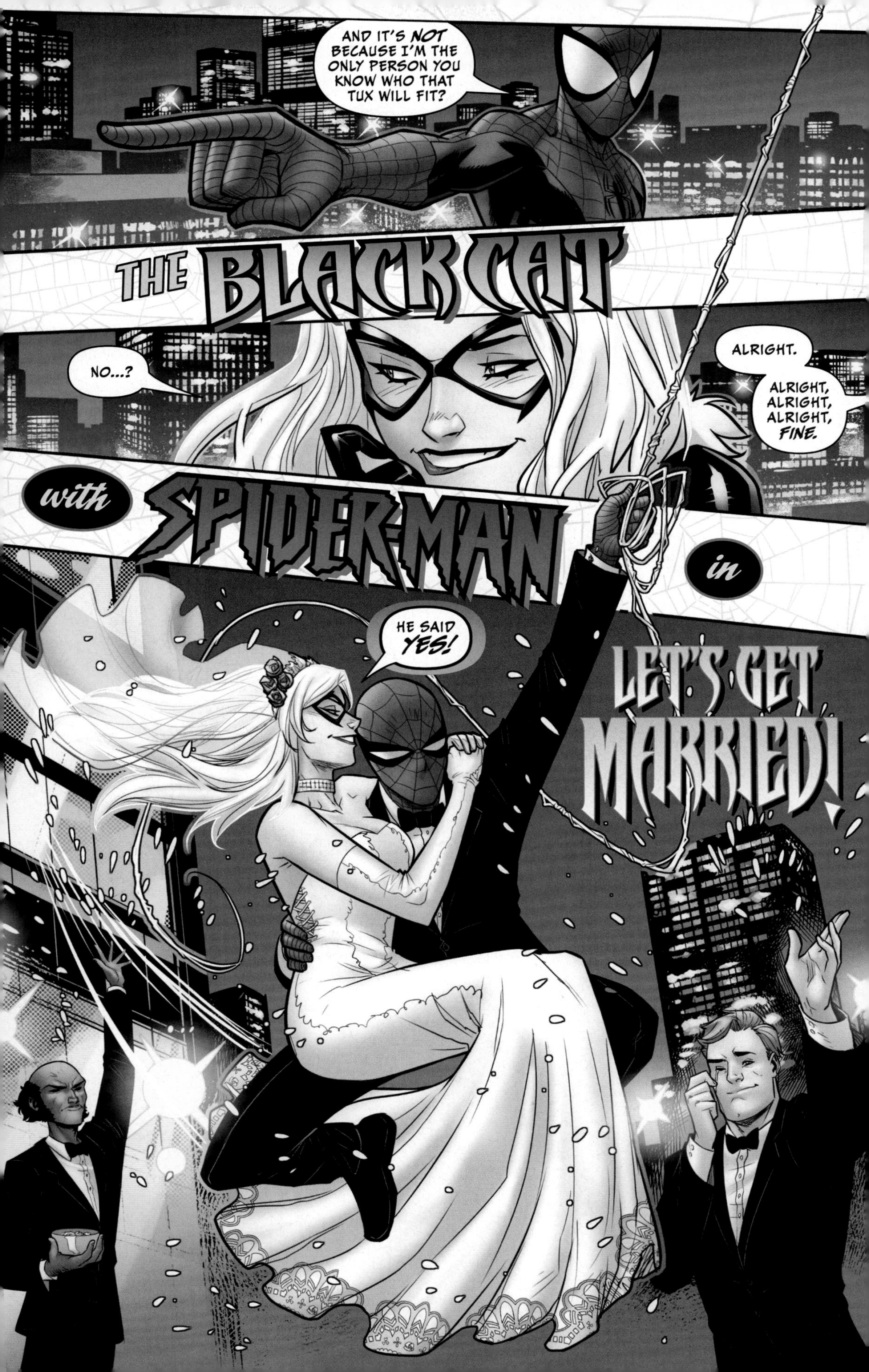
AND IT'S NOT BECAUSE I'M THE ONLY PERSON YOU KNOW WHO THAT TUX WILL FIT?
THE BLACK CAT
NO...?
ALRIGHT.
ALRIGHT, ALRIGHT, ALRIGHT, FINE.
with SPIDER-MAN in
HE SAID YES!
LET'S GET MARRIED!

MARVEL COMICS proudly requests the honor of your presence at the wedding of their daughter and son,

Felicia Sara Hardy,
A.K.A. **Black Cat**

and

Peter Benjamin Parker,
A.K.A. *Spider-Man*

On this day, **Wednesday, November thirteenth,**
in the year two thousand nineteen

At a location to be revealed within the pages of this comic book.
The bride and groom will be accompanied by their wedding party:

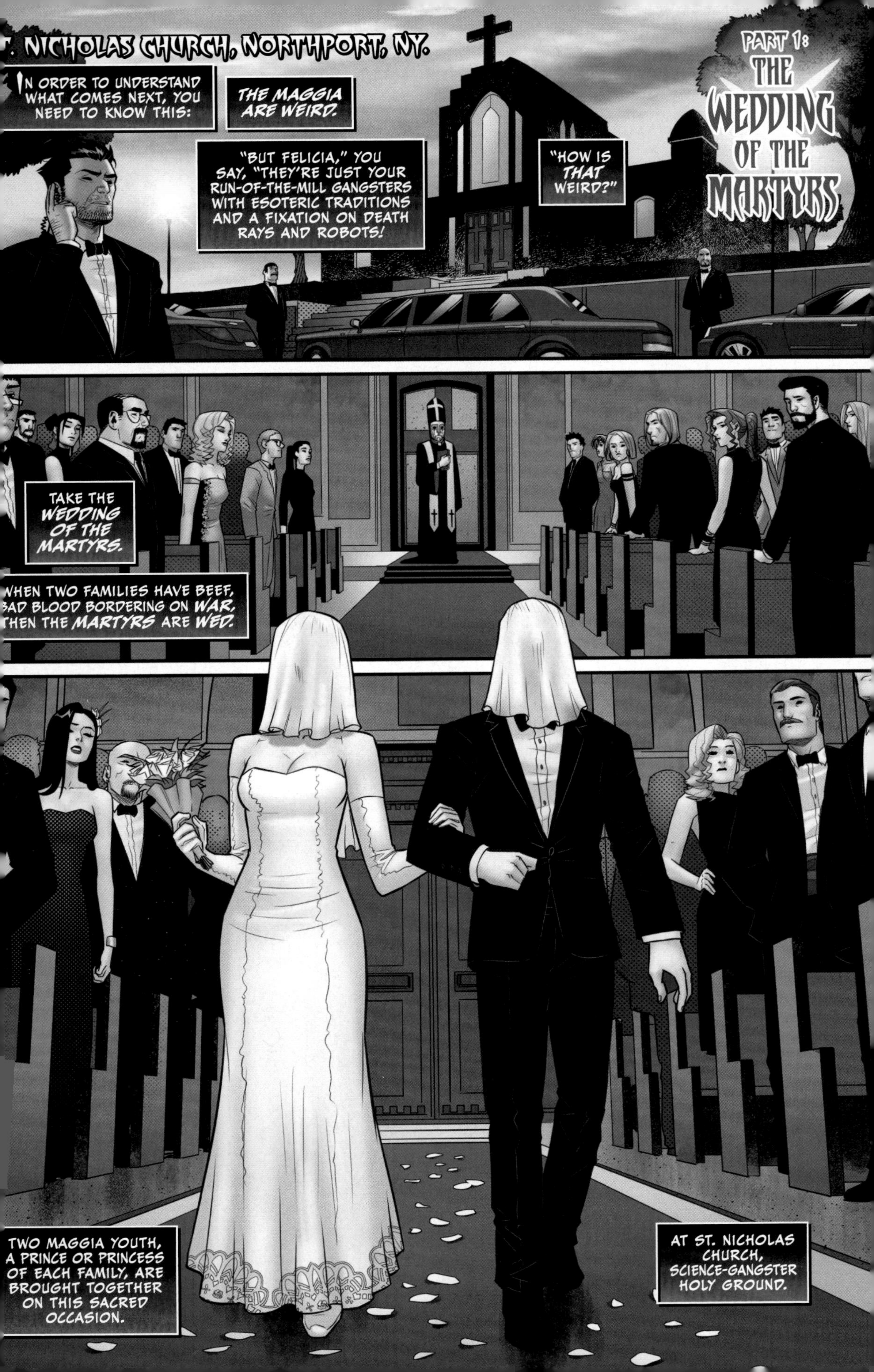

ST. NICHOLAS CHURCH, NORTHPORT, NY.
PART 1: THE WEDDING OF THE MARTYRS
IN ORDER TO UNDERSTAND WHAT COMES NEXT, YOU NEED TO KNOW THIS:
THE MAGGIA ARE WEIRD.
"BUT FELICIA," YOU SAY, "THEY'RE JUST YOUR RUN-OF-THE-MILL GANGSTERS WITH ESOTERIC TRADITIONS AND A FIXATION ON DEATH RAYS AND ROBOTS!
"HOW IS THAT WEIRD?"
TAKE THE WEDDING OF THE MARTYRS.
WHEN TWO FAMILIES HAVE BEEF, BAD BLOOD BORDERING ON WAR, THEN THE MARTYRS ARE WED.
TWO MAGGIA YOUTH, A PRINCE OR PRINCESS OF EACH FAMILY, ARE BROUGHT TOGETHER ON THIS SACRED OCCASION.
AT ST. NICHOLAS CHURCH, SCIENCE-GANGSTER HOLY GROUND.

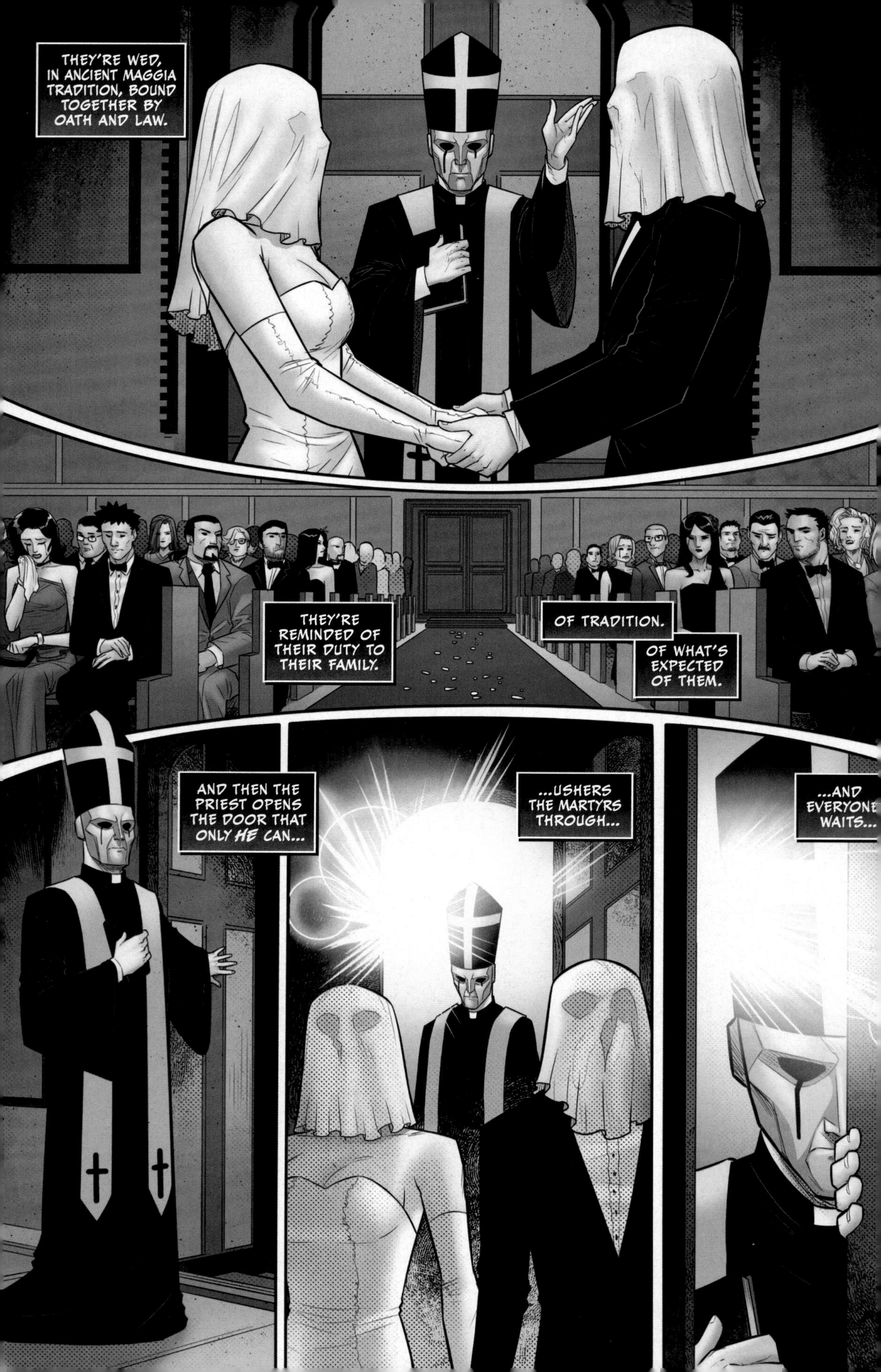
THEY'RE WED, IN ANCIENT MAGGIA TRADITION, BOUND TOGETHER BY OATH AND LAW.
THEY'RE REMINDED OF THEIR DUTY TO THEIR FAMILY.
OF TRADITION.
OF WHAT'S EXPECTED OF THEM.
AND THEN THE PRIEST OPENS THE DOOR THAT ONLY *HE* CAN...
...USHERS THE MARTYRS THROUGH...
...AND EVERYONE WAITS...

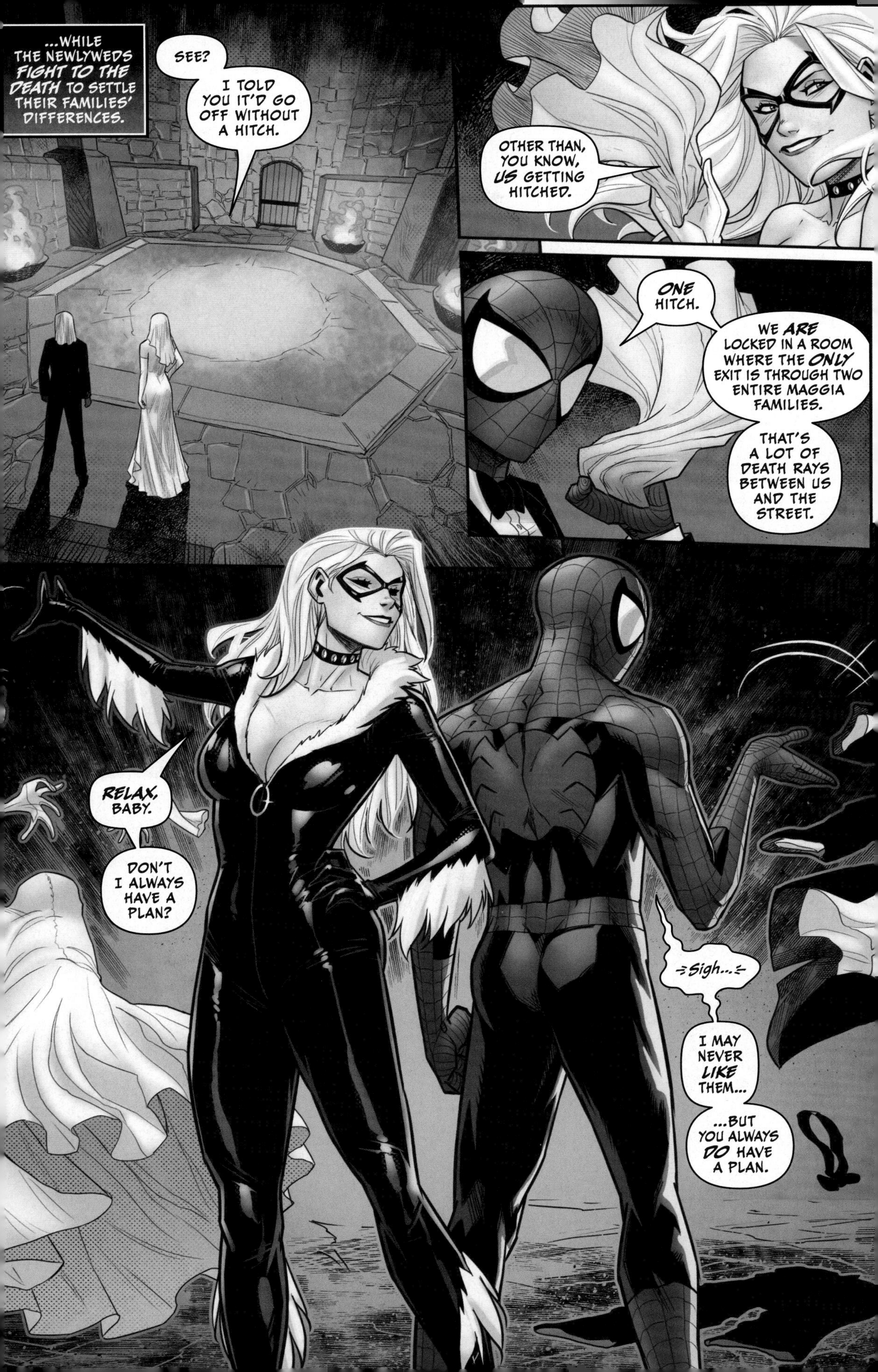
...WHILE THE NEWLYWEDS FIGHT TO THE DEATH TO SETTLE THEIR FAMILIES' DIFFERENCES.
SEE?
I TOLD YOU IT'D GO OFF WITHOUT A HITCH.
OTHER THAN, YOU KNOW, US GETTING HITCHED.
ONE HITCH.
WE ARE LOCKED IN A ROOM WHERE THE ONLY EXIT IS THROUGH TWO ENTIRE MAGGIA FAMILIES.
THAT'S A LOT OF DEATH RAYS BETWEEN US AND THE STREET.
RELAX, BABY.
DON'T I ALWAYS HAVE A PLAN?
Sigh...
I MAY NEVER LIKE THEM...
...BUT YOU ALWAYS DO HAVE A PLAN.

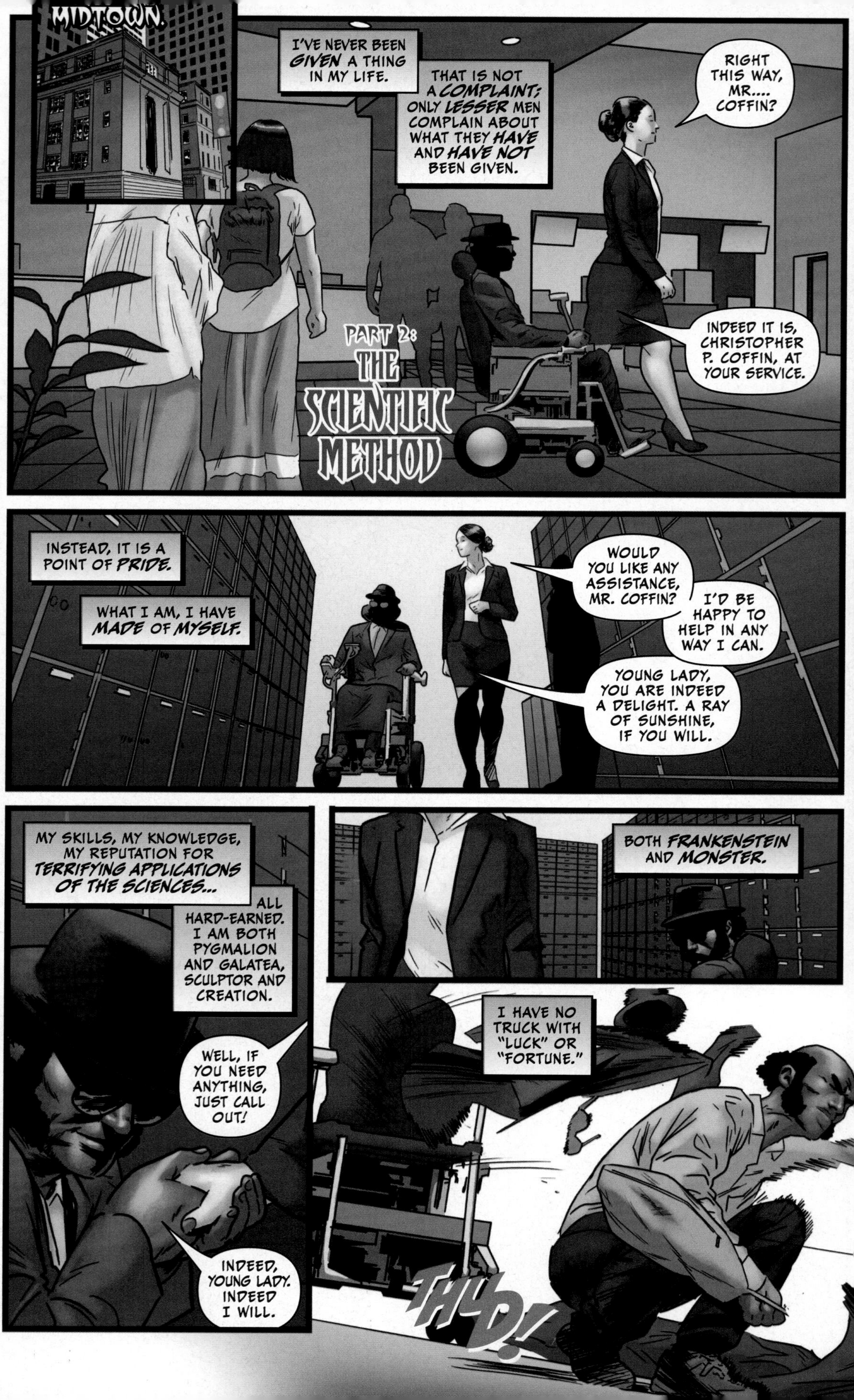
MIDTOWN.
I'VE NEVER BEEN GIVEN A THING IN MY LIFE.
THAT IS NOT A COMPLAINT; ONLY LESSER MEN COMPLAIN ABOUT WHAT THEY HAVE AND HAVE NOT BEEN GIVEN.
RIGHT THIS WAY, MR.... COFFIN?
INDEED IT IS, CHRISTOPHER P. COFFIN, AT YOUR SERVICE.
PART 2: THE SCIENTIFIC METHOD
INSTEAD, IT IS A POINT OF PRIDE.
WHAT I AM, I HAVE MADE OF MYSELF.
WOULD YOU LIKE ANY ASSISTANCE, MR. COFFIN?
I'D BE HAPPY TO HELP IN ANY WAY I CAN.
YOUNG LADY, YOU ARE INDEED A DELIGHT. A RAY OF SUNSHINE, IF YOU WILL.
MY SKILLS, MY KNOWLEDGE, MY REPUTATION FOR TERRIFYING APPLICATIONS OF THE SCIENCES...
ALL HARD-EARNED. I AM BOTH PYGMALION AND GALATEA, SCULPTOR AND CREATION.
BOTH FRANKENSTEIN AND MONSTER.
WELL, IF YOU NEED ANYTHING, JUST CALL OUT!
INDEED, YOUNG LADY. INDEED I WILL.
I HAVE NO TRUCK WITH "LUCK" OR "FORTUNE."
THUD!

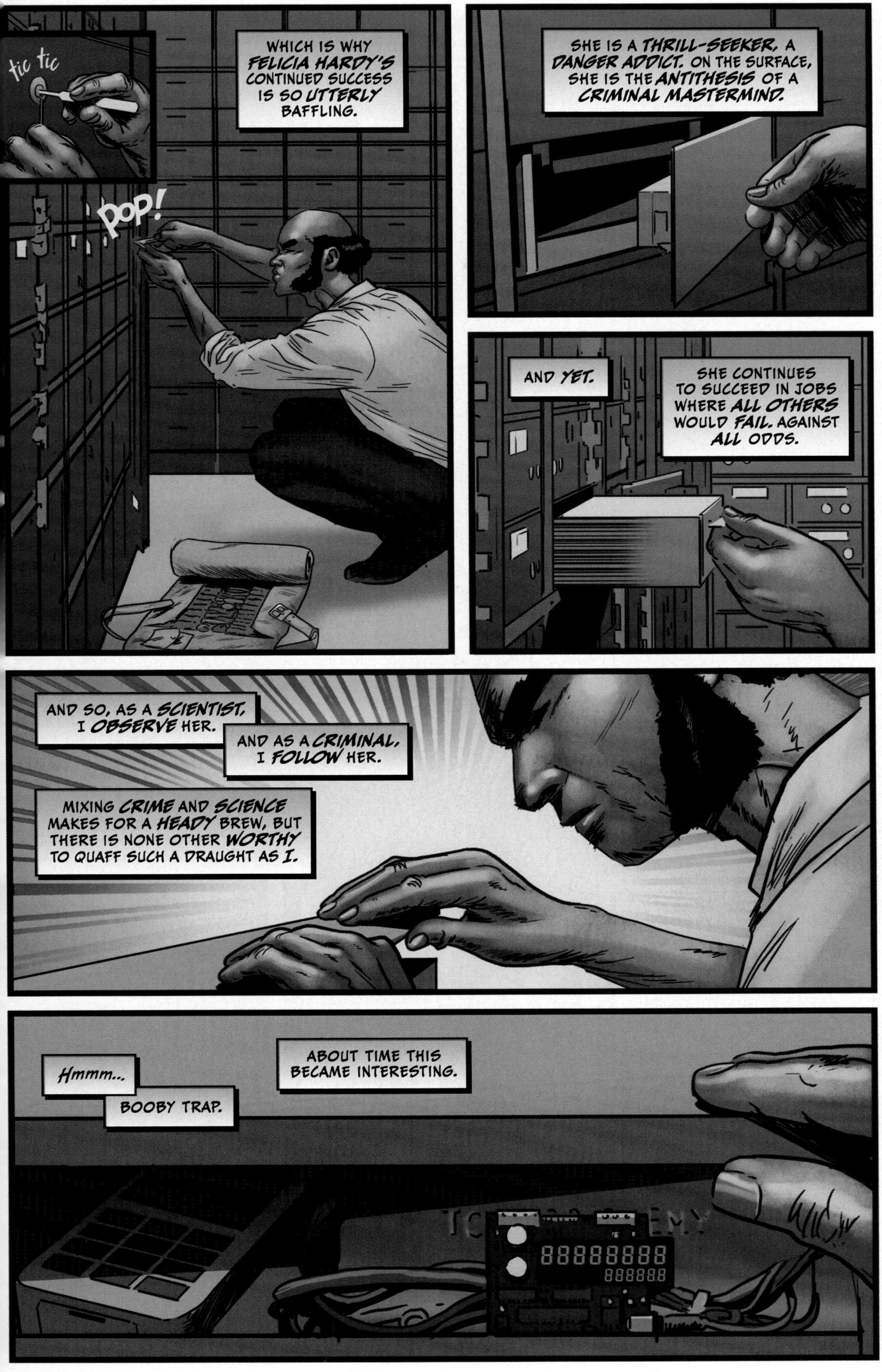

tic tic
WHICH IS WHY FELICIA HARDY'S CONTINUED SUCCESS IS SO UTTERLY BAFFLING.
POP!
SHE IS A THRILL-SEEKER, A DANGER ADDICT. ON THE SURFACE, SHE IS THE ANTITHESIS OF A CRIMINAL MASTERMIND.
AND YET.
SHE CONTINUES TO SUCCEED IN JOBS WHERE ALL OTHERS WOULD FAIL. AGAINST ALL ODDS.
AND SO, AS A SCIENTIST, I OBSERVE HER.
AND AS A CRIMINAL, I FOLLOW HER.
MIXING CRIME AND SCIENCE MAKES FOR A HEADY BREW, BUT THERE IS NONE OTHER WORTHY TO QUAFF SUCH A DRAUGHT AS I.
Hmmm...
BOOBY TRAP.
ABOUT TIME THIS BECAME INTERESTING.

JERSEY.

WHEN YOU'RE A BIG GUY, PEOPLE ASSUME YOU'RE *DUMB.*

PART 3: DUMB GUYS

IF YOU'RE A BIG GUY *AND* YOU DON'T SAY MUCH?

BROTHER, PEOPLE ARE GOING TO THINK YOU GOT THE BRAINS OF A *CACTUS.*

THAT'S OKAY THOUGH.

FOLKS DON'T PAY *ATTENTION* TO DUMB GUYS, THEY GOT *BETTER* THINGS TO WORRY ABOUT. THEY'RE ALWAYS ON THE LOOKOUT FOR THE *SMART GUYS.*

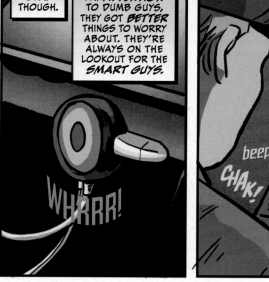

WHRRR!

YOU PUT A DUMB GUY IN *COVERALLS,* WELL, THEY CAN WALK INTO PRETTY MUCH ANYWHERE.

INCLUDING A DECOM YARD IN JERSEY FULL OF EX-S.H.I.E.L.D. HARDWARE.

beep!

CHAK!

SECURITY'S A JOKE AT PLACES LIKE THIS.

AND AFTER S.H.I.E.L.D. FOLDED, THERE'S A *LOT* OF THEM, ALL OVER THE COUNTRY.

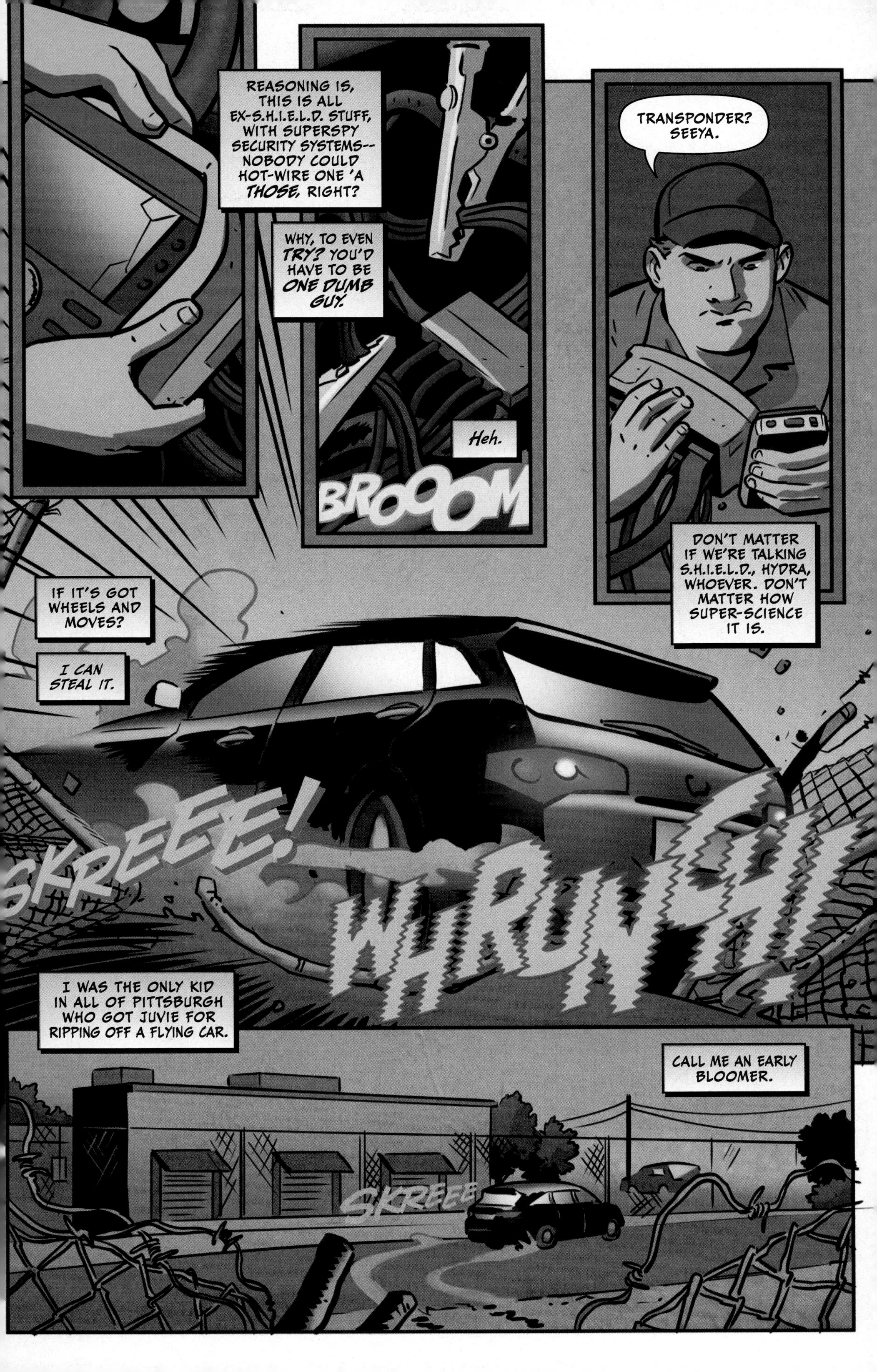
REASONING IS, THIS IS ALL EX-S.H.I.E.L.D. STUFF, WITH SUPERSPY SECURITY SYSTEMS-- NOBODY COULD HOT-WIRE ONE 'A THOSE, RIGHT?
WHY, TO EVEN TRY? YOU'D HAVE TO BE ONE DUMB GUY.
Heh.
BROOOOM
TRANSPONDER? SEEYA.
DON'T MATTER IF WE'RE TALKING S.H.I.E.L.D., HYDRA, WHOEVER. DON'T MATTER HOW SUPER-SCIENCE IT IS.
IF IT'S GOT WHEELS AND MOVES?
I CAN STEAL IT.
SKREEE!
WHRUNCH!
I WAS THE ONLY KID IN ALL OF PITTSBURGH WHO GOT JUVIE FOR RIPPING OFF A FLYING CAR.
CALL ME AN EARLY BLOOMER.
SKREEE

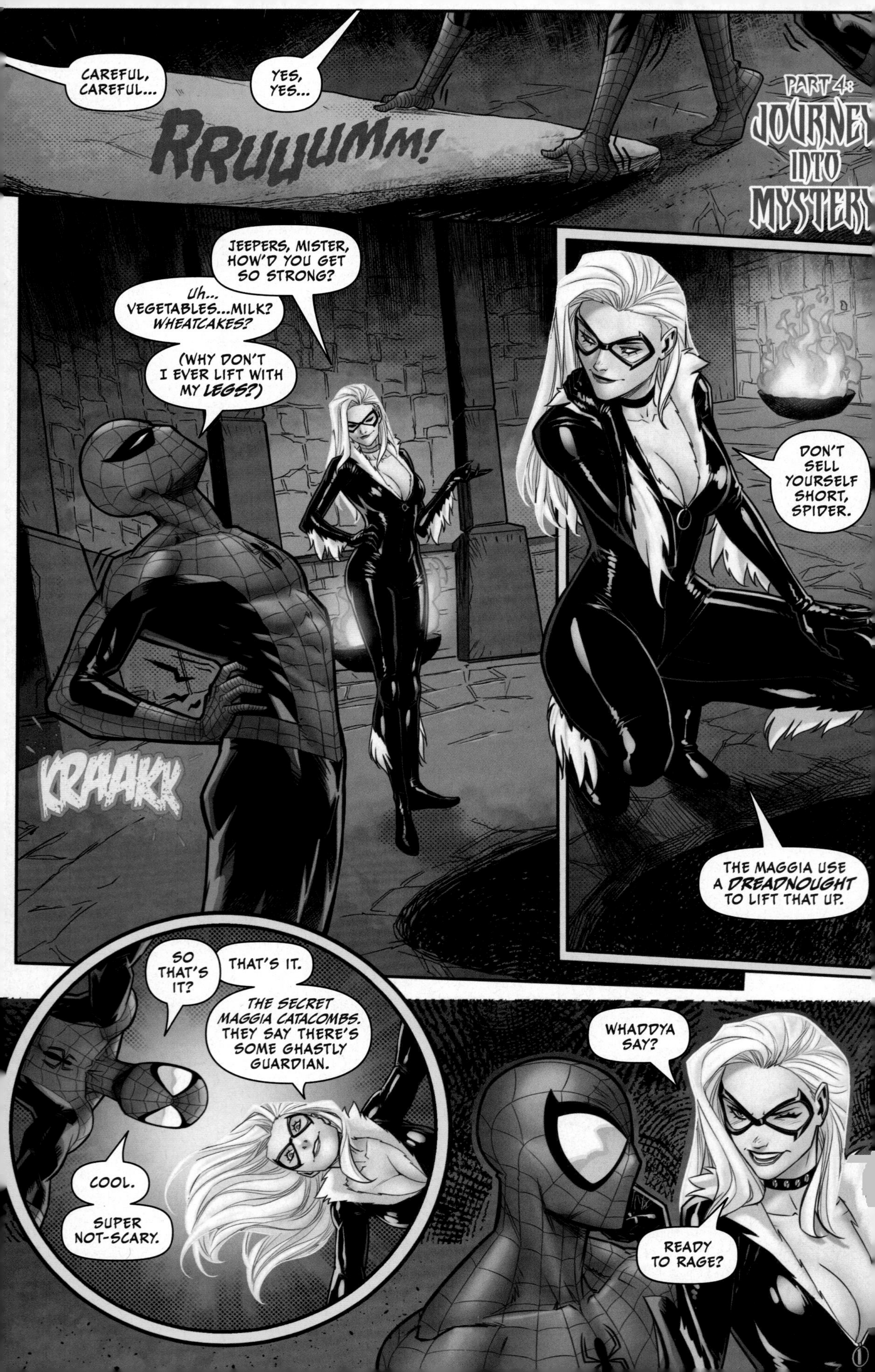
CAREFUL, CAREFUL...
YES, YES...
RRUUUMM!
PART 4:
JOURNEY INTO MYSTERY
JEEPERS, MISTER, HOW'D YOU GET SO STRONG?
Uh... VEGETABLES...MILK? WHEATCAKES?
(WHY DON'T I EVER LIFT WITH MY LEGS?)
KRAAK!
DON'T SELL YOURSELF SHORT, SPIDER.
THE MAGGIA USE A DREADNOUGHT TO LIFT THAT UP.
SO THAT'S IT?
THAT'S IT.
THE SECRET MAGGIA CATACOMBS. THEY SAY THERE'S SOME GHASTLY GUARDIAN.
COOL.
SUPER NOT-SCARY.
WHADDYA SAY?
READY TO RAGE?

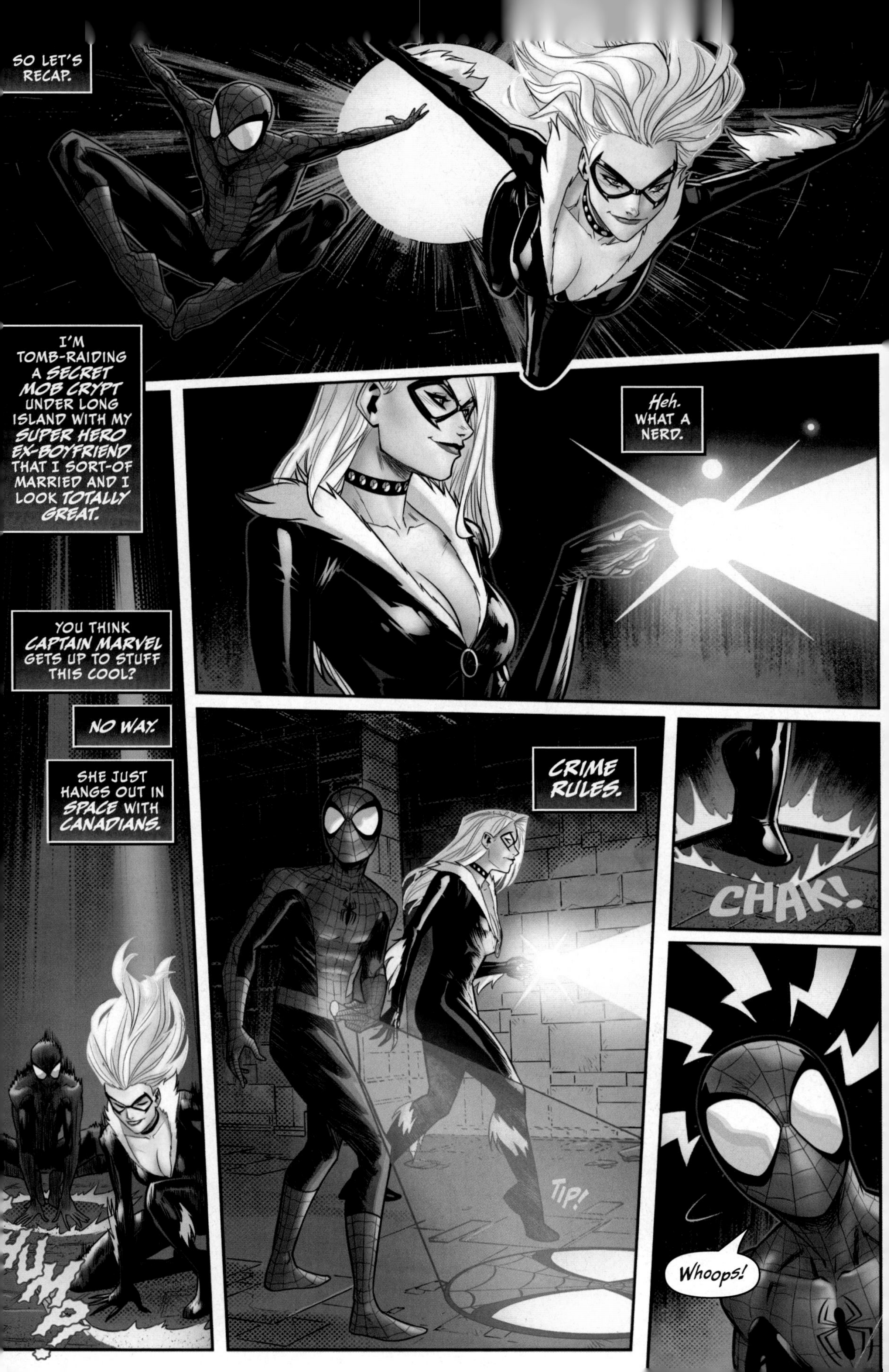
SO LET'S RECAP.
I'M TOMB-RAIDING A SECRET MOB CRYPT UNDER LONG ISLAND WITH MY SUPER HERO EX-BOYFRIEND THAT I SORT-OF MARRIED AND I LOOK TOTALLY GREAT.
Heh. WHAT A NERD.
YOU THINK CAPTAIN MARVEL GETS UP TO STUFF THIS COOL?
NO WAY.
SHE JUST HANGS OUT IN SPACE WITH CANADIANS.
CRIME RULES.
TIP!
CHAK!
Whoops!

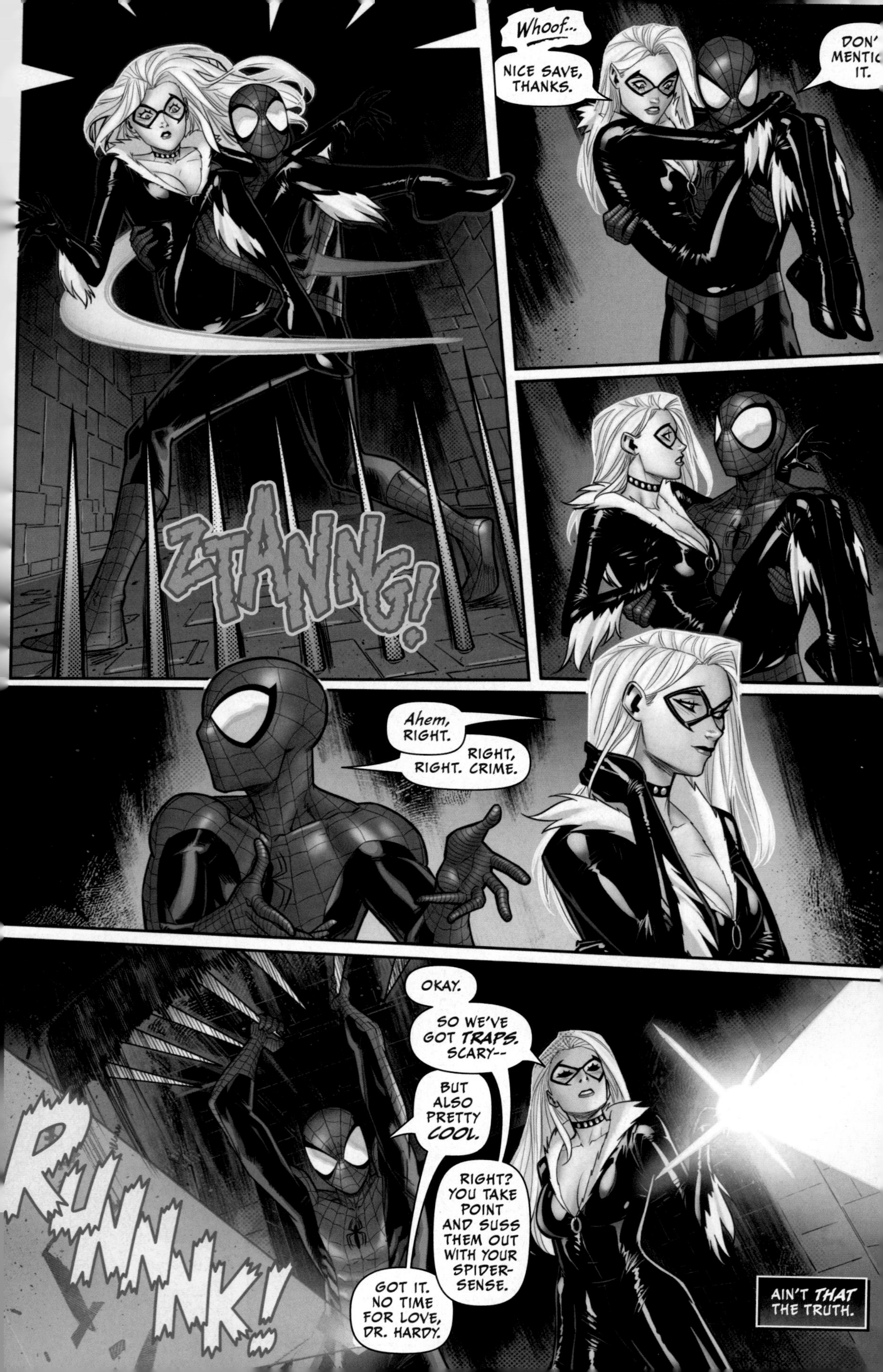
ZTANNG!
Whoof...
NICE SAVE, THANKS.
DON'T MENTIC IT.
Ahem, RIGHT.
RIGHT, RIGHT. CRIME.
RUNNK!
OKAY.
SO WE'VE GOT TRAPS. SCARY--
BUT ALSO PRETTY COOL.
RIGHT? YOU TAKE POINT AND SUSS THEM OUT WITH YOUR SPIDER-SENSE.
GOT IT. NO TIME FOR LOVE, DR. HARDY.
AIN'T THAT THE TRUTH.

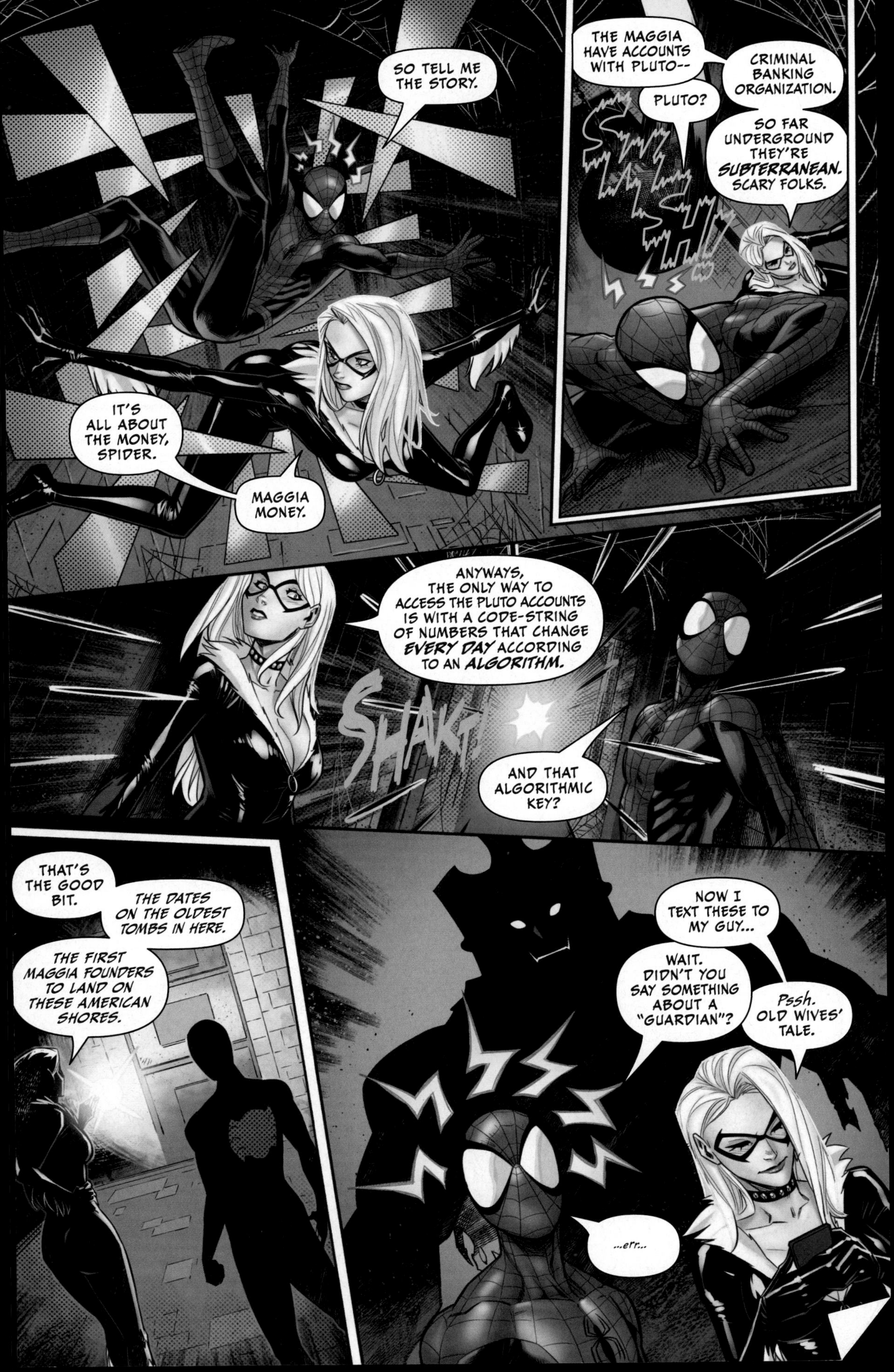
SO TELL ME THE STORY.
IT'S ALL ABOUT THE MONEY, SPIDER.
MAGGIA MONEY.
THE MAGGIA HAVE ACCOUNTS WITH PLUTO--
CRIMINAL BANKING ORGANIZATION.
PLUTO?
SO FAR UNDERGROUND THEY'RE SUBTERRANEAN. SCARY FOLKS.
ANYWAYS, THE ONLY WAY TO ACCESS THE PLUTO ACCOUNTS IS WITH A CODE-STRING OF NUMBERS THAT CHANGE EVERY DAY ACCORDING TO AN ALGORITHM.
AND THAT ALGORITHMIC KEY?
THAT'S THE GOOD BIT.
THE DATES ON THE OLDEST TOMBS IN HERE.
THE FIRST MAGGIA FOUNDERS TO LAND ON THESE AMERICAN SHORES.
NOW I TEXT THESE TO MY GUY...
WAIT. DIDN'T YOU SAY SOMETHING ABOUT A "GUARDIAN"?
Pssh. OLD WIVES' TALE.
...err...

THE BOMB IS RUDIMENTARY.

BUT IN *DISARMING* IT, IT MUST FIRST BE *ARMED.*

AND ONCE *ARMED,* THE SLIGHTEST BREAK IN CONCENTRATION...

Bee-deep!

Pffft!

IT WOULD APPEAR HARDY AND THE *BUG* HAVE DELIVERED.

Inbox

1 NEW MESSAGE

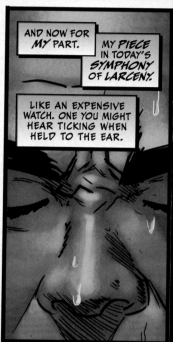

AND NOW FOR *MY* PART. MY *PIECE* IN TODAY'S *SYMPHONY* OF *LARCENY.*

LIKE AN EXPENSIVE WATCH. ONE YOU MIGHT HEAR TICKING WHEN HELD TO THE EAR.

EVERY PART WORKING IN *UNISON.*

TICK-TICK-TICK-*TICK.*

SNIP

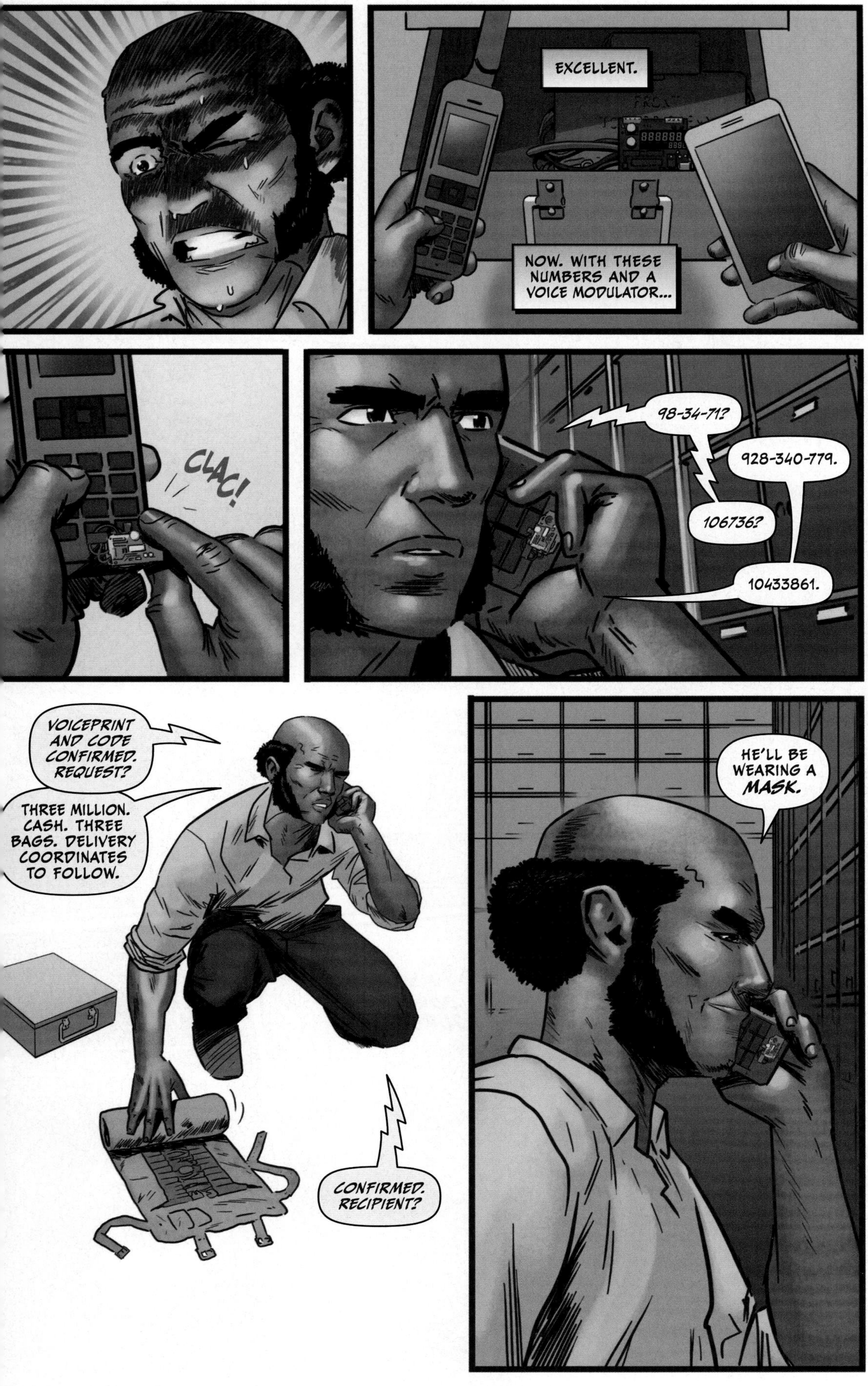
EXCELLENT.
NOW. WITH THESE NUMBERS AND A VOICE MODULATOR...
CLAC!
98-34-71?
928-340-779.
106736?
10433861.
VOICEPRINT AND CODE CONFIRMED. REQUEST?
THREE MILLION. CASH. THREE BAGS. DELIVERY COORDINATES TO FOLLOW.
CONFIRMED. RECIPIENT?
HE'LL BE WEARING A MASK.

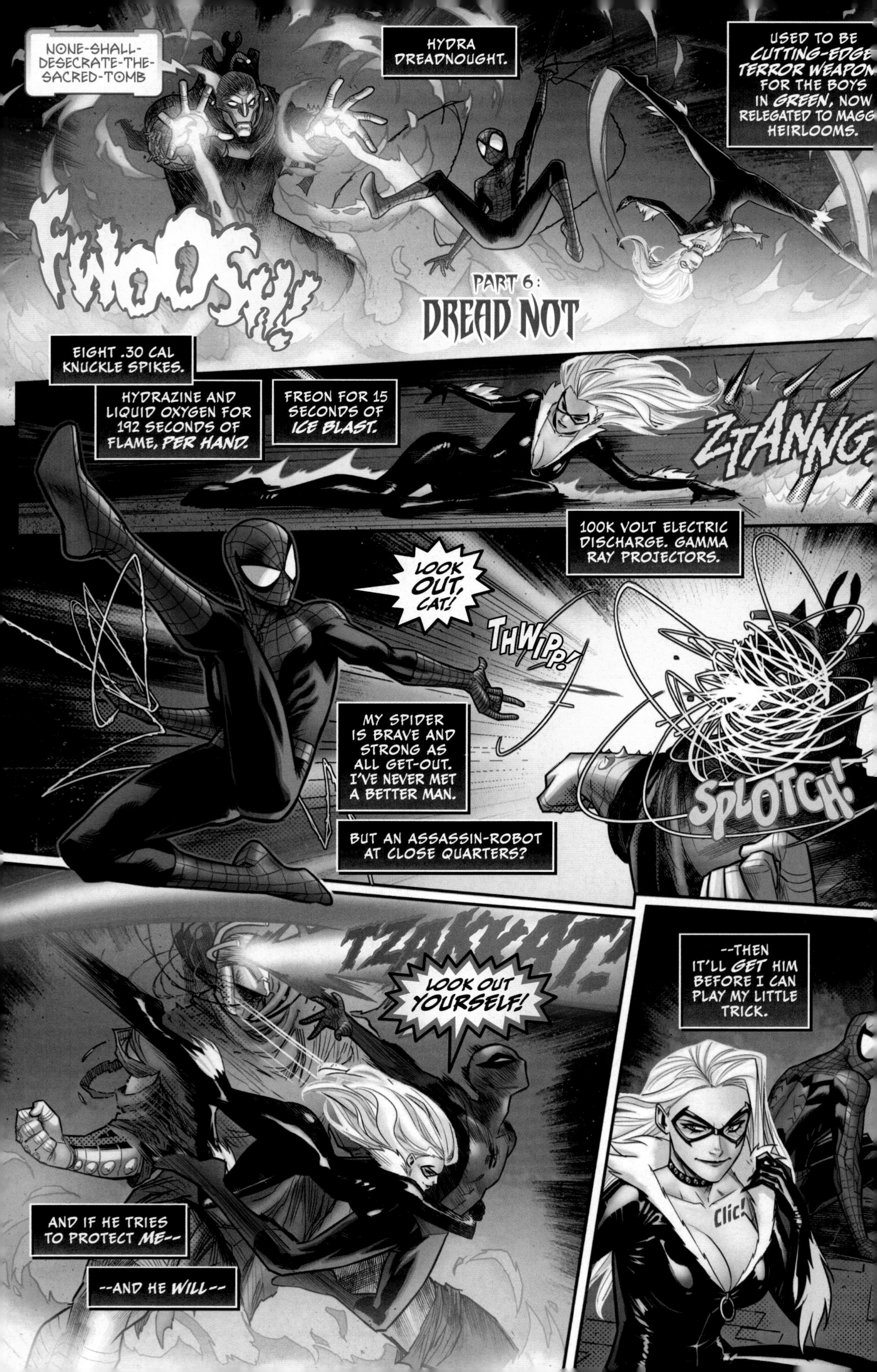
NONE-SHALL-DESECRATE-THE-SACRED-TOMB
FWOOSH!
HYDRA DREADNOUGHT.
USED TO BE CUTTING-EDGE TERROR WEAPON FOR THE BOYS IN GREEN, NOW RELEGATED TO MAGG HEIRLOOMS.
PART 6:
DREAD NOT
EIGHT .30 CAL KNUCKLE SPIKES.
HYDRAZINE AND LIQUID OXYGEN FOR 192 SECONDS OF FLAME, PER HAND.
FREON FOR 15 SECONDS OF ICE BLAST.
ZTANNG!
100K VOLT ELECTRIC DISCHARGE. GAMMA RAY PROJECTORS.
LOOK OUT, CAT!
THWIPP!
MY SPIDER IS BRAVE AND STRONG AS ALL GET-OUT. I'VE NEVER MET A BETTER MAN.
BUT AN ASSASSIN-ROBOT AT CLOSE QUARTERS?
SPLOTCH!
TZAKKAT!
LOOK OUT YOURSELF!
--THEN IT'LL GET HIM BEFORE I CAN PLAY MY LITTLE TRICK.
AND IF HE TRIES TO PROTECT ME--
--AND HE WILL--
Clic!

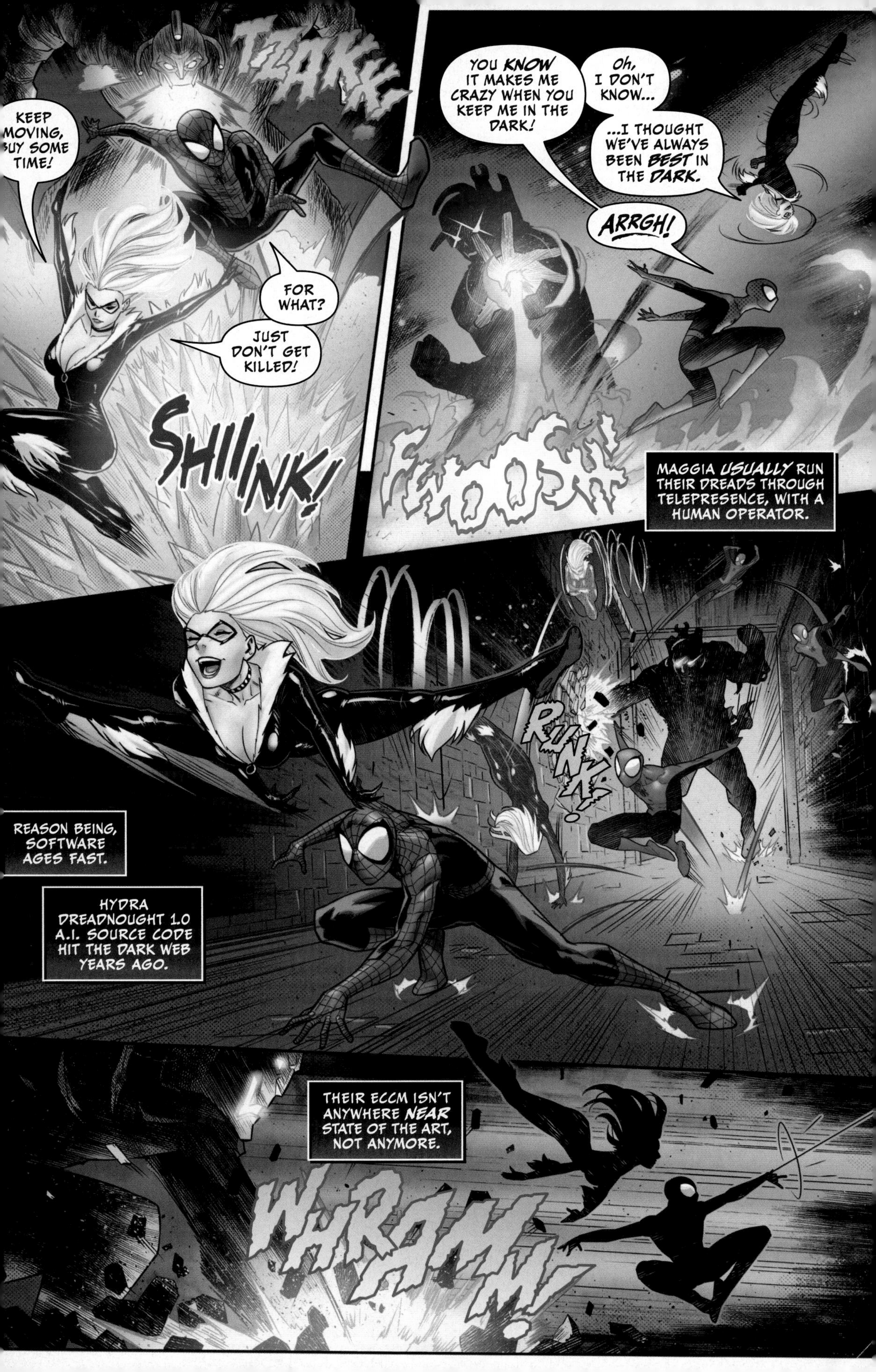
TZAKK
KEEP MOVING, UY SOME TIME!
FOR WHAT?
JUST DON'T GET KILLED!
SHIIINK!
YOU KNOW IT MAKES ME CRAZY WHEN YOU KEEP ME IN THE DARK!
Oh, I DON'T KNOW...
...I THOUGHT WE'VE ALWAYS BEEN BEST IN THE DARK.
ARRGH!
MAGGIA USUALLY RUN THEIR DREADS THROUGH TELEPRESENCE, WITH A HUMAN OPERATOR.
REASON BEING, SOFTWARE AGES FAST.
HYDRA DREADNOUGHT 1.0 A.I. SOURCE CODE HIT THE DARK WEB YEARS AGO.
RUNK!
THEIR ECCM ISN'T ANYWHERE NEAR STATE OF THE ART, NOT ANYMORE.
WHRAM!

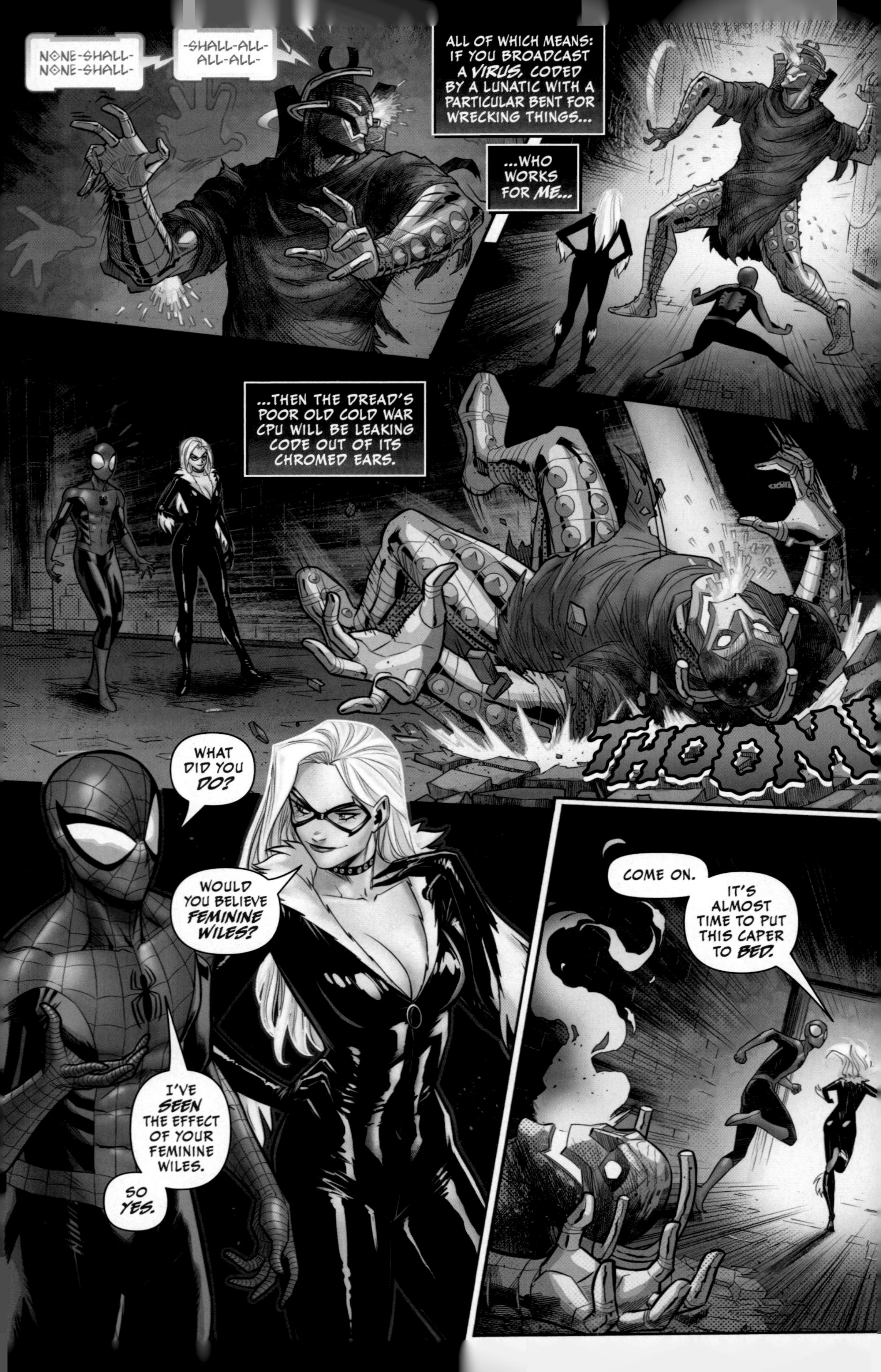
NONE-SHALL-
NONE-SHALL-
-SHALL-ALL-
ALL-ALL-
ALL OF WHICH MEANS: IF YOU BROADCAST A VIRUS, CODED BY A LUNATIC WITH A PARTICULAR BENT FOR WRECKING THINGS...
...WHO WORKS FOR ME...
...THEN THE DREAD'S POOR OLD COLD WAR CPU WILL BE LEAKING CODE OUT OF ITS CHROMED EARS.
THOOM!
WHAT DID YOU DO?
WOULD YOU BELIEVE FEMININE WILES?
I'VE SEEN THE EFFECT OF YOUR FEMININE WILES.
SO YES.
COME ON.
IT'S ALMOST TIME TO PUT THIS CAPER TO BED.

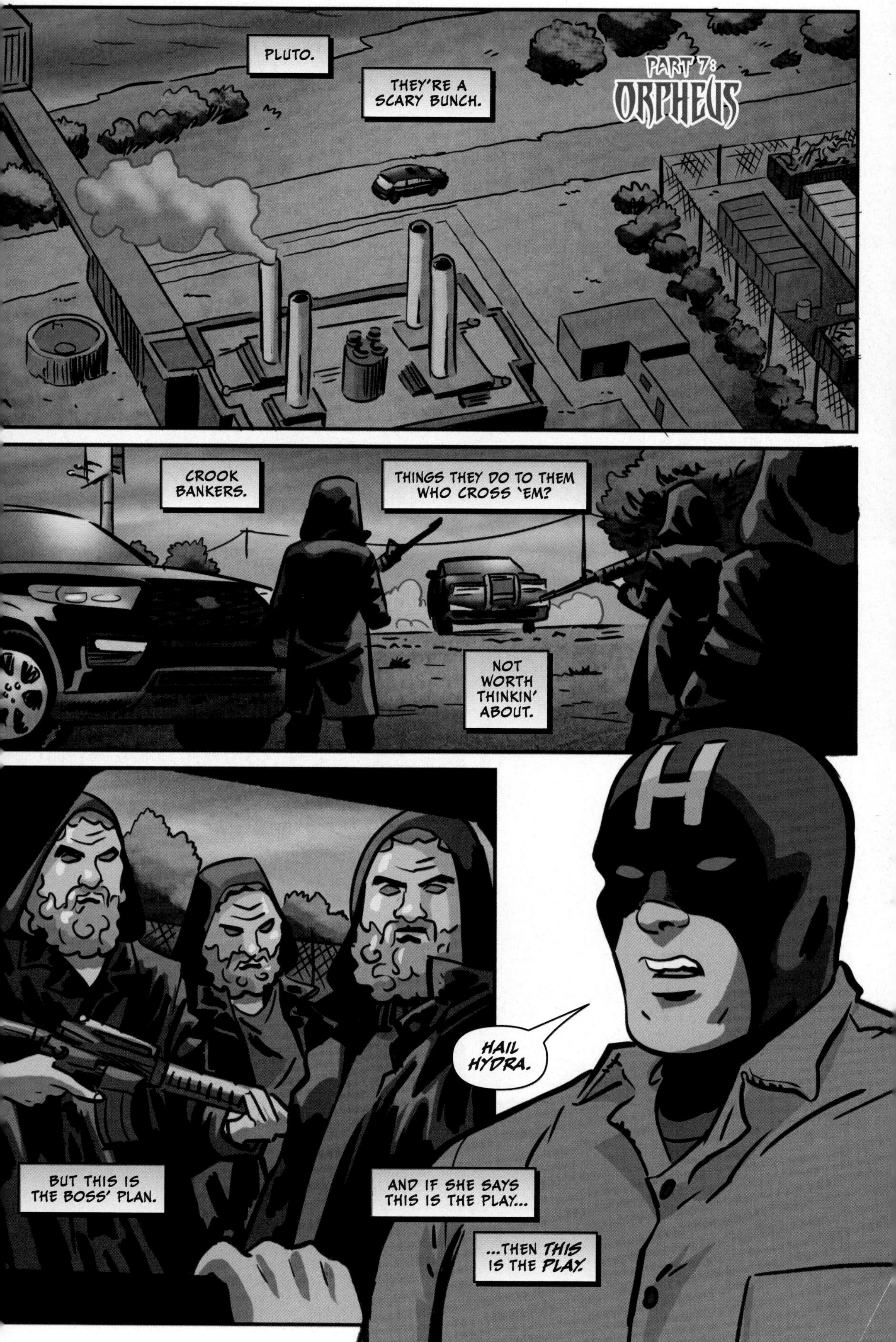
PLUTO.
THEY'RE A SCARY BUNCH.
PART 7: ORPHEUS
CROOK BANKERS.
THINGS THEY DO TO THEM WHO CROSS 'EM?
NOT WORTH THINKIN' ABOUT.
HAIL HYDRA.
BUT THIS IS THE BOSS' PLAN.
AND IF SHE SAYS THIS IS THE PLAY...
...THEN THIS IS THE PLAY.

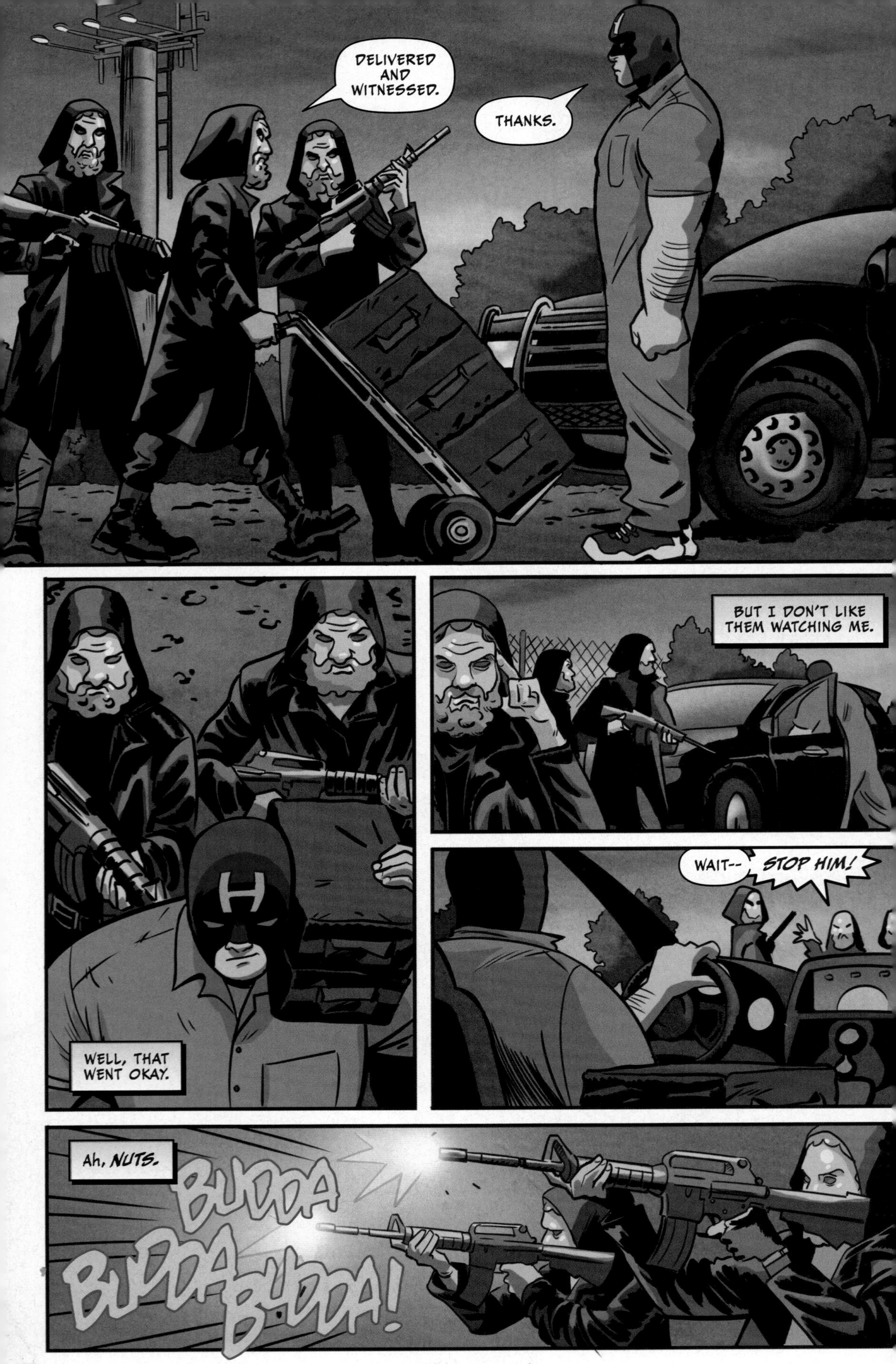
DELIVERED AND WITNESSED.
THANKS.
WELL, THAT WENT OKAY.
BUT I DON'T LIKE THEM WATCHING ME.
WAIT--
STOP HIM!
Ah, NUTS.
BUDDA
BUDDA BUDDA!

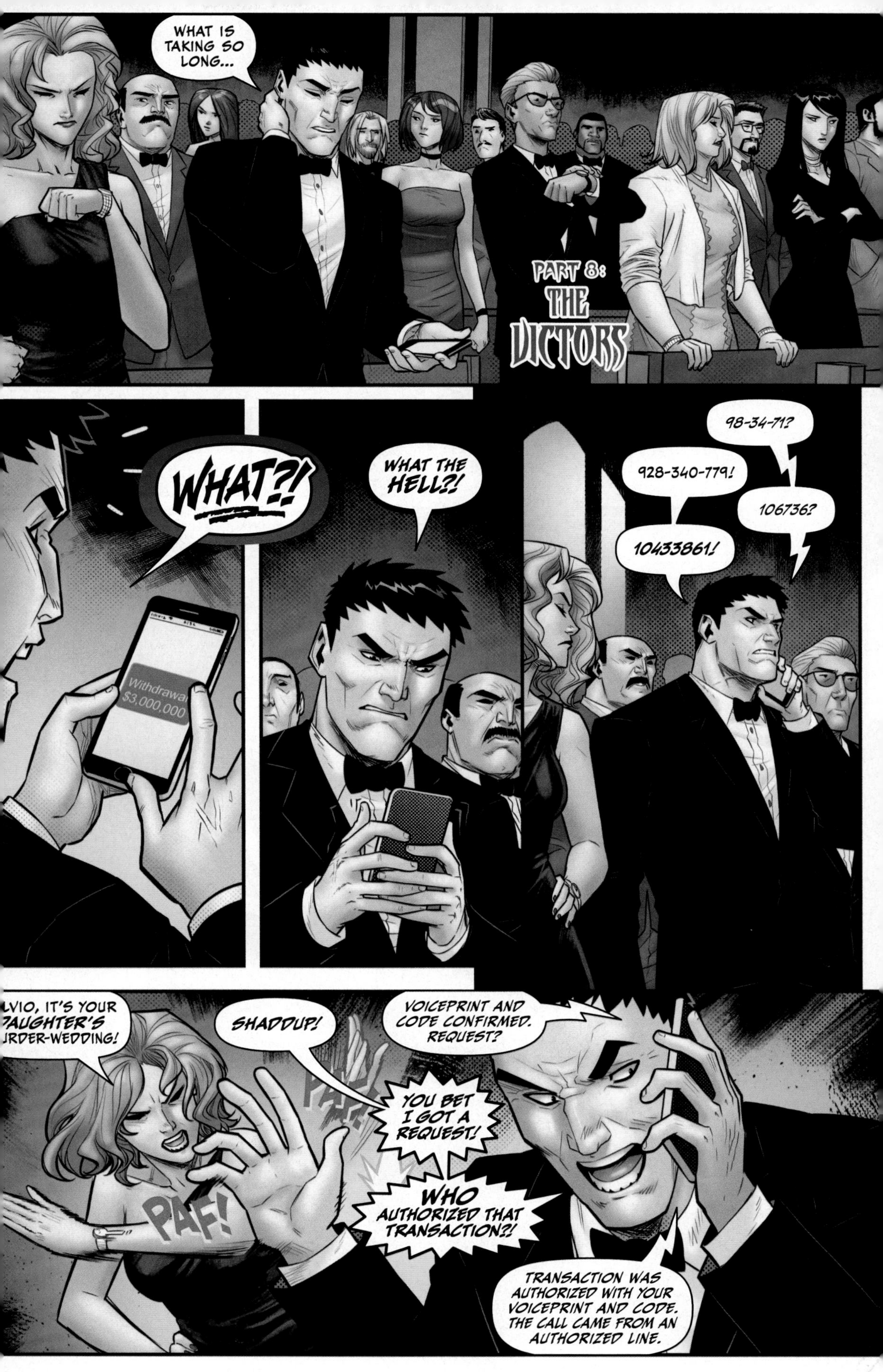

WHAT IS TAKING SO LONG...
PART 8: THE VICTORS
WHAT?!
Withdrawal $3,000,000
WHAT THE HELL?!
98-34-71?
928-340-779!
106736?
10433861!
LVIO, IT'S YOUR DAUGHTER'S URDER-WEDDING!
SHADDUP!
PAF!
PAF!
VOICEPRINT AND CODE CONFIRMED. REQUEST?
YOU BET I GOT A REQUEST!
WHO AUTHORIZED THAT TRANSACTION?!
TRANSACTION WAS AUTHORIZED WITH YOUR VOICEPRINT AND CODE. THE CALL CAME FROM AN AUTHORIZED LINE.

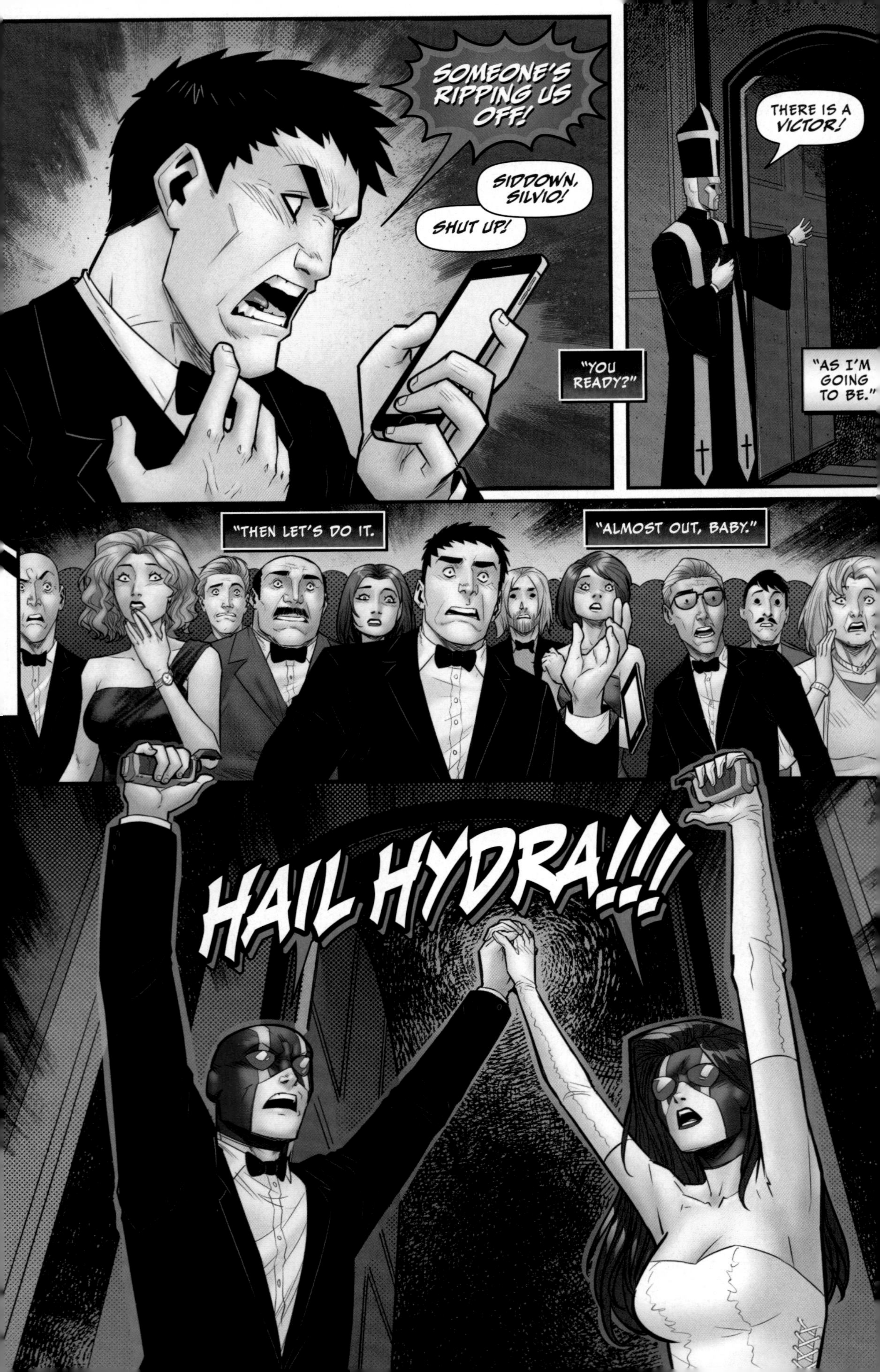
SOMEONE'S RIPPING US OFF!
SIDDOWN, SILVIO!
SHUT UP!
THERE IS A VICTOR!
"YOU READY?"
"AS I'M GOING TO BE."
"THEN LET'S DO IT.
"ALMOST OUT, BABY."
HAIL HYDRA!!!

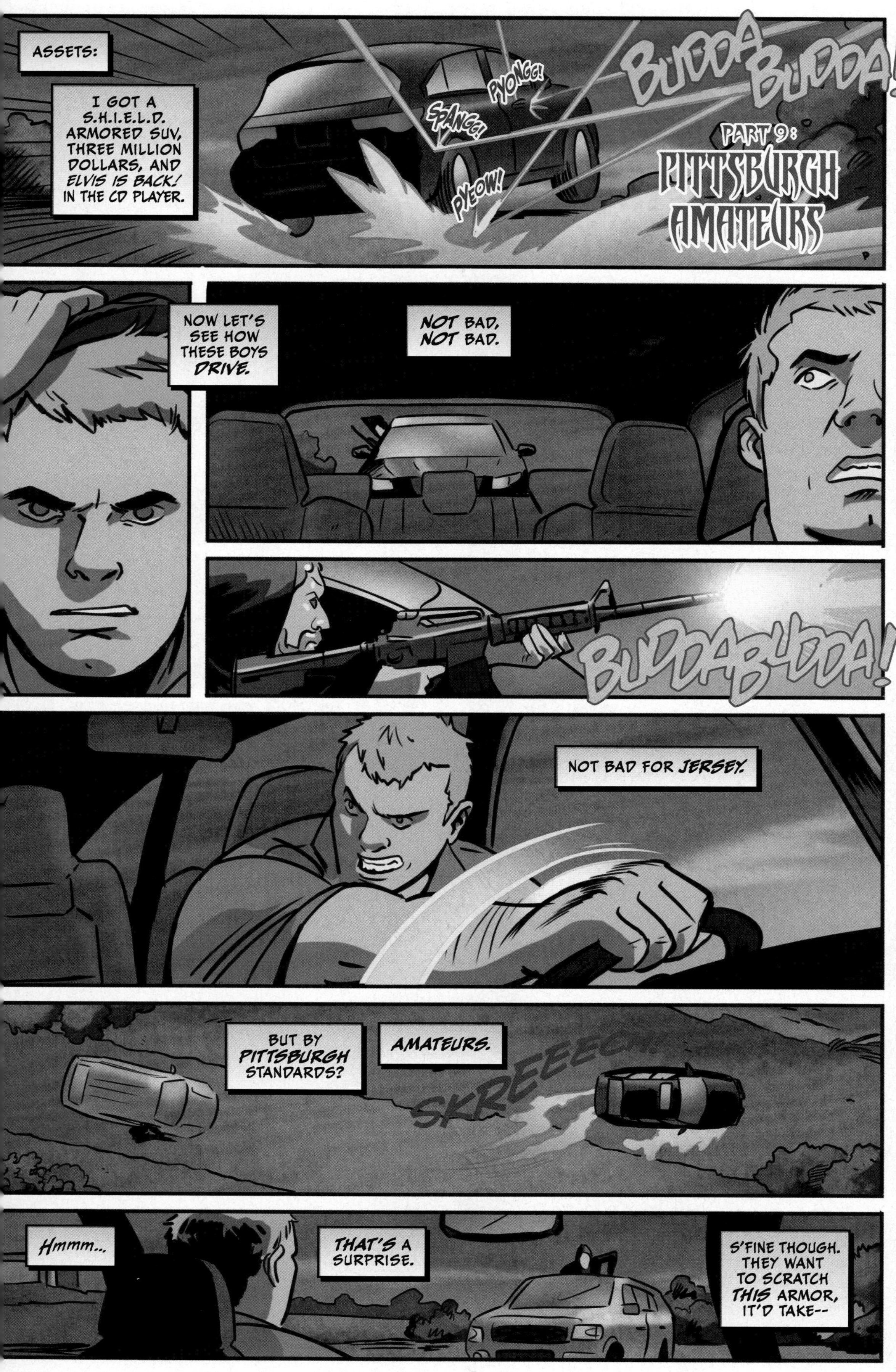

ASSETS:
I GOT A S.H.I.E.L.D. ARMORED SUV, THREE MILLION DOLLARS, AND ELVIS IS BACK! IN THE CD PLAYER.
BUDDA BUDDA!
PYONGG!
SPANGG!
PYEOW!
PART 9:
PITTSBURGH AMATEURS
NOW LET'S SEE HOW THESE BOYS DRIVE.
NOT BAD, NOT BAD.
BUDDABUDDA!
NOT BAD FOR JERSEY.
BUT BY PITTSBURGH STANDARDS?
AMATEURS.
SKREEEECH!
Hmmm...
THAT'S A SURPRISE.
S'FINE THOUGH. THEY WANT TO SCRATCH THIS ARMOR, IT'D TAKE--

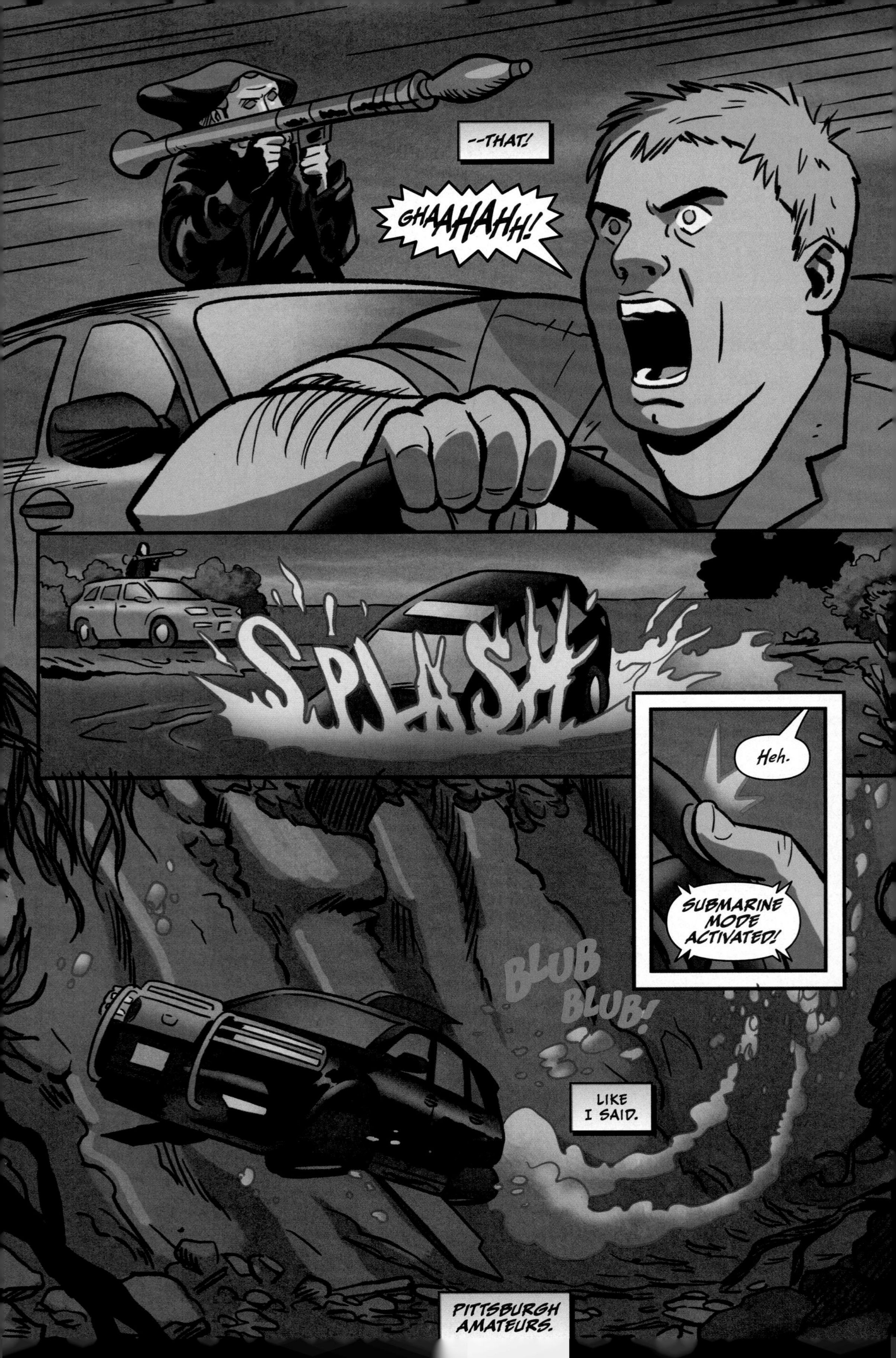
--THAT!
GHAAHAHH!
SPLASH
Heh.
SUBMARINE MODE ACTIVATED!
BLUB BLUB!
LIKE I SAID.
PITTSBURGH AMATEURS.

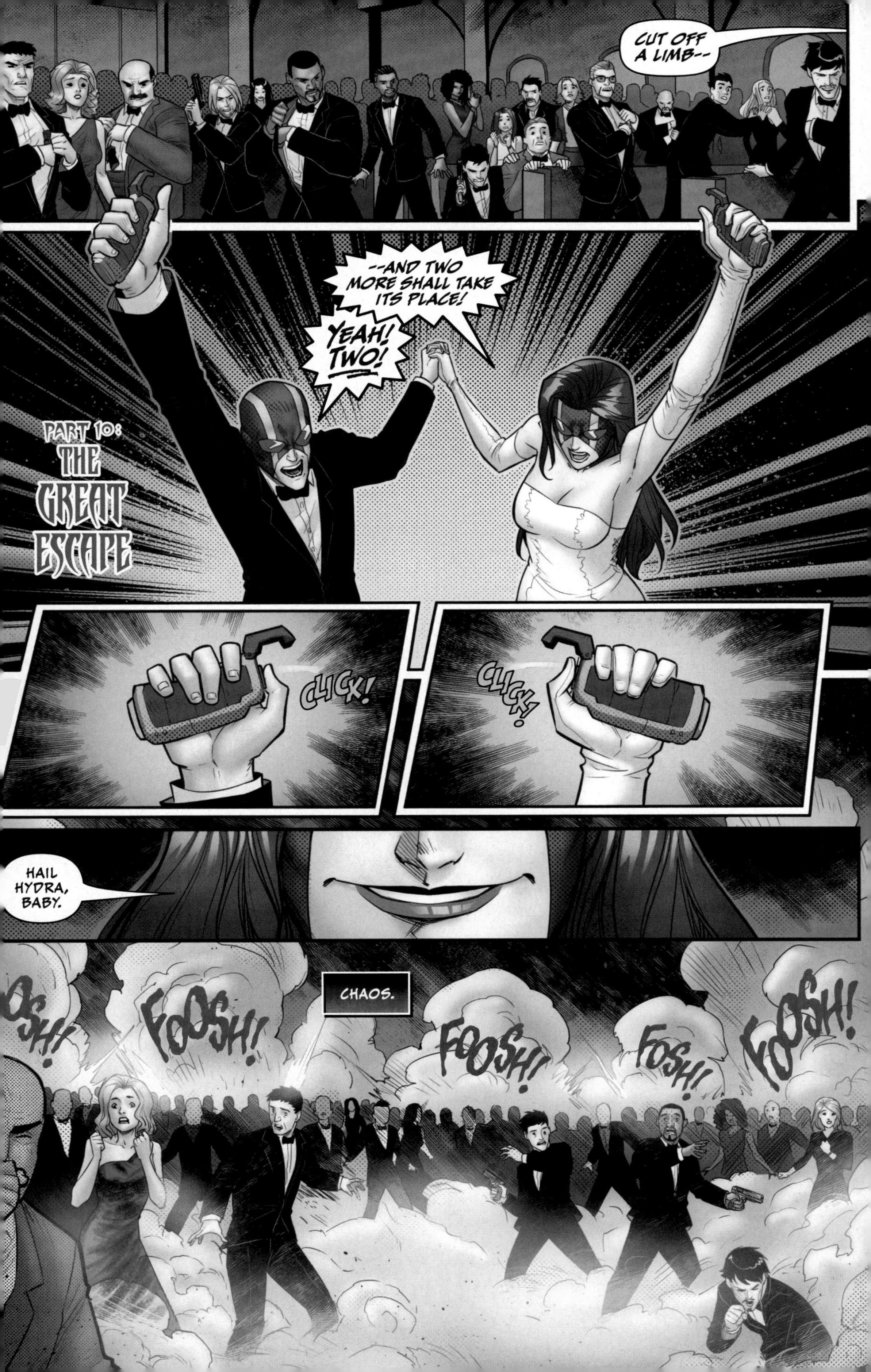
CUT OFF A LIMB--
--AND TWO MORE SHALL TAKE ITS PLACE!
YEAH! TWO!
PART 10: THE GREAT ESCAPE
CLICK!
CLICK!
HAIL HYDRA, BABY.
CHAOS.
FOOSH!
FOOSH!
FOSH!
FOOSH!

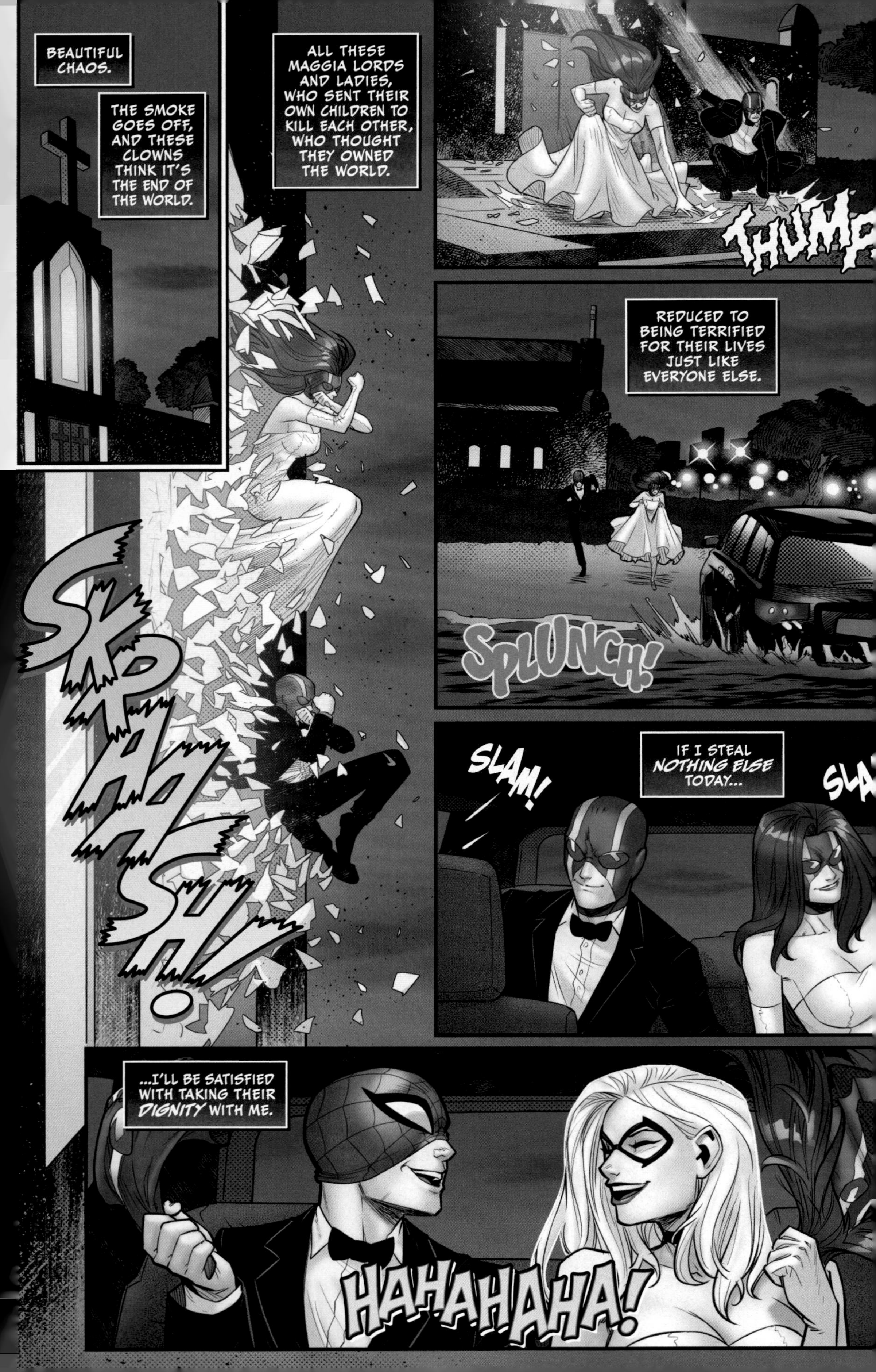
BEAUTIFUL CHAOS.
THE SMOKE GOES OFF, AND THESE CLOWNS THINK IT'S THE END OF THE WORLD.
ALL THESE MAGGIA LORDS AND LADIES, WHO SENT THEIR OWN CHILDREN TO KILL EACH OTHER, WHO THOUGHT THEY OWNED THE WORLD.
SKRASSH!
THUMP
REDUCED TO BEING TERRIFIED FOR THEIR LIVES JUST LIKE EVERYONE ELSE.
SPLUNCH!
SLAM!
IF I STEAL NOTHING ELSE TODAY...
...I'LL BE SATISFIED WITH TAKING THEIR DIGNITY WITH ME.
HAHAHAHA!

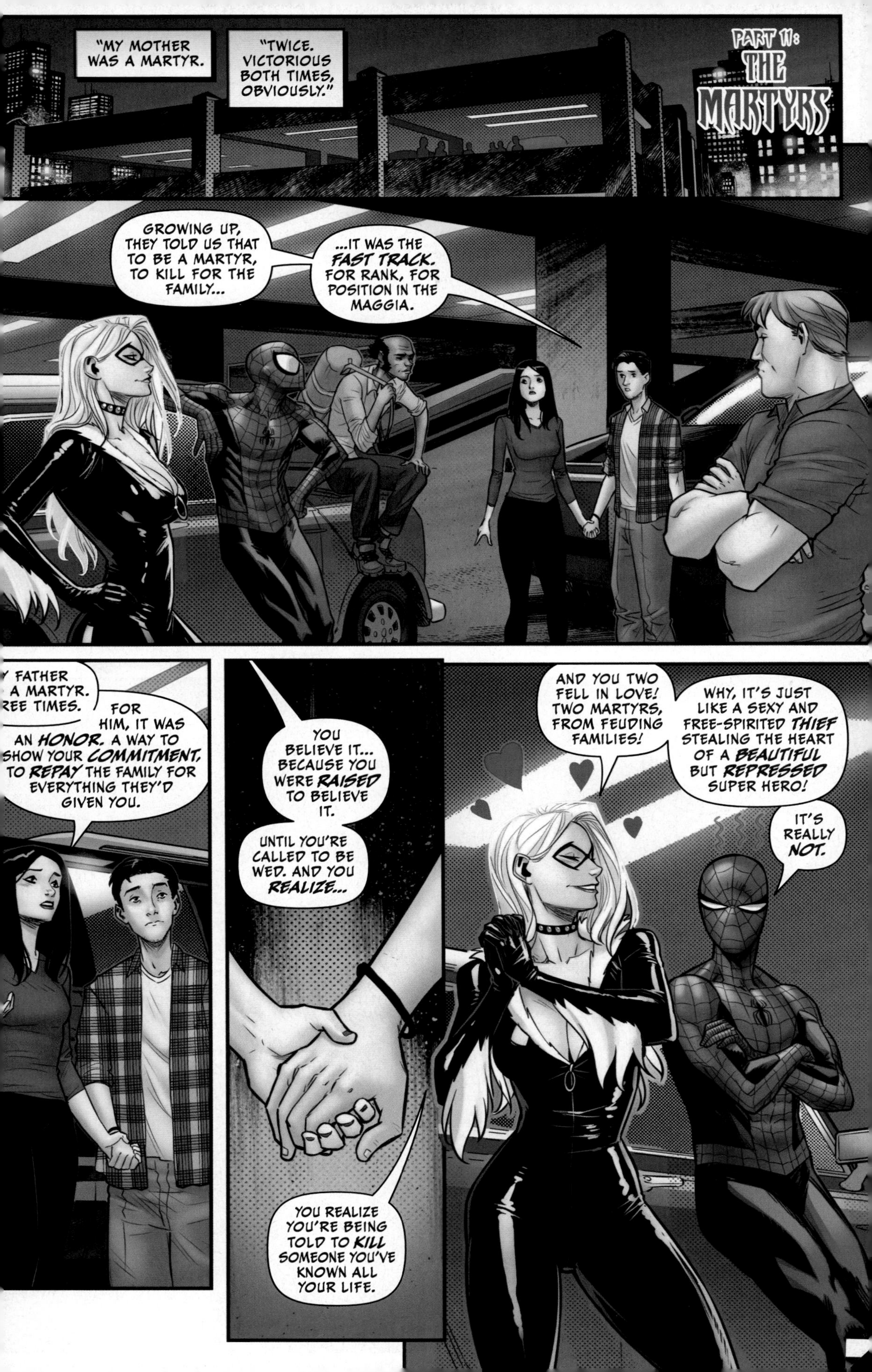
PART 11: THE MARTYRS
"MY MOTHER WAS A MARTYR.
"TWICE. VICTORIOUS BOTH TIMES, OBVIOUSLY."
GROWING UP, THEY TOLD US THAT TO BE A MARTYR, TO KILL FOR THE FAMILY...
...IT WAS THE FAST TRACK. FOR RANK, FOR POSITION IN THE MAGGIA.
FATHER A MARTYR. REE TIMES.
FOR HIM, IT WAS AN HONOR. A WAY TO SHOW YOUR COMMITMENT. TO REPAY THE FAMILY FOR EVERYTHING THEY'D GIVEN YOU.
YOU BELIEVE IT... BECAUSE YOU WERE RAISED TO BELIEVE IT.
UNTIL YOU'RE CALLED TO BE WED. AND YOU REALIZE...
YOU REALIZE YOU'RE BEING TOLD TO KILL SOMEONE YOU'VE KNOWN ALL YOUR LIFE.
AND YOU TWO FELL IN LOVE! TWO MARTYRS, FROM FEUDING FAMILIES!
WHY, IT'S JUST LIKE A SEXY AND FREE-SPIRITED THIEF STEALING THE HEART OF A BEAUTIFUL BUT REPRESSED SUPER HERO!
IT'S REALLY NOT.

REGARDLESS.

YOU KIDS CAME TO THE RIGHT PERSON.

ONE MILLION IN CASH AND A BULLETPROOF CAR--

THAT'S ABOUT AS GOOD A START ON A NEW LIFE TOGETHER AS I CAN THINK OF.

THUMP!

AND *OUR* DEAL, FELICIA?

FIIIIINE.

THE OTHER HALF, ALL *ONE MILLION* DOLLARS OF IT--

--WILL GO TO CHARITIES THROUGHOUT NEW YORK.

I'LL GET RECEIPTS AND EVERYTHING.

YOU'RE GIVING YOUR CUT TO *CHARITY?*

ONLY WAY TO GET YOUR FRIENDLY NEIGHBORHOOD SPIDER-MAN ON THE JOB. IT'S ALL GOT TO BE STRICTLY *PRO BONO.*

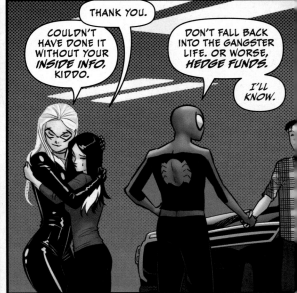

THANK YOU.

COULDN'T HAVE DONE IT WITHOUT YOUR *INSIDE INFO,* KIDDO.

DON'T FALL BACK INTO THE GANGSTER LIFE. OR WORSE, *HEDGE FUNDS.*

I'LL KNOW.

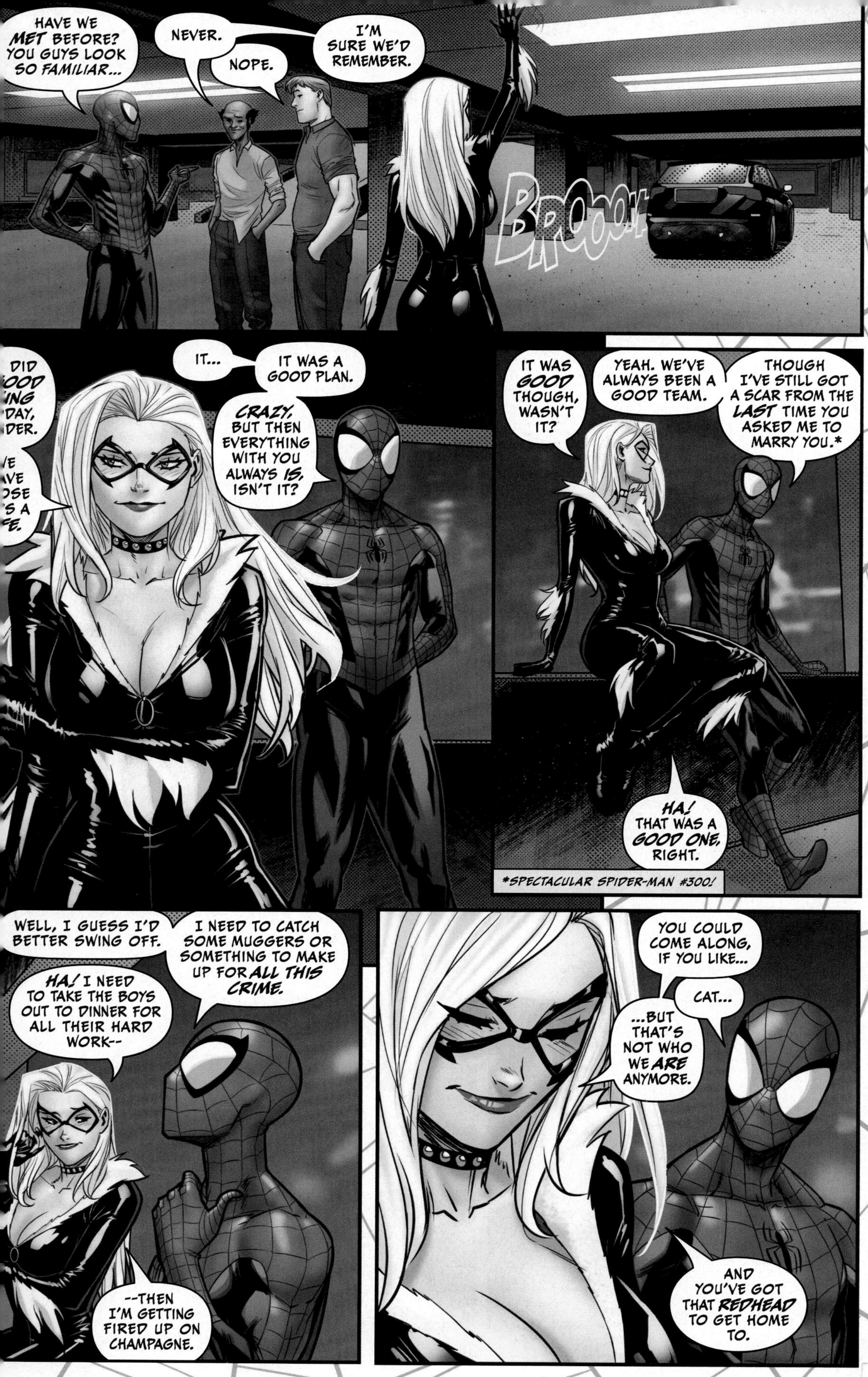
HAVE WE MET BEFORE? YOU GUYS LOOK SO FAMILIAR...
NEVER.
NOPE.
I'M SURE WE'D REMEMBER.
BRROOOM
IT...
IT WAS A GOOD PLAN.
CRAZY. BUT THEN EVERYTHING WITH YOU ALWAYS IS, ISN'T IT?
IT WAS GOOD THOUGH, WASN'T IT?
YEAH. WE'VE ALWAYS BEEN A GOOD TEAM.
THOUGH I'VE STILL GOT A SCAR FROM THE LAST TIME YOU ASKED ME TO MARRY YOU.*
HA! THAT WAS A GOOD ONE, RIGHT.
*SPECTACULAR SPIDER-MAN #300!
WELL, I GUESS I'D BETTER SWING OFF.
I NEED TO CATCH SOME MUGGERS OR SOMETHING TO MAKE UP FOR ALL THIS CRIME.
HA! I NEED TO TAKE THE BOYS OUT TO DINNER FOR ALL THEIR HARD WORK--
--THEN I'M GETTING FIRED UP ON CHAMPAGNE.
YOU COULD COME ALONG, IF YOU LIKE...
CAT...
...BUT THAT'S NOT WHO WE ARE ANYMORE.
AND YOU'VE GOT THAT REDHEAD TO GET HOME TO.

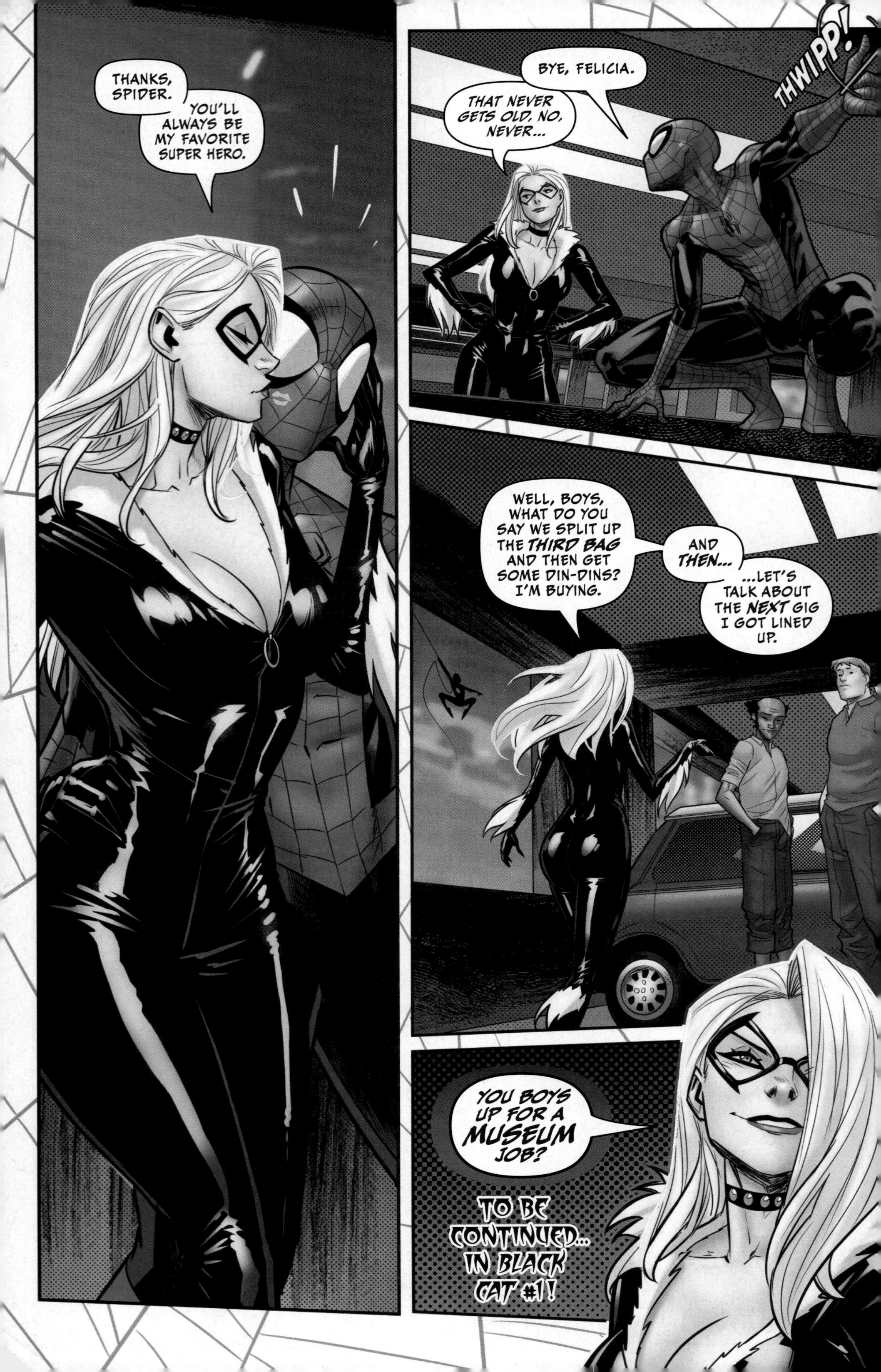
THANKS, SPIDER.
YOU'LL ALWAYS BE MY FAVORITE SUPER HERO.
THAT NEVER GETS OLD, NO, NEVER...
BYE, FELICIA.
THWIPP!
WELL, BOYS, WHAT DO YOU SAY WE SPLIT UP THE THIRD BAG AND THEN GET SOME DIN-DINS? I'M BUYING.
AND THEN...
...LET'S TALK ABOUT THE NEXT GIG I GOT LINED UP.
YOU BOYS UP FOR A MUSEUM JOB?
TO BE CONTINUED... IN BLACK CAT #1!

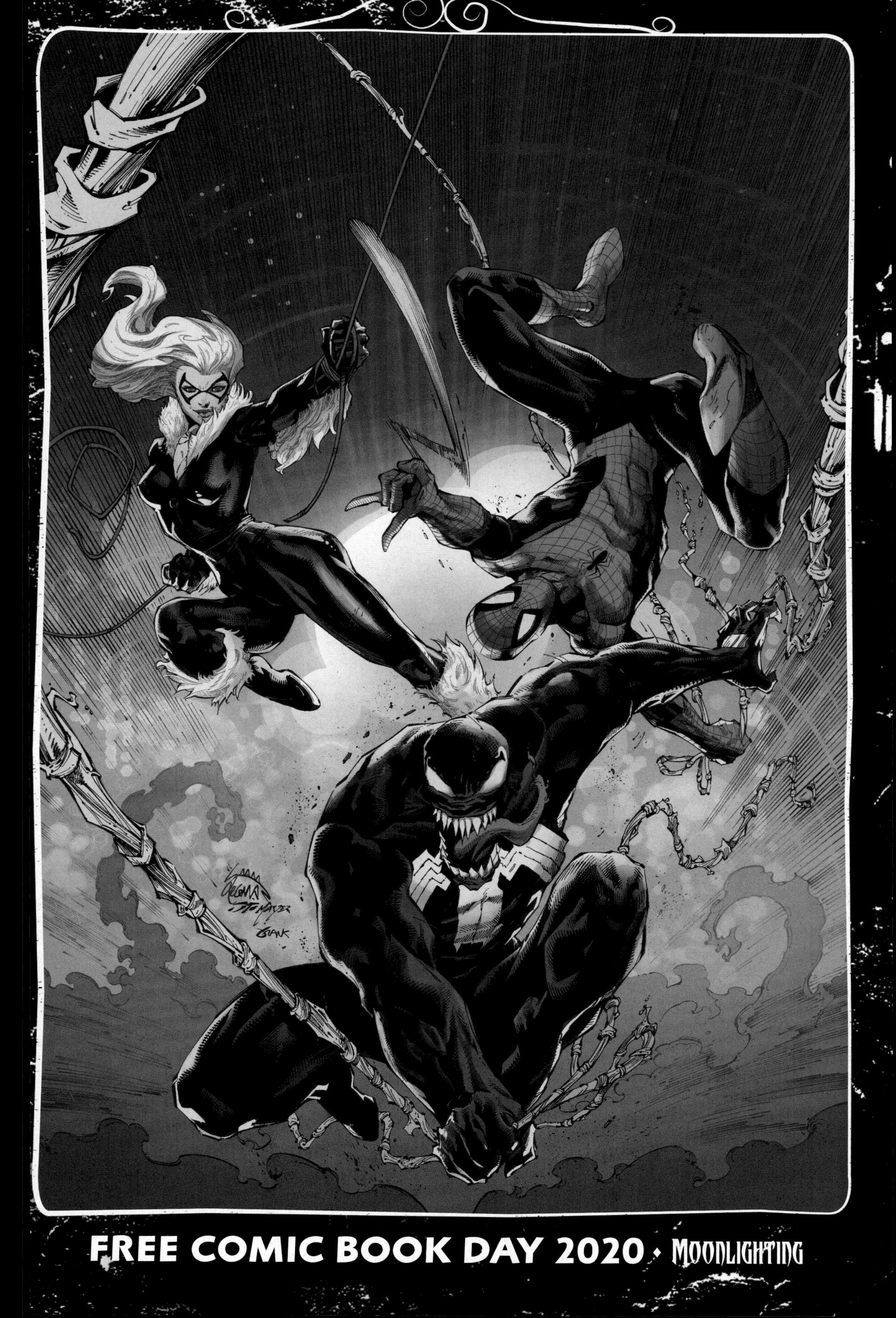

FREE COMIC BOOK DAY 2020 • MOONLIGHTING

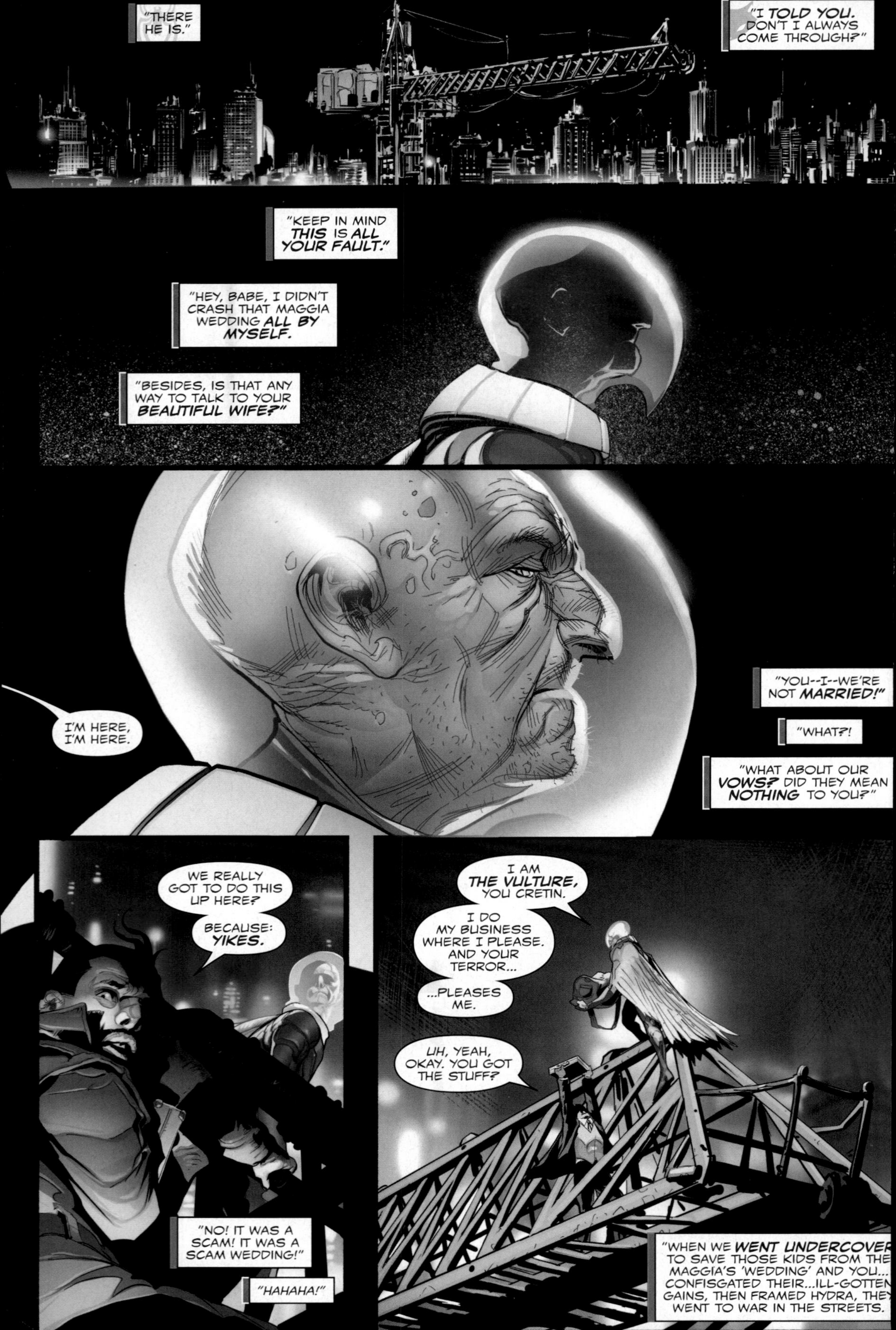
"THERE HE IS."
"I TOLD YOU. DON'T I ALWAYS COME THROUGH?"
"KEEP IN MIND THIS IS ALL YOUR FAULT."
"HEY, BABE, I DIDN'T CRASH THAT MAGGIA WEDDING ALL BY MYSELF.
"BESIDES, IS THAT ANY WAY TO TALK TO YOUR BEAUTIFUL WIFE?"
I'M HERE, I'M HERE.
"YOU--I--WE'RE NOT MARRIED!"
"WHAT?!
"WHAT ABOUT OUR VOWS? DID THEY MEAN NOTHING TO YOU?"
WE REALLY GOT TO DO THIS UP HERE?
BECAUSE: YIKES.
"NO! IT WAS A SCAM! IT WAS A SCAM WEDDING!"
"HAHAHA!"
I AM THE VULTURE, YOU CRETIN.
I DO MY BUSINESS WHERE I PLEASE. AND YOUR TERROR...
...PLEASES ME.
UH, YEAH, OKAY. YOU GOT THE STUFF?
"WHEN WE WENT UNDERCOVER TO SAVE THOSE KIDS FROM THE MAGGIA'S 'WEDDING' AND YOU... CONFISCATED THEIR...ILL-GOTTEN GAINS, THEN FRAMED HYDRA, THEY WENT TO WAR IN THE STREETS.

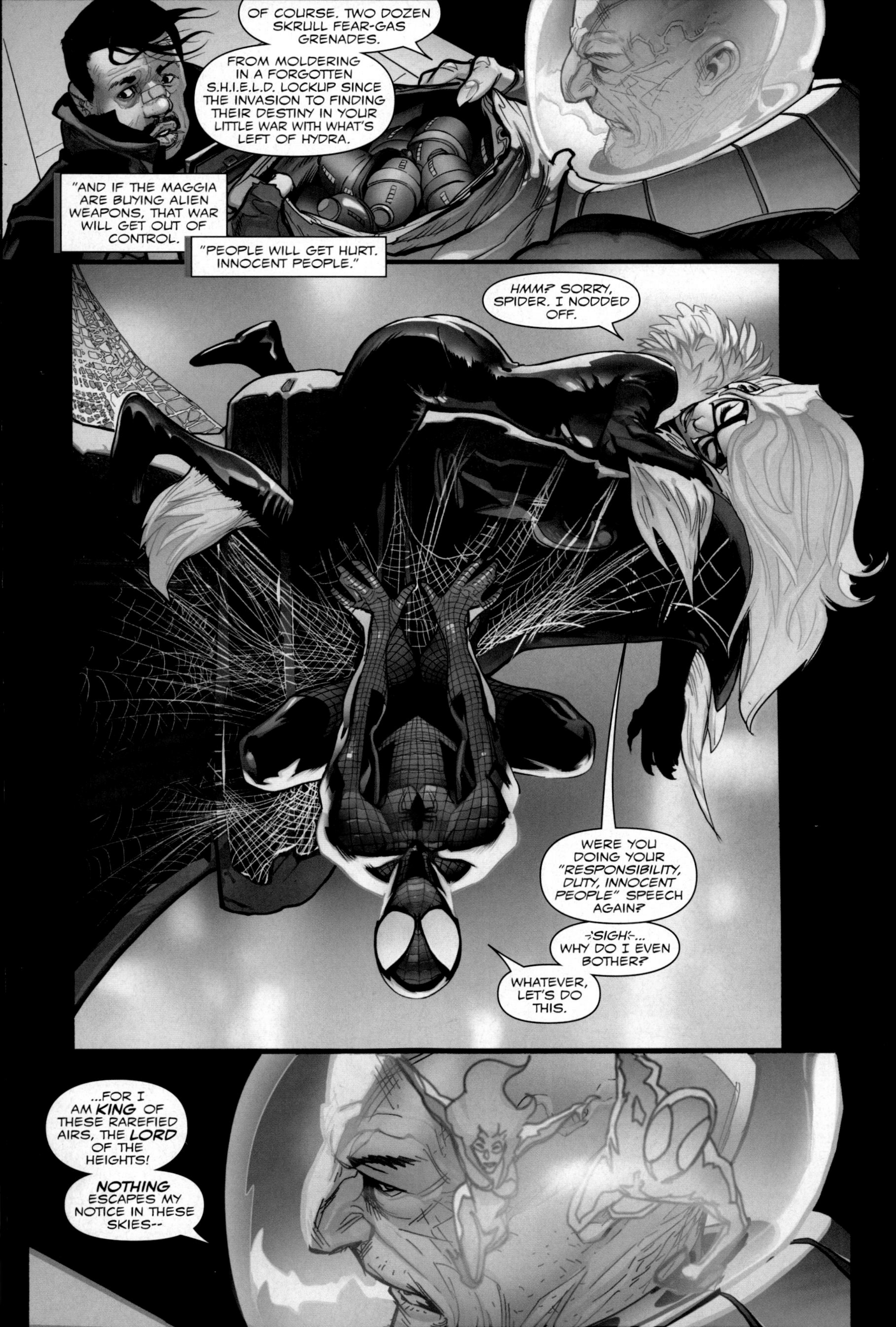
OF COURSE. TWO DOZEN SKRULL FEAR-GAS GRENADES.
FROM MOLDERING IN A FORGOTTEN S.H.I.E.L.D. LOCKUP SINCE THE INVASION TO FINDING THEIR DESTINY IN YOUR LITTLE WAR WITH WHAT'S LEFT OF HYDRA.
"AND IF THE MAGGIA ARE BUYING ALIEN WEAPONS, THAT WAR WILL GET OUT OF CONTROL.
"PEOPLE WILL GET HURT. INNOCENT PEOPLE."
HMM? SORRY, SPIDER. I NODDED OFF.
WERE YOU DOING YOUR "RESPONSIBILITY, DUTY, INNOCENT PEOPLE" SPEECH AGAIN?
SIGH... WHY DO I EVEN BOTHER?
WHATEVER, LET'S DO THIS.
...FOR I AM **KING** OF THESE RAREFIED AIRS, THE **LORD** OF THE HEIGHTS!
NOTHING ESCAPES MY NOTICE IN THESE SKIES--

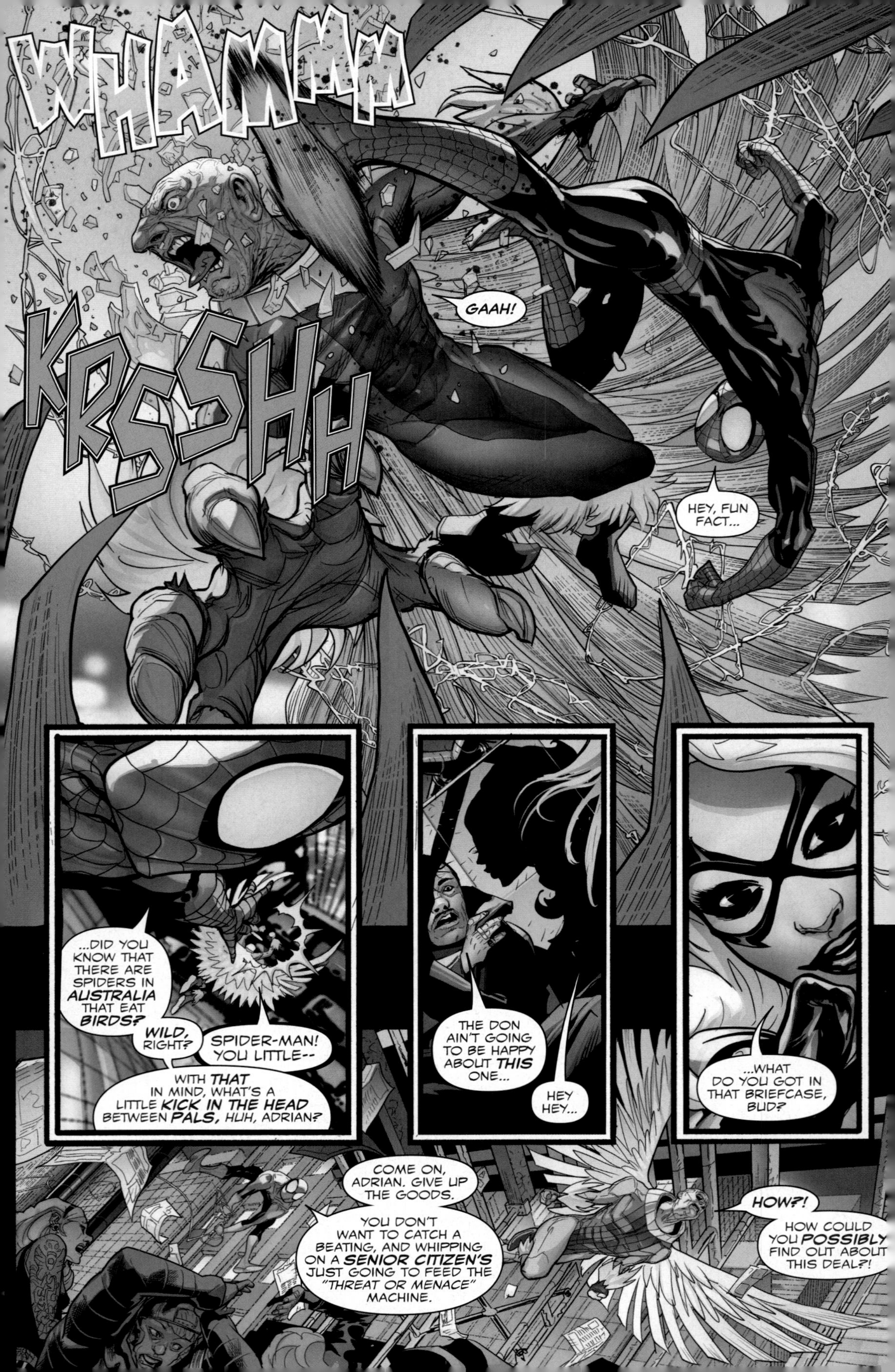
WHAMMM
KRSSHH
GAAH!
HEY, FUN FACT...
...DID YOU KNOW THAT THERE ARE SPIDERS IN AUSTRALIA THAT EAT BIRDS?
WILD, RIGHT?
SPIDER-MAN! YOU LITTLE--
WITH THAT IN MIND, WHAT'S A LITTLE KICK IN THE HEAD BETWEEN PALS, HUH, ADRIAN?
THE DON AIN'T GOING TO BE HAPPY ABOUT THIS ONE...
HEY HEY...
...WHAT DO YOU GOT IN THAT BRIEFCASE, BUD?
COME ON, ADRIAN. GIVE UP THE GOODS.
YOU DON'T WANT TO CATCH A BEATING, AND WHIPPING ON A SENIOR CITIZEN'S JUST GOING TO FEED THE "THREAT OR MENACE" MACHINE.
HOW?!
HOW COULD YOU POSSIBLY FIND OUT ABOUT THIS DEAL?!

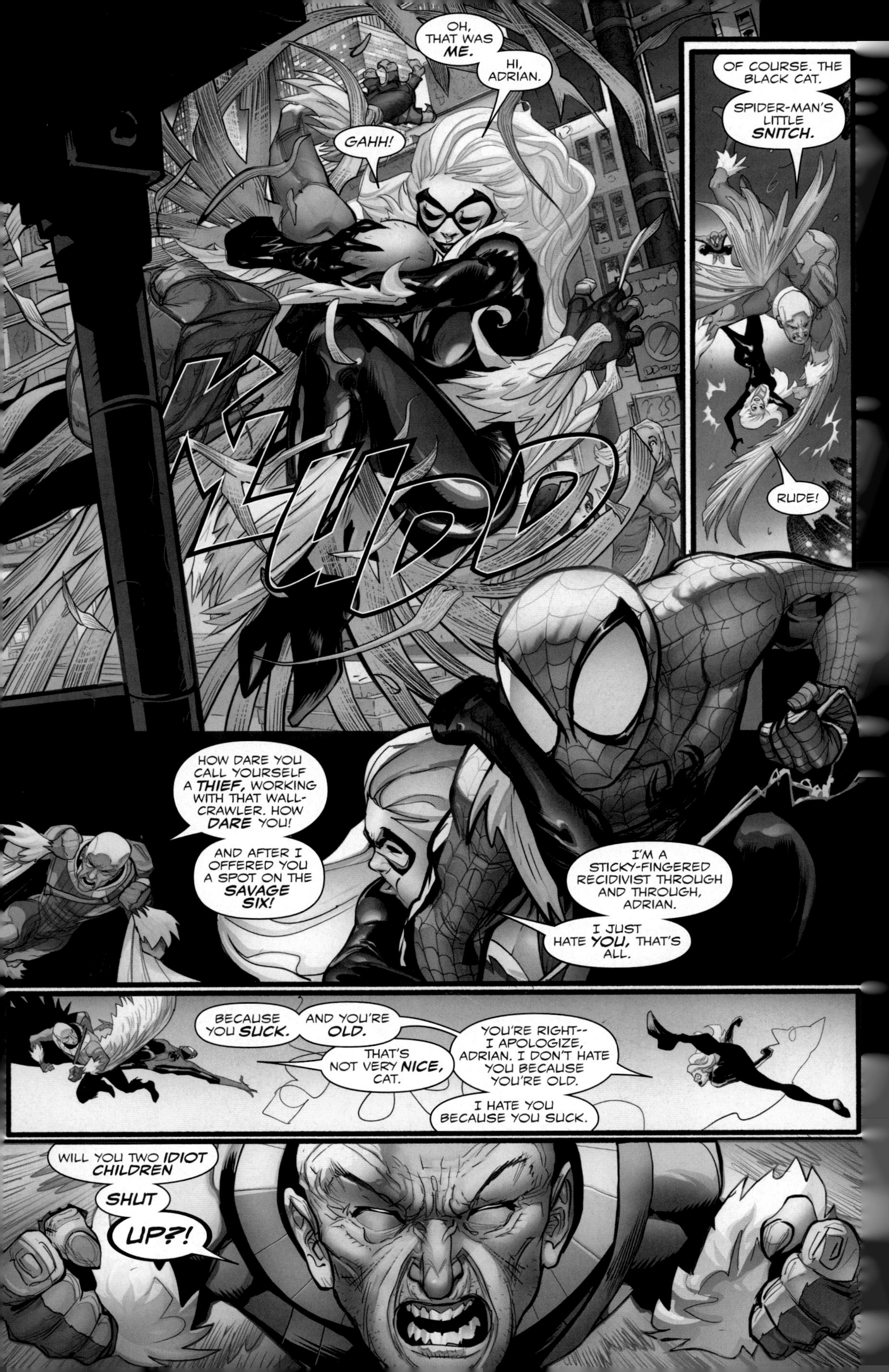

OH, THAT WAS ME.
HI, ADRIAN.
GAHH!
KLUDD
OF COURSE. THE BLACK CAT.
SPIDER-MAN'S LITTLE SNITCH.
RUDE!
HOW DARE YOU CALL YOURSELF A THIEF, WORKING WITH THAT WALL-CRAWLER. HOW DARE YOU!
AND AFTER I OFFERED YOU A SPOT ON THE SAVAGE SIX!
I'M A STICKY-FINGERED RECIDIVIST THROUGH AND THROUGH, ADRIAN.
I JUST HATE YOU, THAT'S ALL.
BECAUSE YOU SUCK.
AND YOU'RE OLD.
THAT'S NOT VERY NICE, CAT.
YOU'RE RIGHT-- I APOLOGIZE, ADRIAN. I DON'T HATE YOU BECAUSE YOU'RE OLD.
I HATE YOU BECAUSE YOU SUCK.
WILL YOU TWO IDIOT CHILDREN
SHUT
UP?!

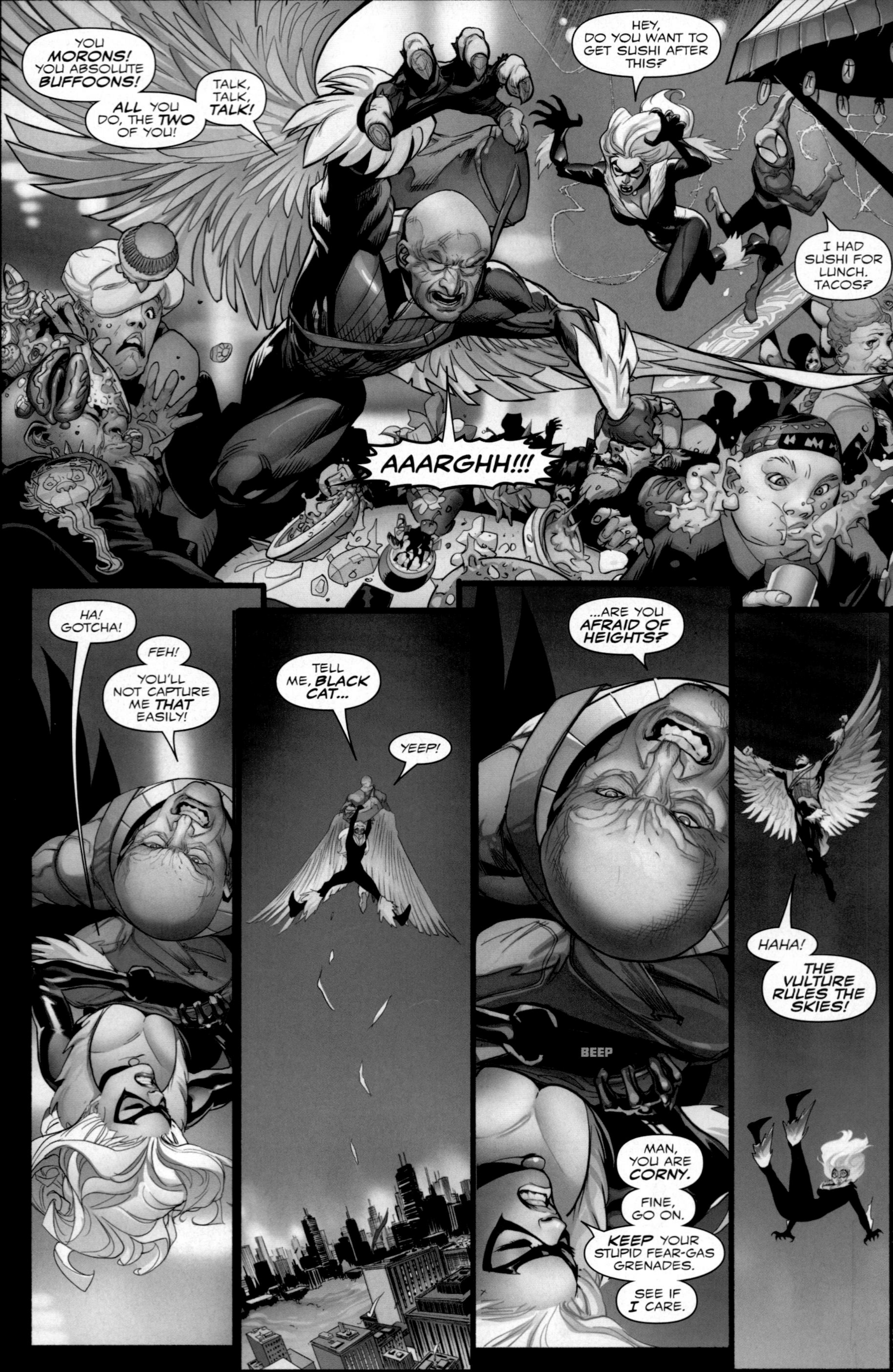
YOU MORONS! YOU ABSOLUTE BUFFOONS!
ALL YOU DO, THE TWO OF YOU!
TALK, TALK, TALK!
HEY, DO YOU WANT TO GET SUSHI AFTER THIS?
I HAD SUSHI FOR LUNCH. TACOS?
AAARGHH!!!
HA! GOTCHA!
FEH!
YOU'LL NOT CAPTURE ME THAT EASILY!
TELL ME, BLACK CAT...
YEEP!
...ARE YOU AFRAID OF HEIGHTS?
BEEP
MAN, YOU ARE CORNY.
FINE, GO ON.
KEEP YOUR STUPID FEAR-GAS GRENADES.
SEE IF I CARE.
HAHA!
THE VULTURE RULES THE SKIES!

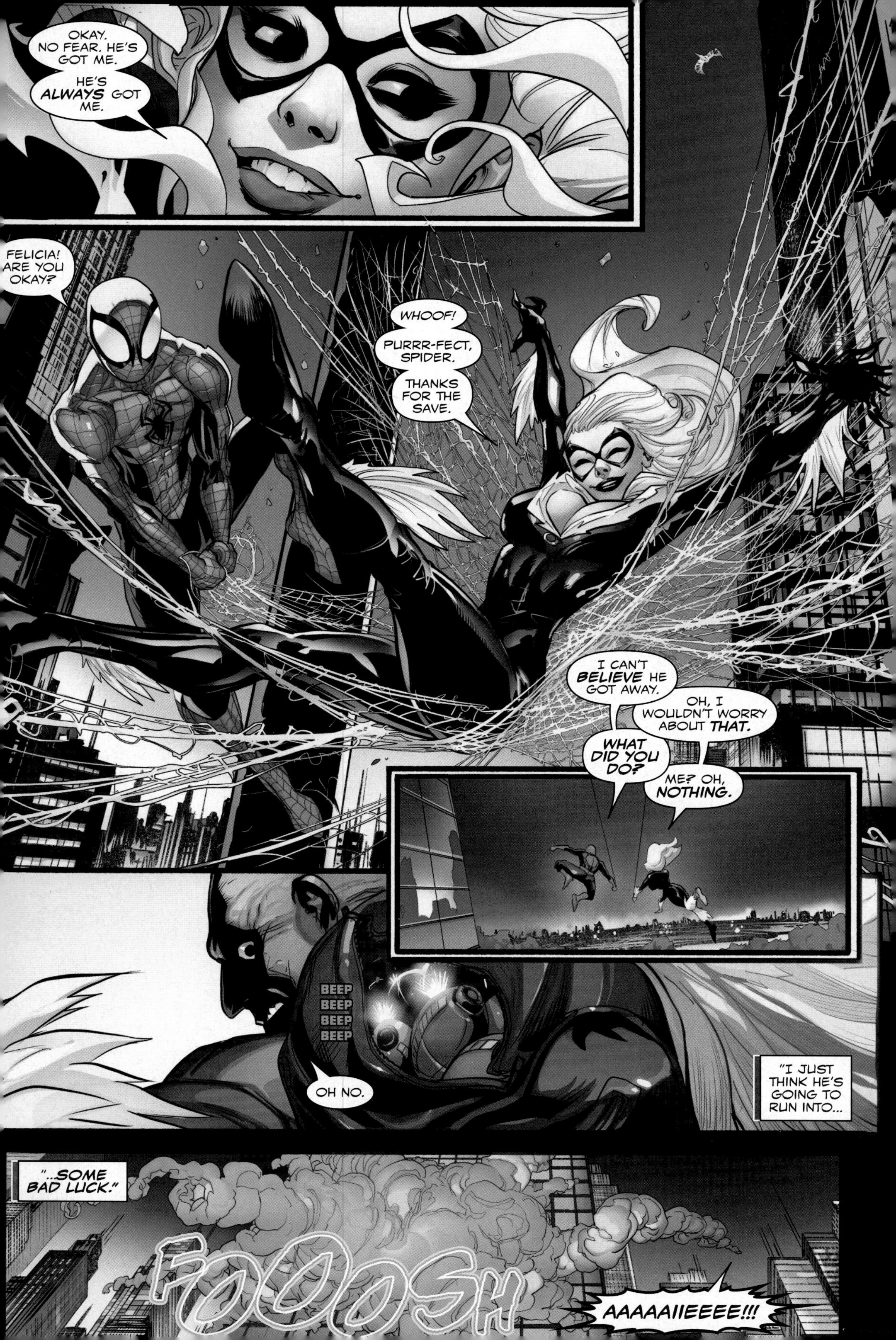
OKAY. NO FEAR. HE'S GOT ME.
HE'S ALWAYS GOT ME.
FELICIA! ARE YOU OKAY?
WHOOF!
PURRR-FECT, SPIDER.
THANKS FOR THE SAVE.
I CAN'T BELIEVE HE GOT AWAY.
OH, I WOULDN'T WORRY ABOUT THAT.
WHAT DID YOU DO?
ME? OH, NOTHING.
BEEP BEEP BEEP BEEP
OH NO.
"I JUST THINK HE'S GOING TO RUN INTO...
"...SOME BAD LUCK."
FOOOOSH
AAAAAIIEEEE!!!

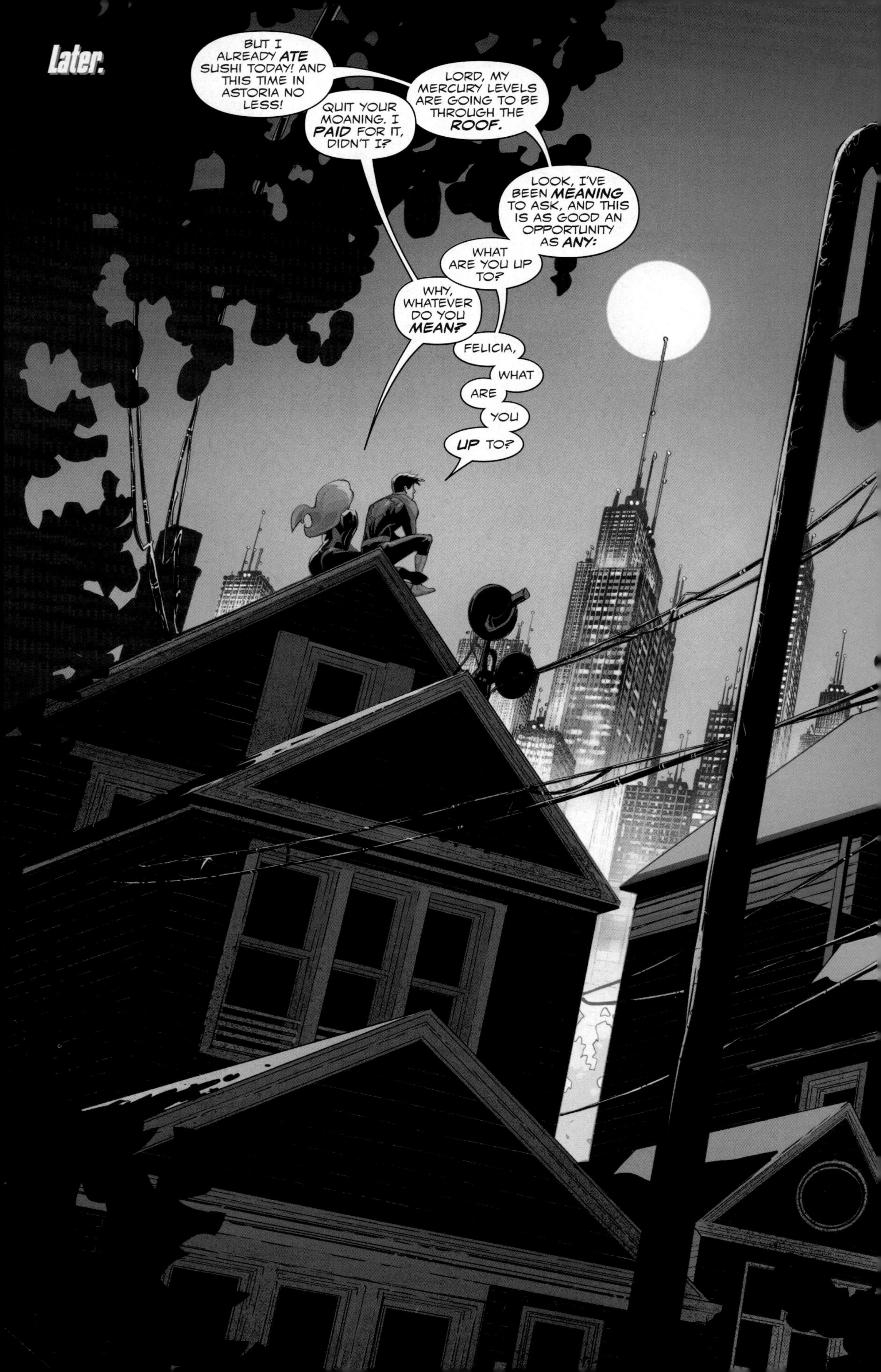
Later.
BUT I ALREADY ATE SUSHI TODAY! AND THIS TIME IN ASTORIA NO LESS!
LORD, MY MERCURY LEVELS ARE GOING TO BE THROUGH THE ROOF.
QUIT YOUR MOANING. I PAID FOR IT, DIDN'T I?
LOOK, I'VE BEEN MEANING TO ASK, AND THIS IS AS GOOD AN OPPORTUNITY AS ANY:
WHAT ARE YOU UP TO?
WHY, WHATEVER DO YOU MEAN?
FELICIA, WHAT ARE YOU UP TO?

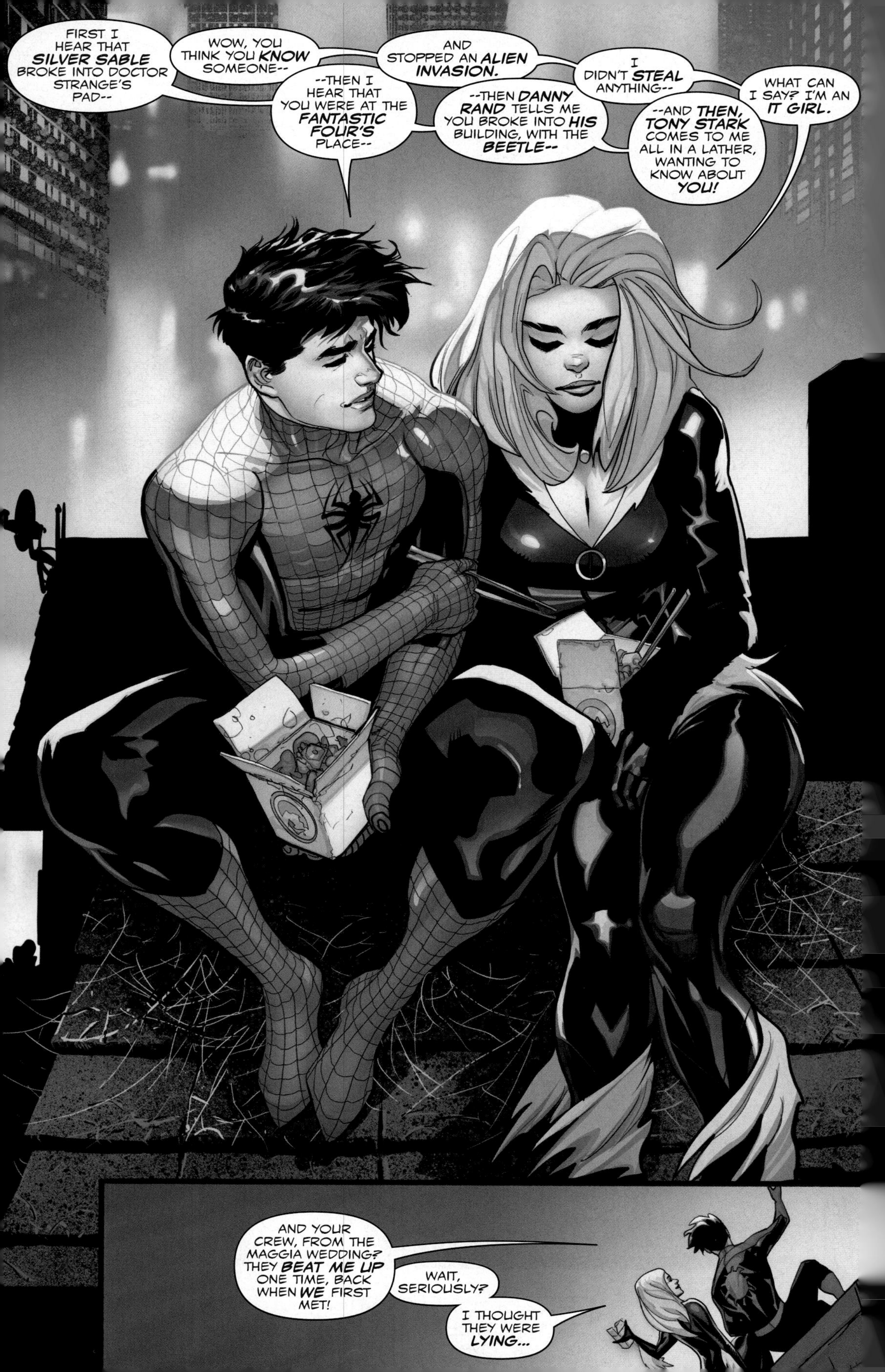
FIRST I HEAR THAT SILVER SABLE BROKE INTO DOCTOR STRANGE'S PAD--
WOW, YOU THINK YOU KNOW SOMEONE--
--THEN I HEAR THAT YOU WERE AT THE FANTASTIC FOUR'S PLACE--
AND STOPPED AN ALIEN INVASION.
--THEN DANNY RAND TELLS ME YOU BROKE INTO HIS BUILDING, WITH THE BEETLE--
I DIDN'T STEAL ANYTHING--
--AND THEN, TONY STARK COMES TO ME ALL IN A LATHER, WANTING TO KNOW ABOUT YOU!
WHAT CAN I SAY? I'M AN IT GIRL.
AND YOUR CREW, FROM THE MAGGIA WEDDING? THEY BEAT ME UP ONE TIME, BACK WHEN WE FIRST MET!
WAIT, SERIOUSLY?
I THOUGHT THEY WERE LYING...

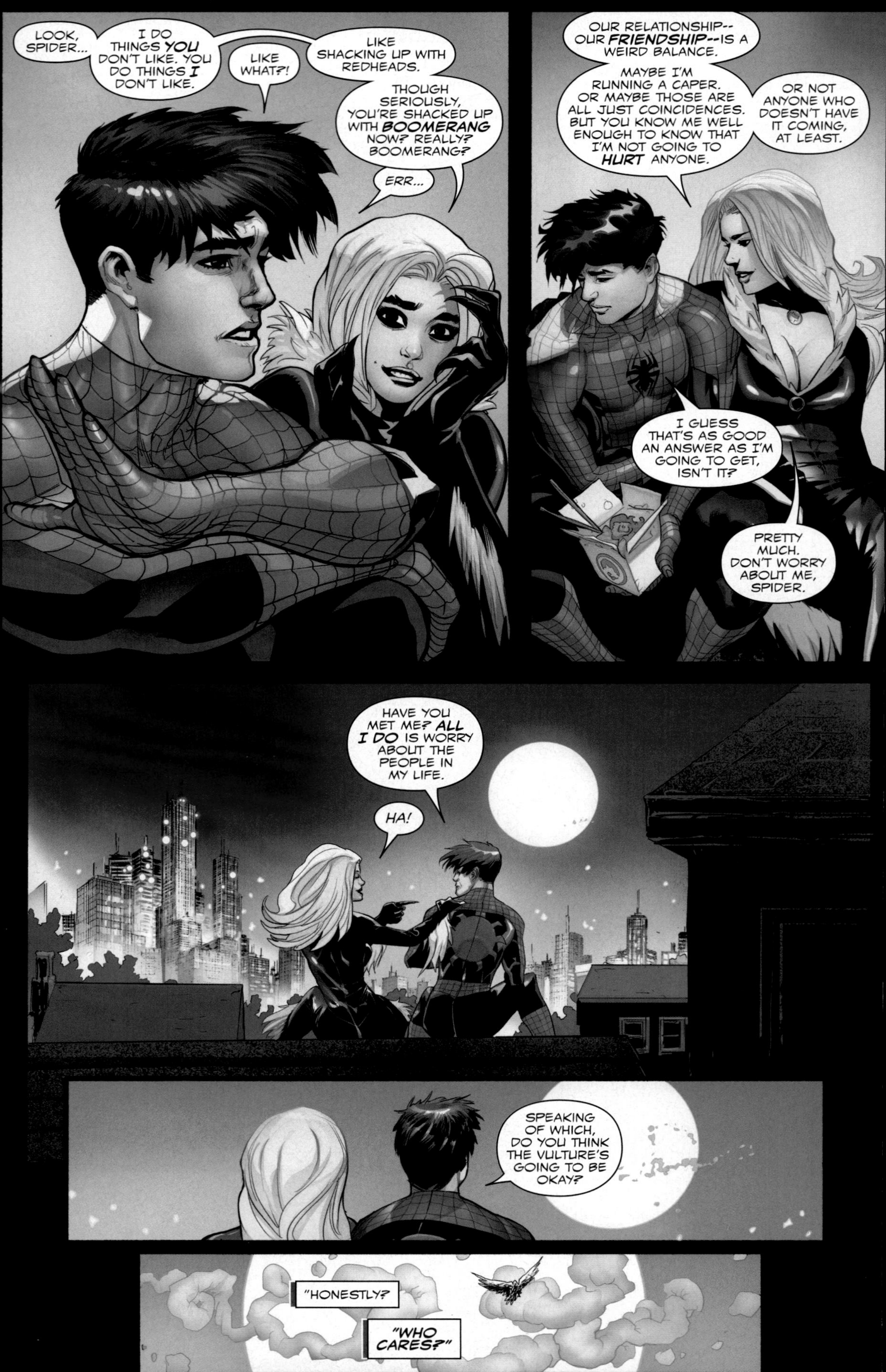
LOOK, SPIDER...
I DO THINGS YOU DON'T LIKE. YOU DO THINGS I DON'T LIKE.
LIKE WHAT?!
LIKE SHACKING UP WITH REDHEADS.
THOUGH SERIOUSLY, YOU'RE SHACKED UP WITH BOOMERANG NOW? REALLY? BOOMERANG?
ERR...
OUR RELATIONSHIP-- OUR FRIENDSHIP--IS A WEIRD BALANCE.
MAYBE I'M RUNNING A CAPER. OR MAYBE THOSE ARE ALL JUST COINCIDENCES. BUT YOU KNOW ME WELL ENOUGH TO KNOW THAT I'M NOT GOING TO HURT ANYONE.
OR NOT ANYONE WHO DOESN'T HAVE IT COMING, AT LEAST.
I GUESS THAT'S AS GOOD AN ANSWER AS I'M GOING TO GET, ISN'T IT?
PRETTY MUCH. DON'T WORRY ABOUT ME, SPIDER.
HAVE YOU MET ME? ALL I DO IS WORRY ABOUT THE PEOPLE IN MY LIFE.
HA!
SPEAKING OF WHICH, DO YOU THINK THE VULTURE'S GOING TO BE OKAY?
"HONESTLY?
"WHO CARES?"

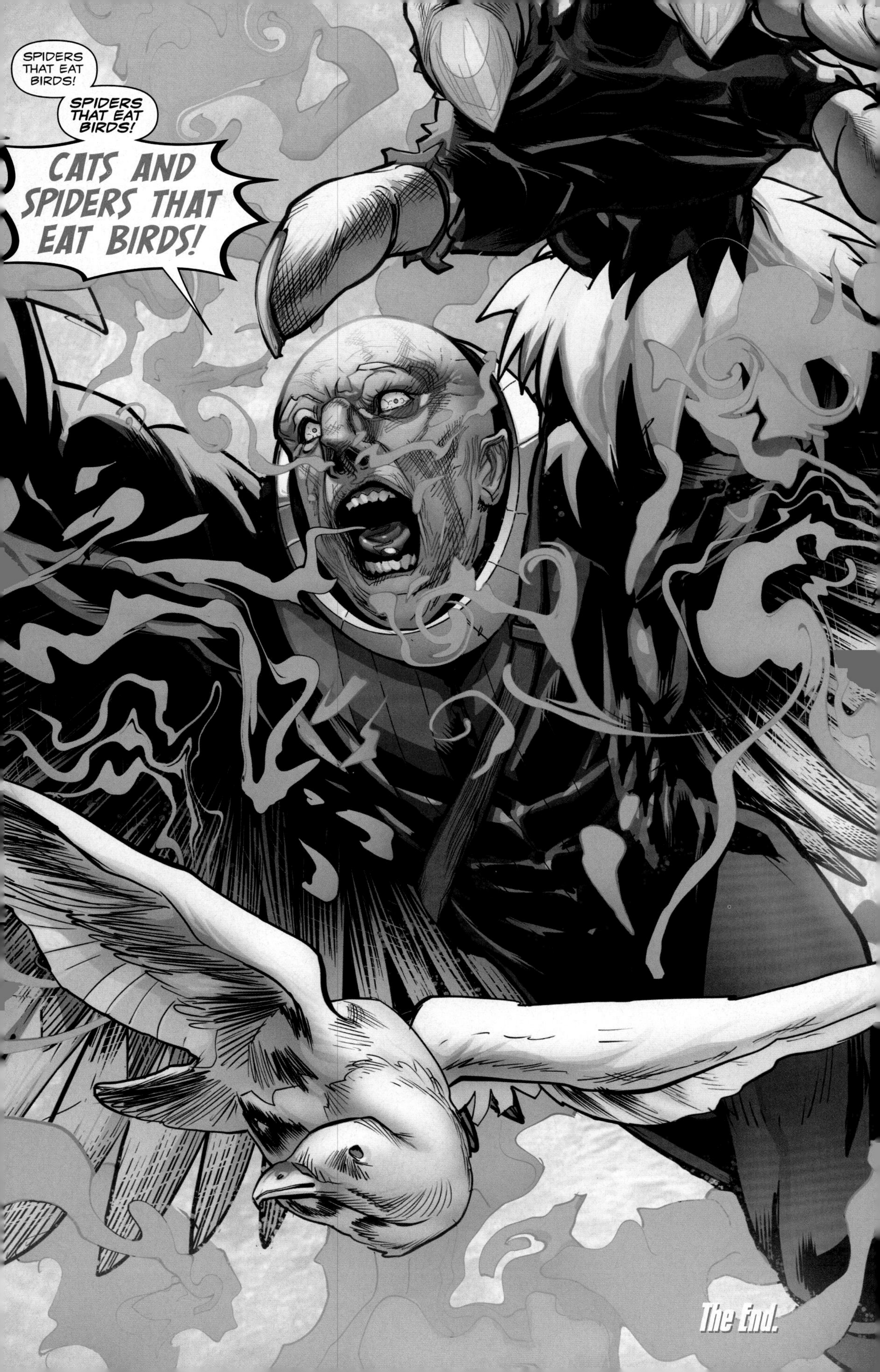
SPIDERS THAT EAT BIRDS!
SPIDERS THAT EAT BIRDS!
CATS AND SPIDERS THAT EAT BIRDS!
The End.

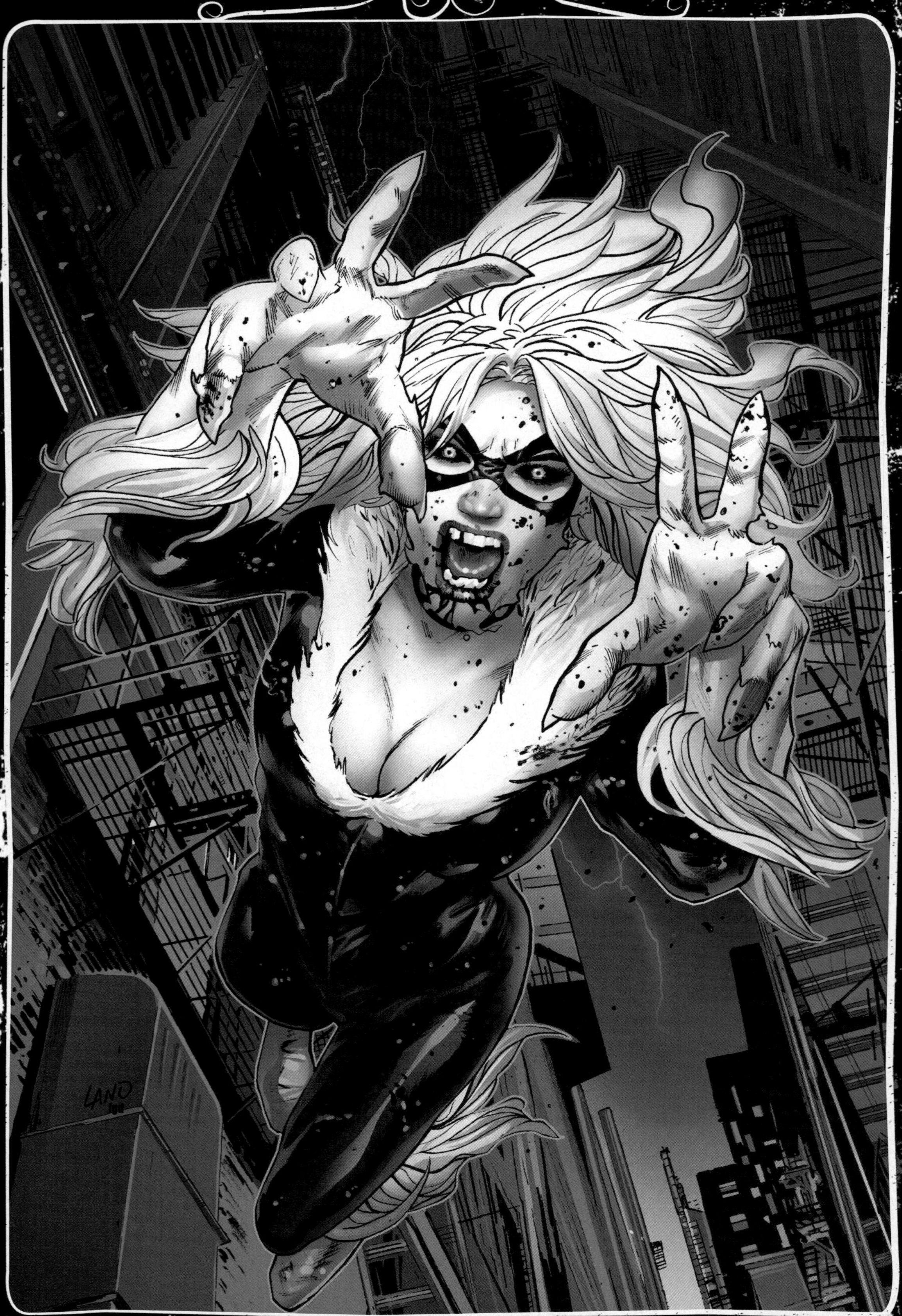
LAND

#11 variant by **GREG LAND** and **FRANK D'ARMATA**

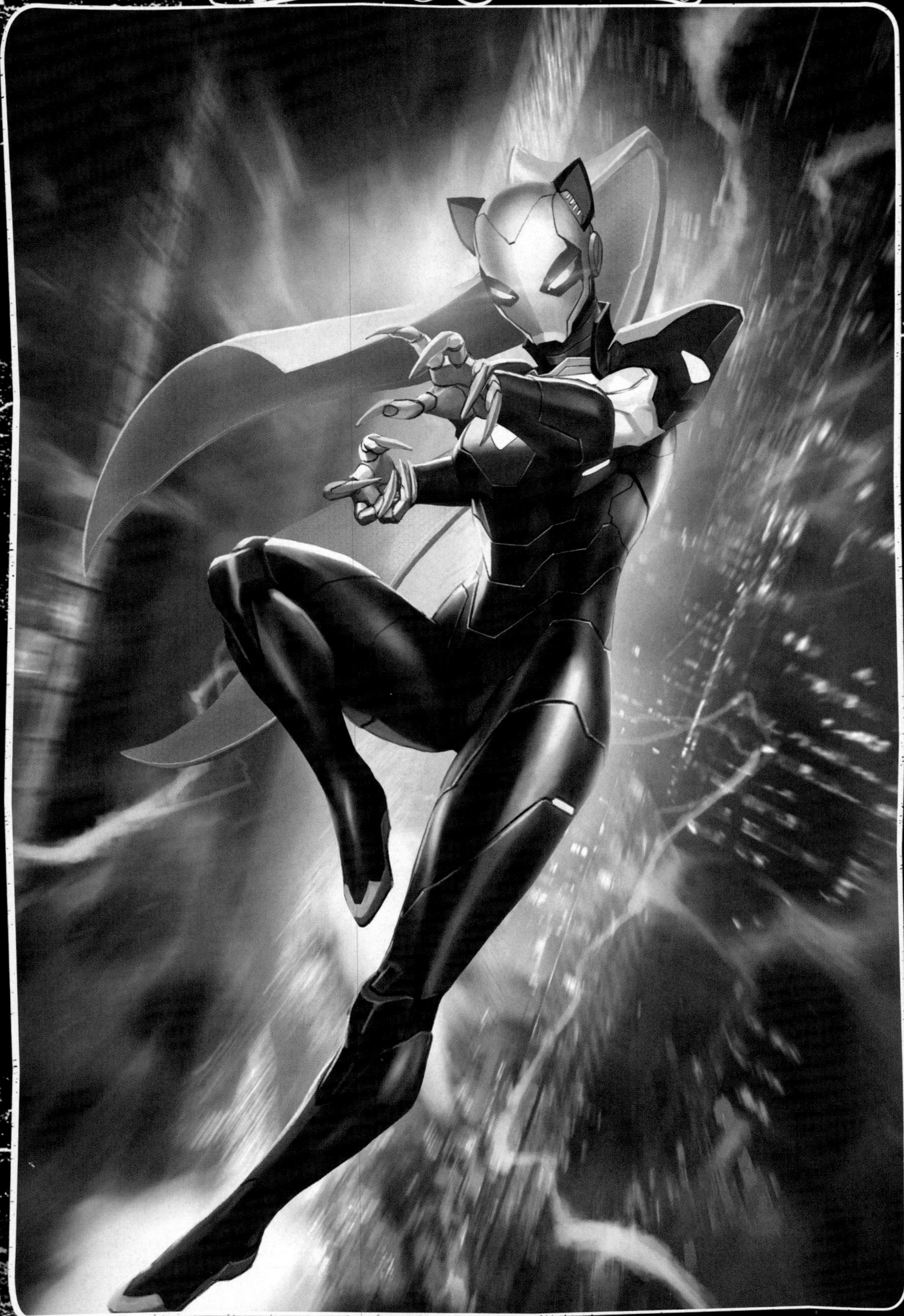

#12 variant by **SKAN**

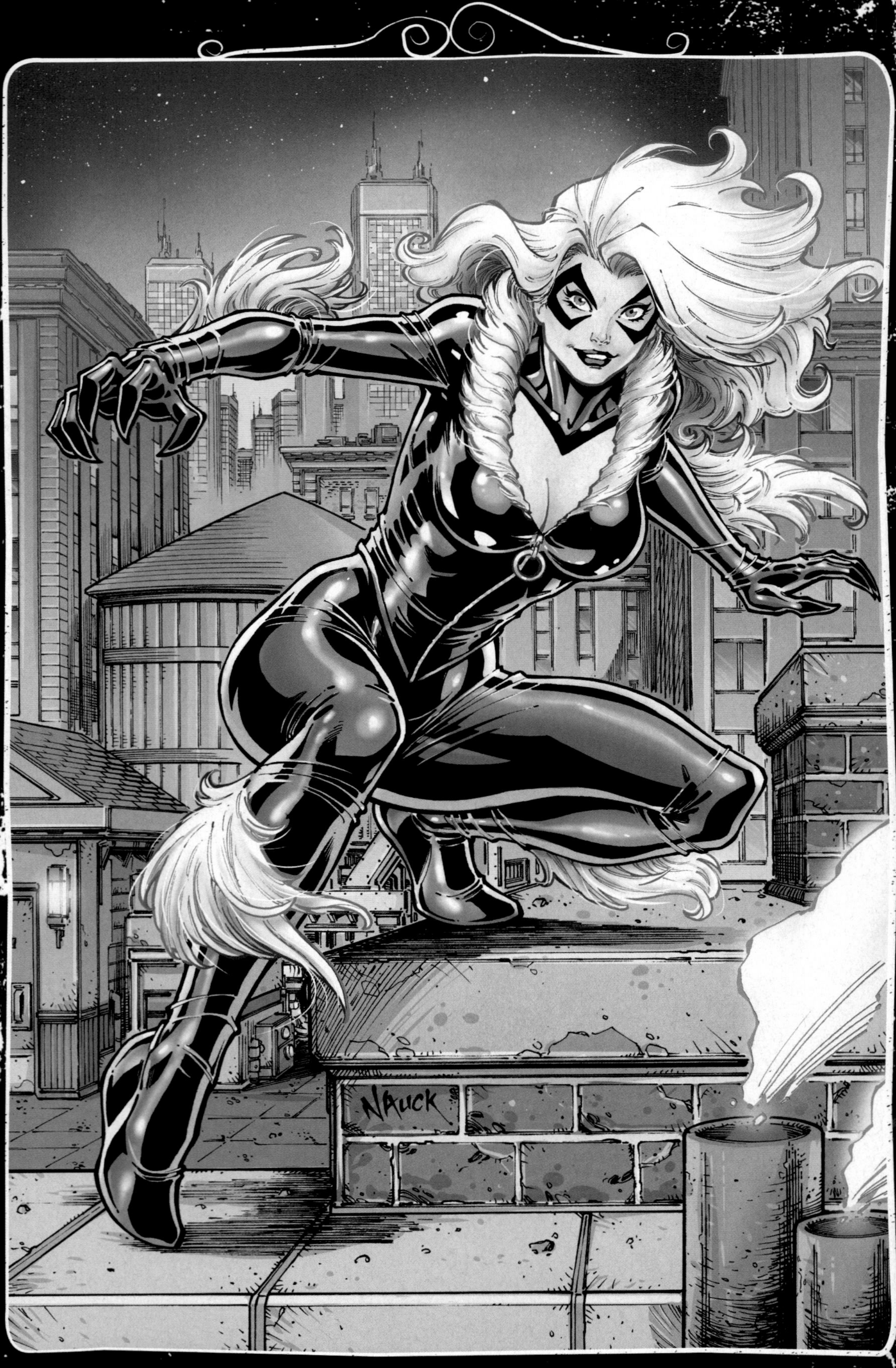
NAUCK

Annual #1 variant by **TODD NAUCK**

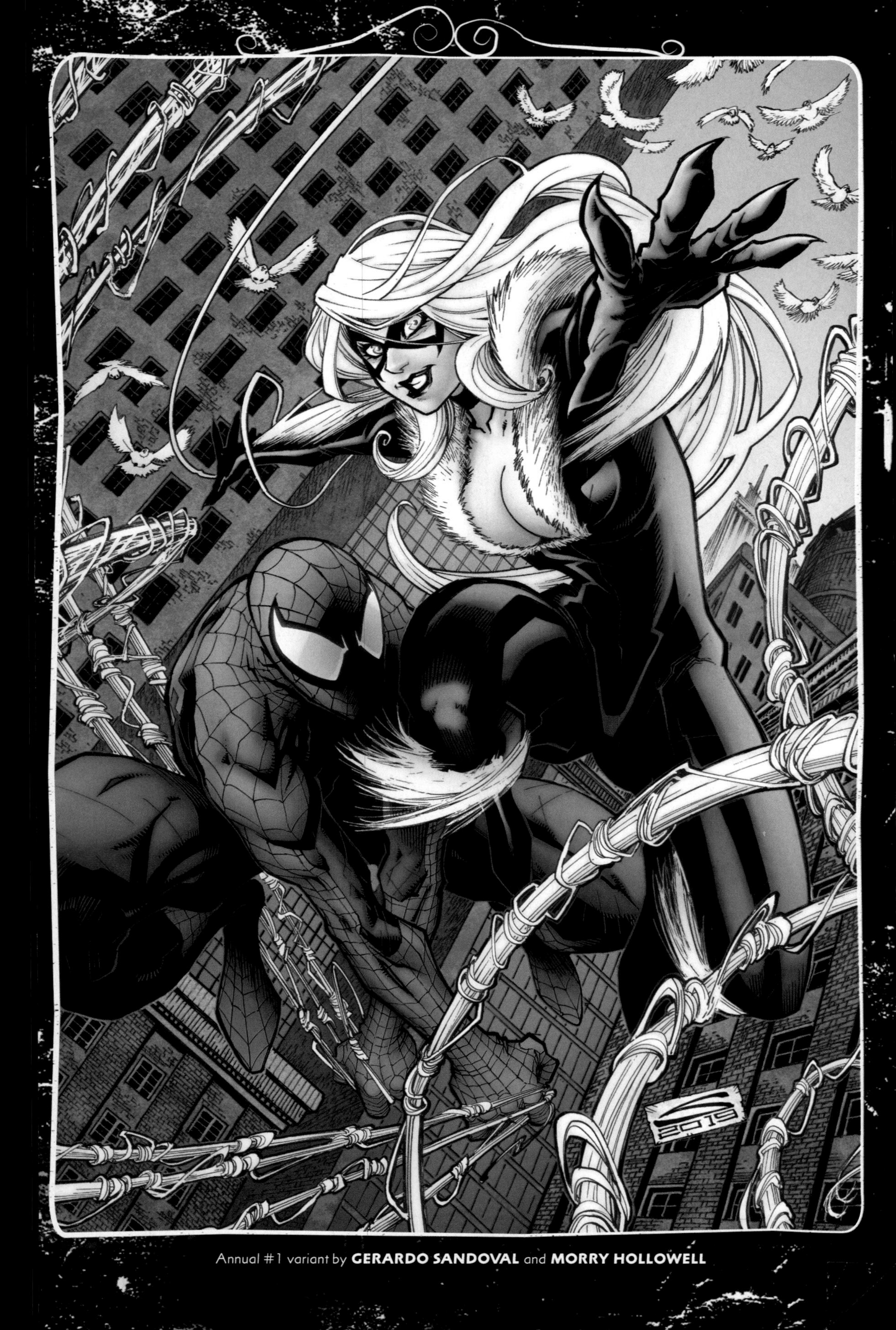

Annual #1 variant by **GERARDO SANDOVAL** and **MORRY HOLLOWELL**

BLACK CAT #11
IRON CAT ARMOR

BLACK CAT #11
IRON CAT ARMOR

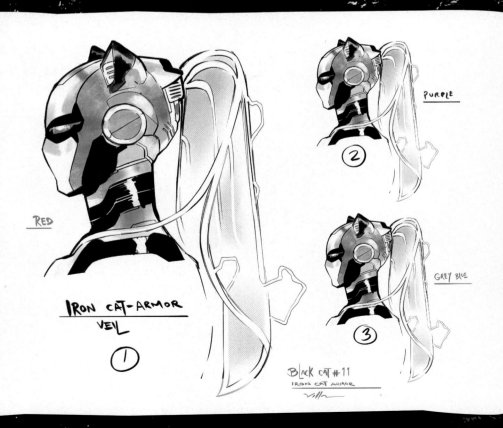

RED

PURPLE

IRON CAT-ARMOR
VEIL

① ② ③

GREY BLUE

BLACK CAT #11
IRON CAT ARMOR

Iron Cat designs by **C.F. VILLA**

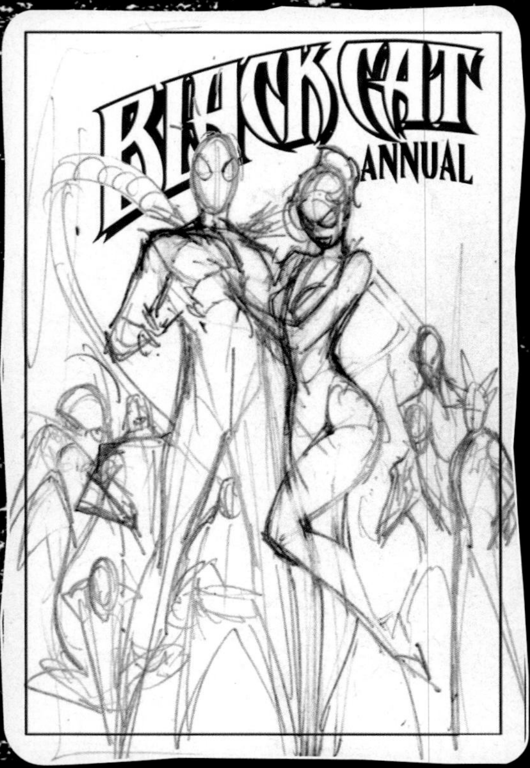
BLACK CAT
ANNUAL
Annual #1 cover sketch by **J. SCOTT CAMPBELL**

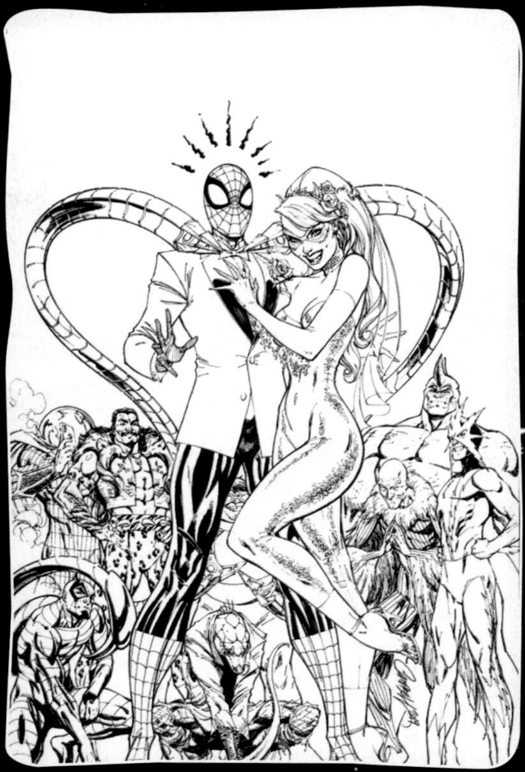
Annual #1 cover art by **J. SCOTT CAMPBELL**

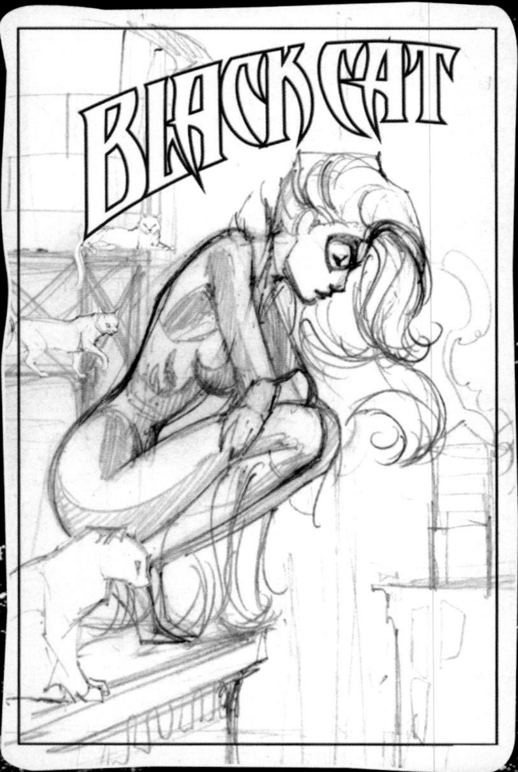
BLACK CAT
#11 cover sketch by **J. SCOTT CAMPBELL**

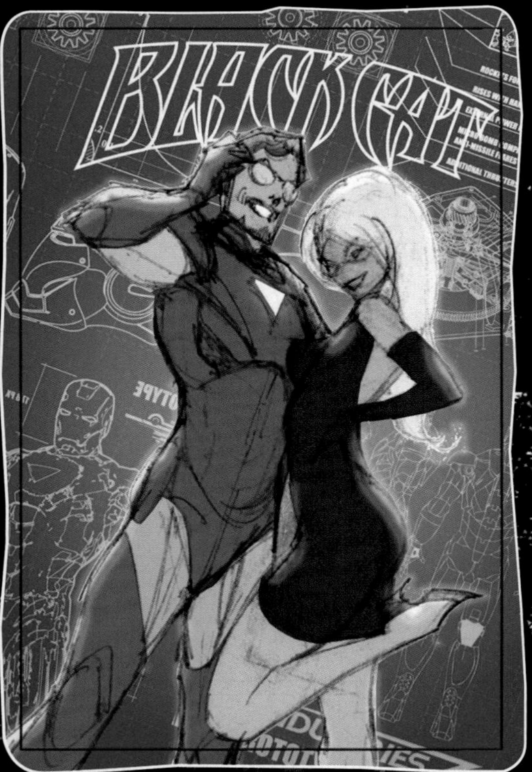
BLACK CAT
#12 cover sketch by **J. SCOTT CAMPBELL**

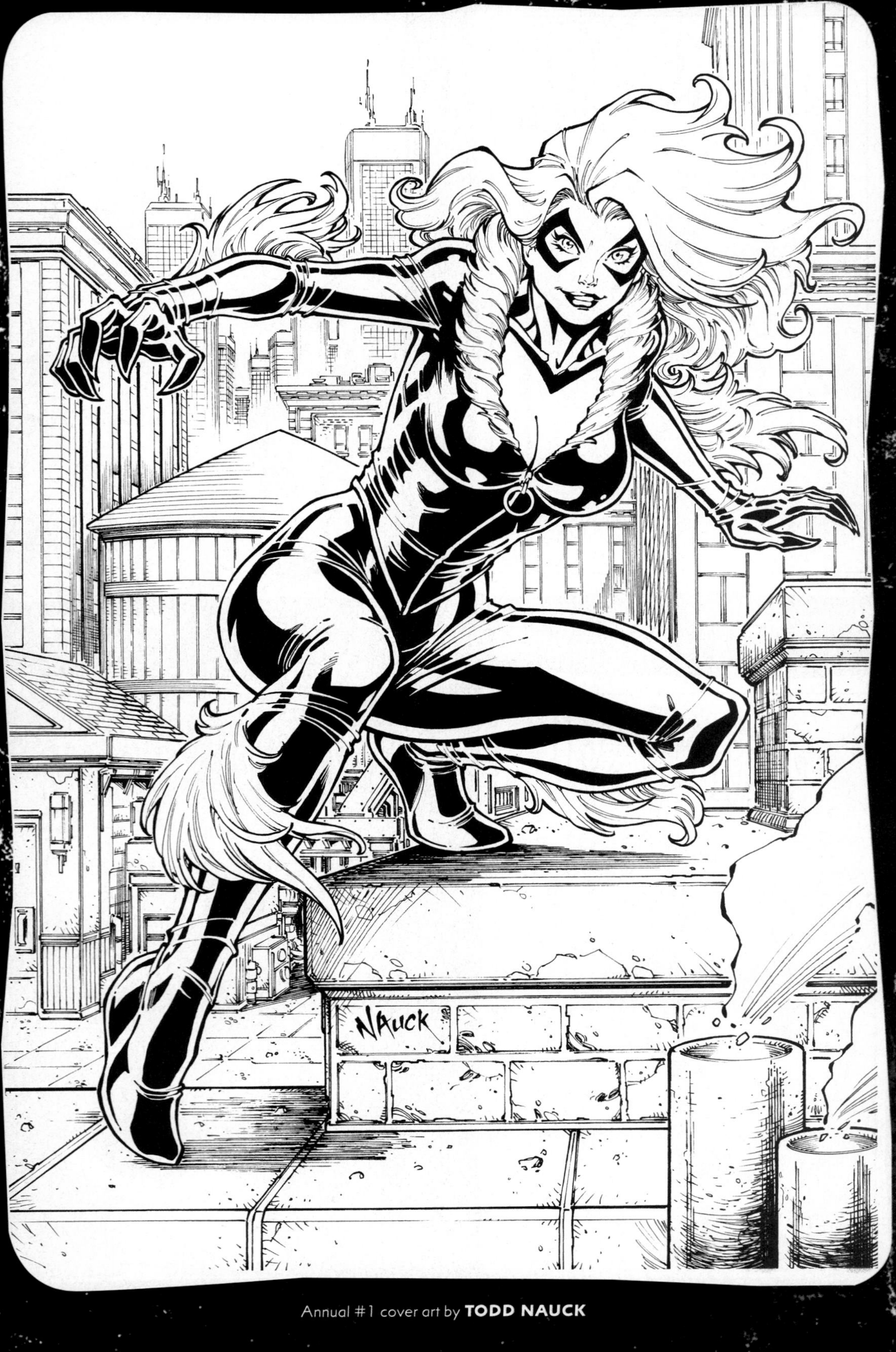
NAUCK
Annual #1 cover art by **TODD NAUCK**

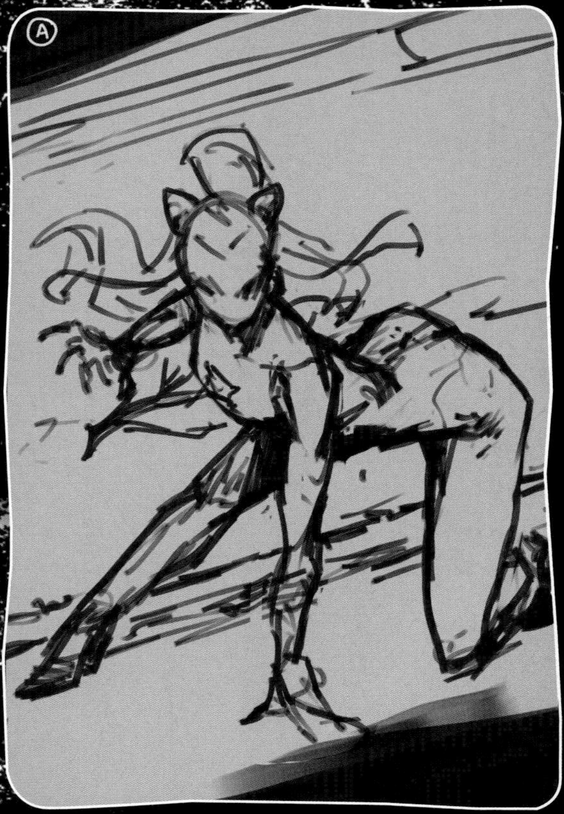
A

#12 variant cover sketch by **SKAN**

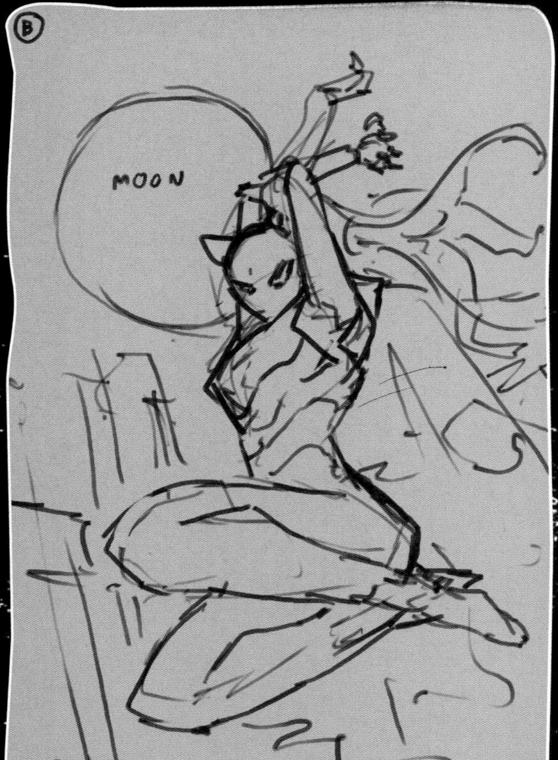
B
MOON
CITY BG.

#12 variant cover sketch by **SKAN**

Annual #1 cover sketch by **GERARDO SANDOVAL**

Annual #1 cover sketch by **GERARDO SANDOVAL**

Annual #1 cover sketch by **GERARDO SANDOVAL**

Annual #1 cover sketch by **GERARDO SANDOVAL**

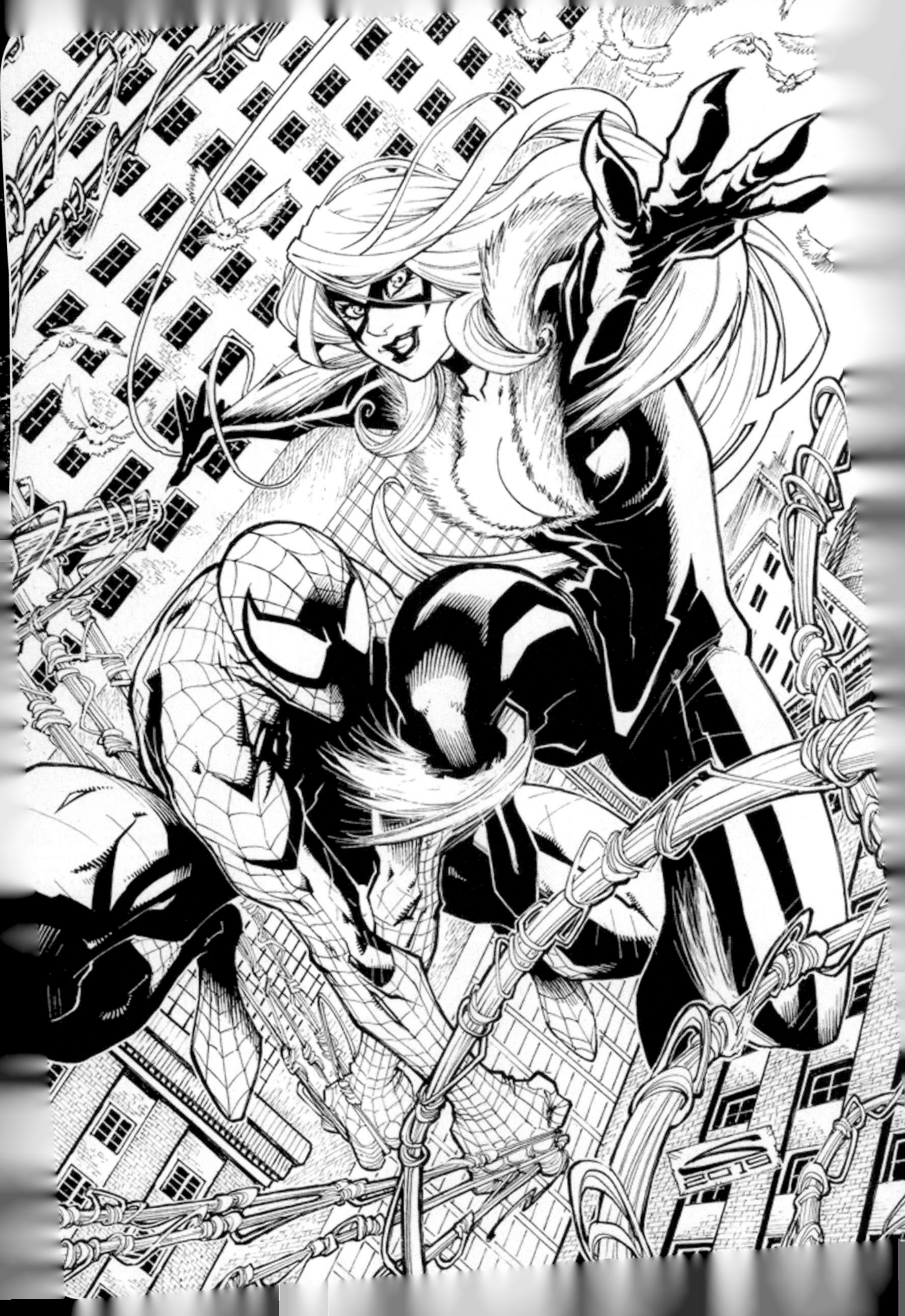

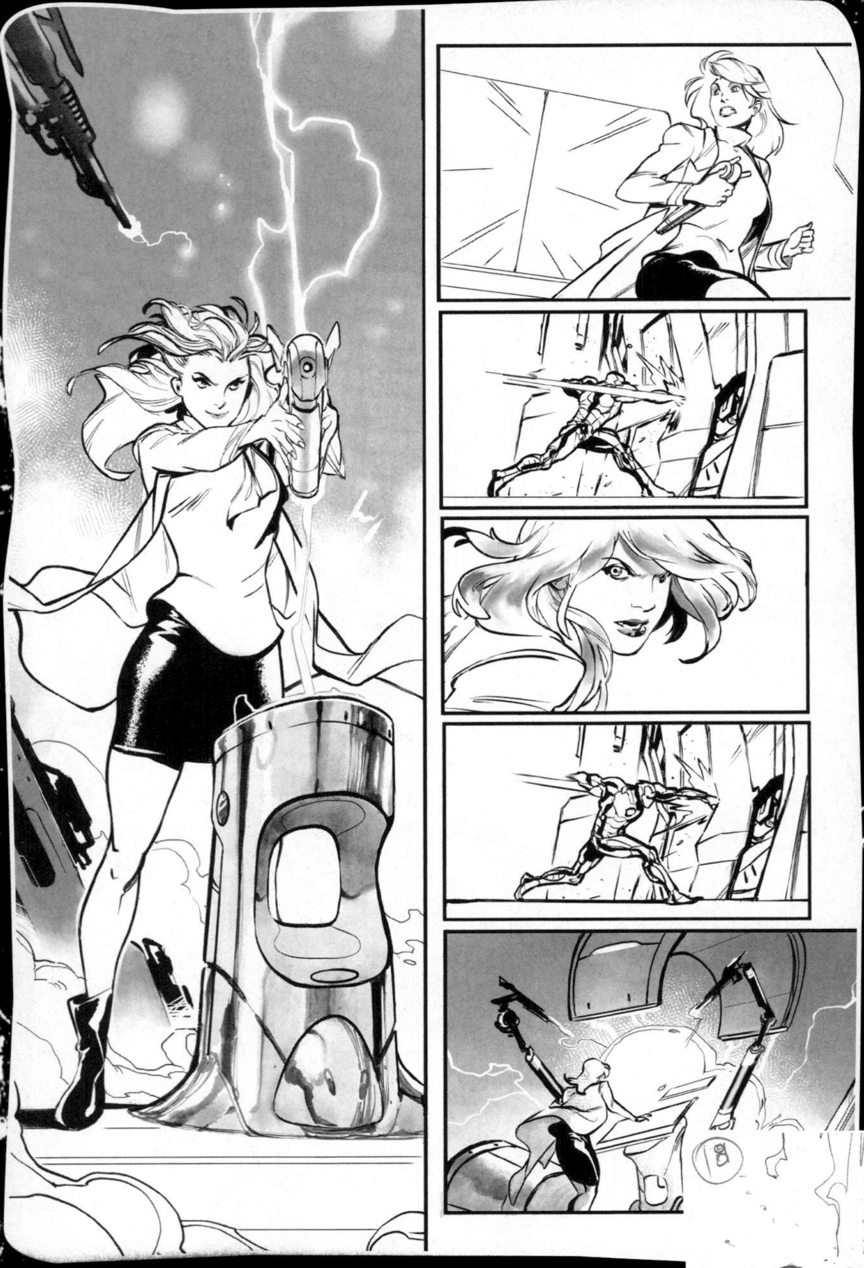

#11, page 18 art by **C.F. VILLA**

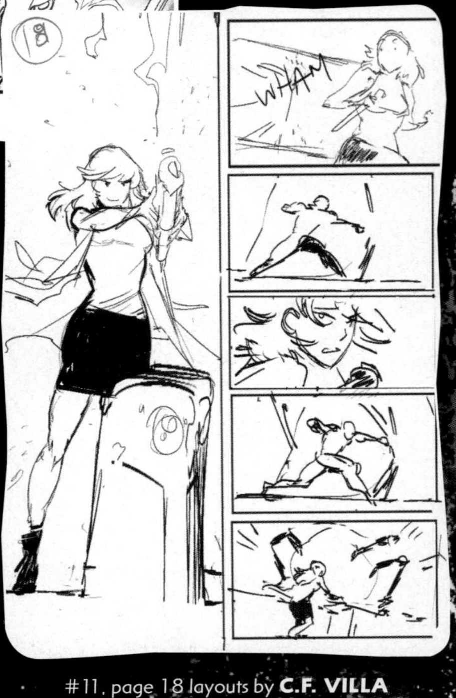
18
WHAM

#11, page 18 layouts by **C.F. VILLA**

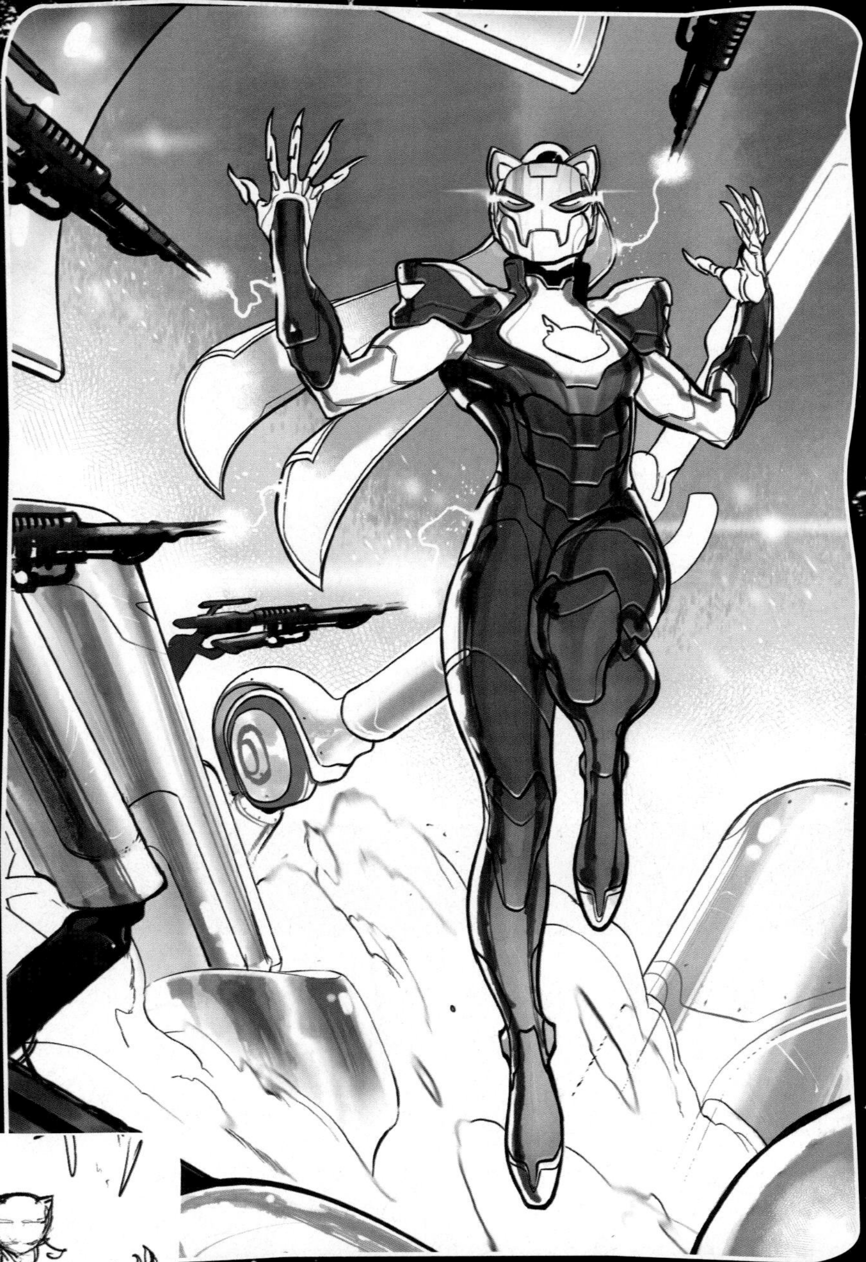

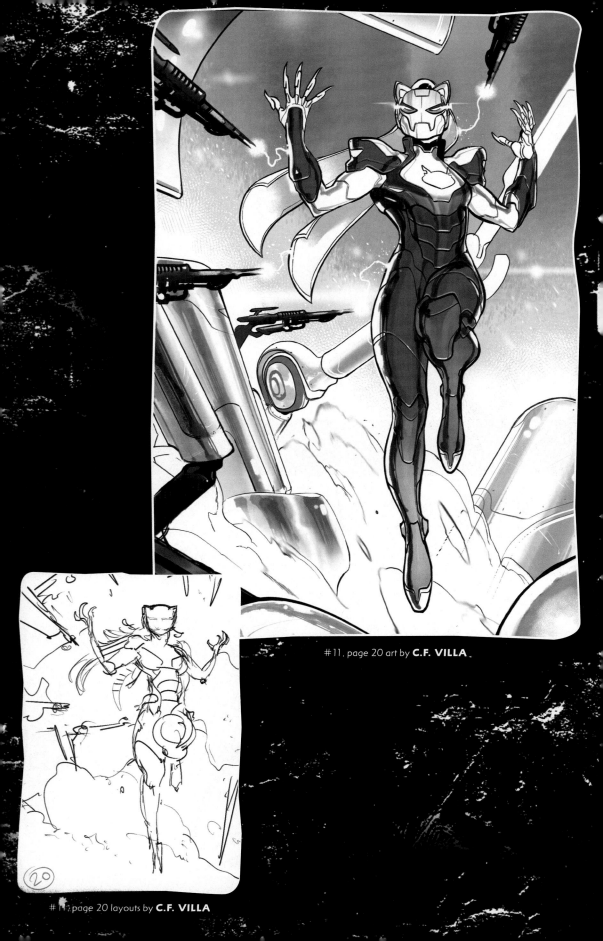

#11, page 20 art by **C.F. VILLA**

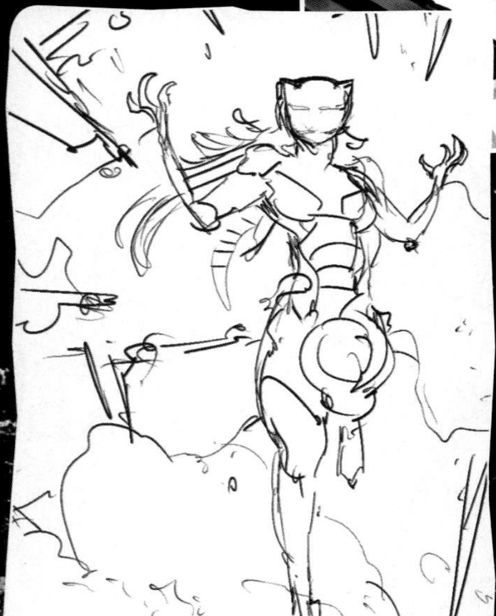

#11, page 20 layouts by **C.F. VILLA**

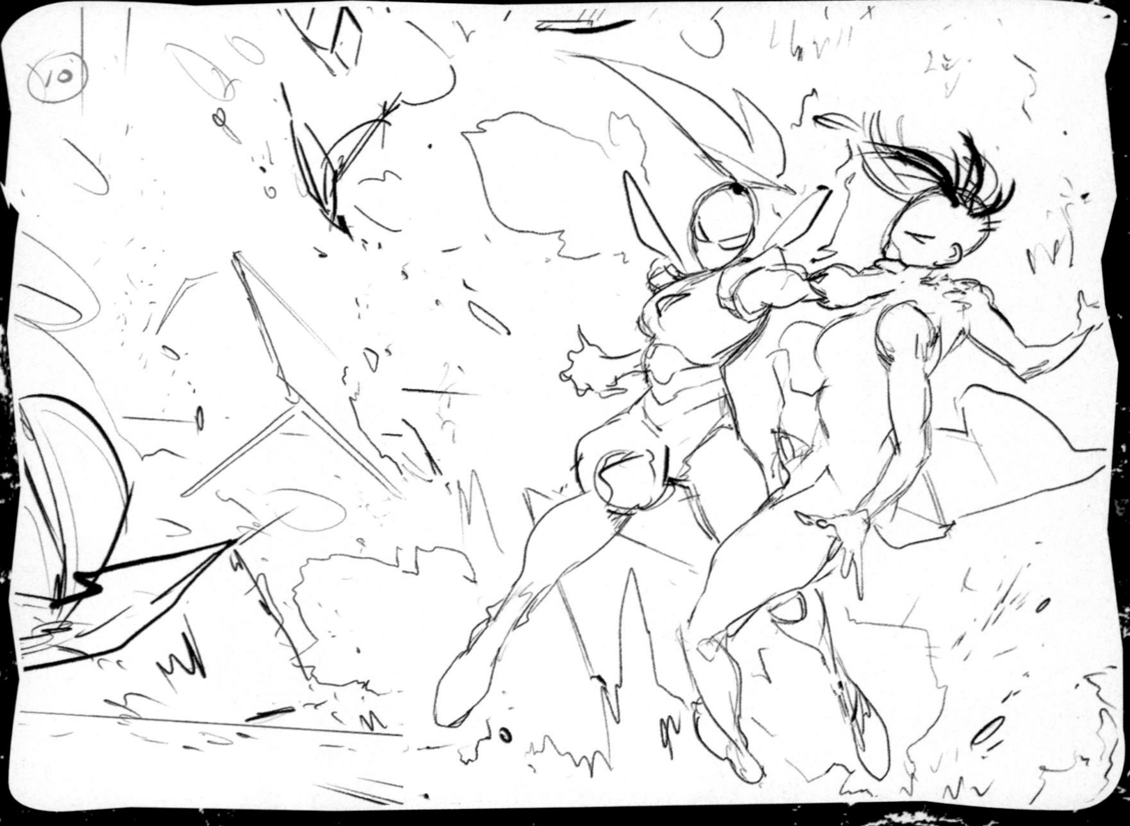

#12, page 10 layouts by **C.F. VILLA**

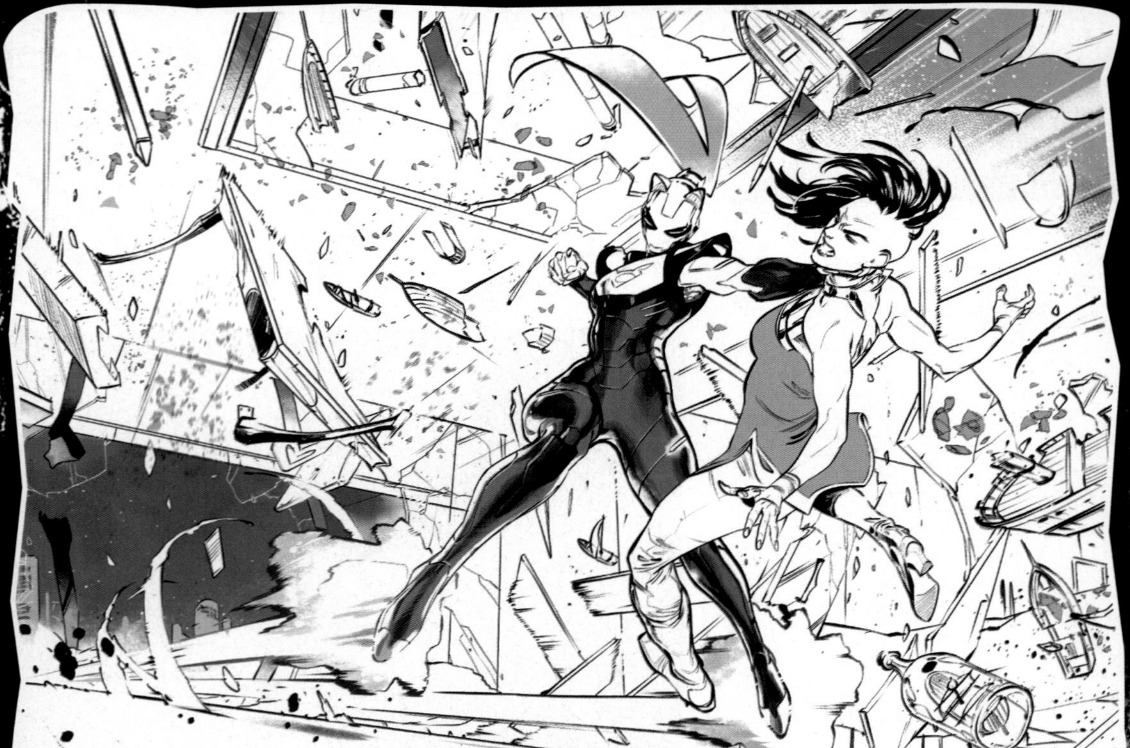

#12, page 10 art by **C.F. VILLA**

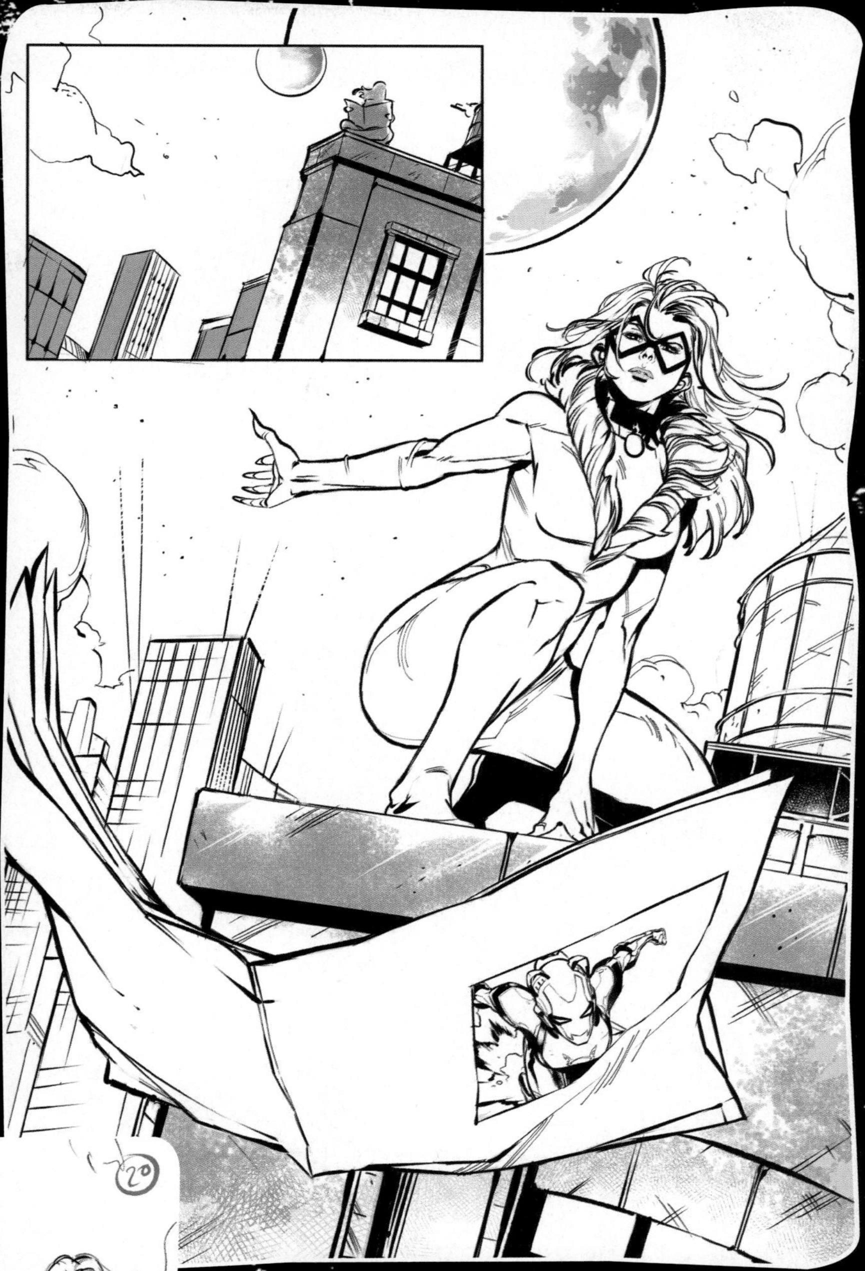

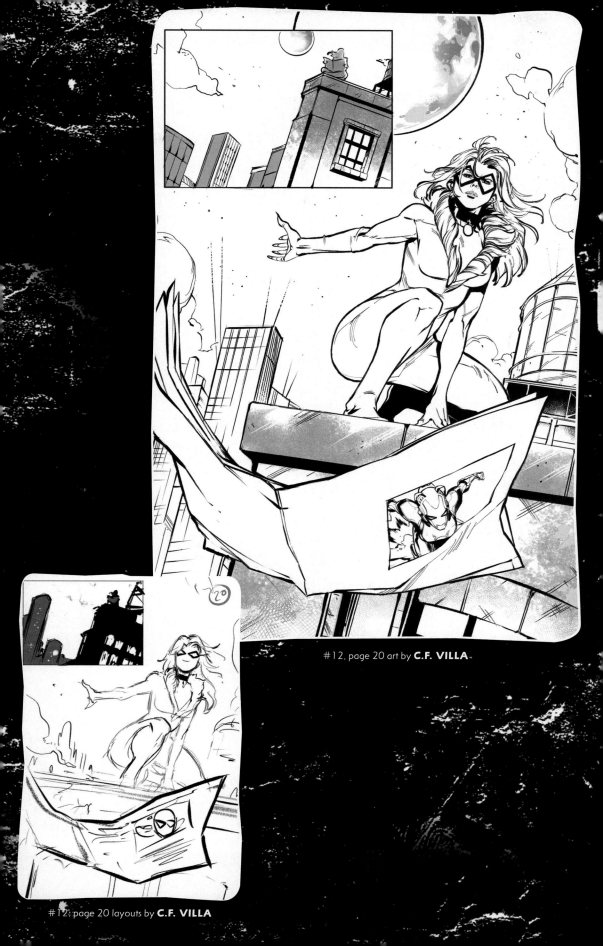

#12, page 20 art by **C.F. VILLA**

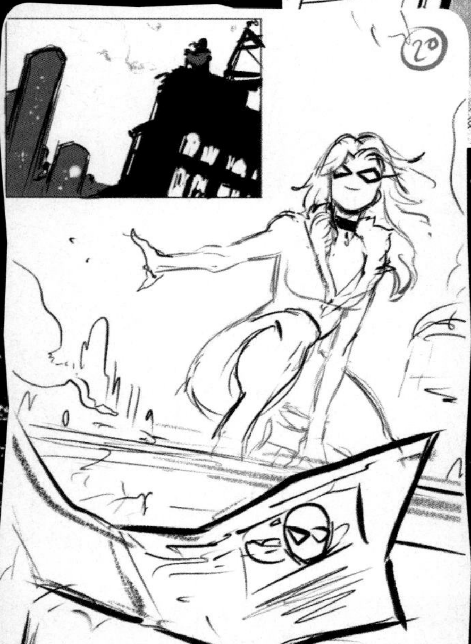

#12, page 20 layouts by **C.F. VILLA**

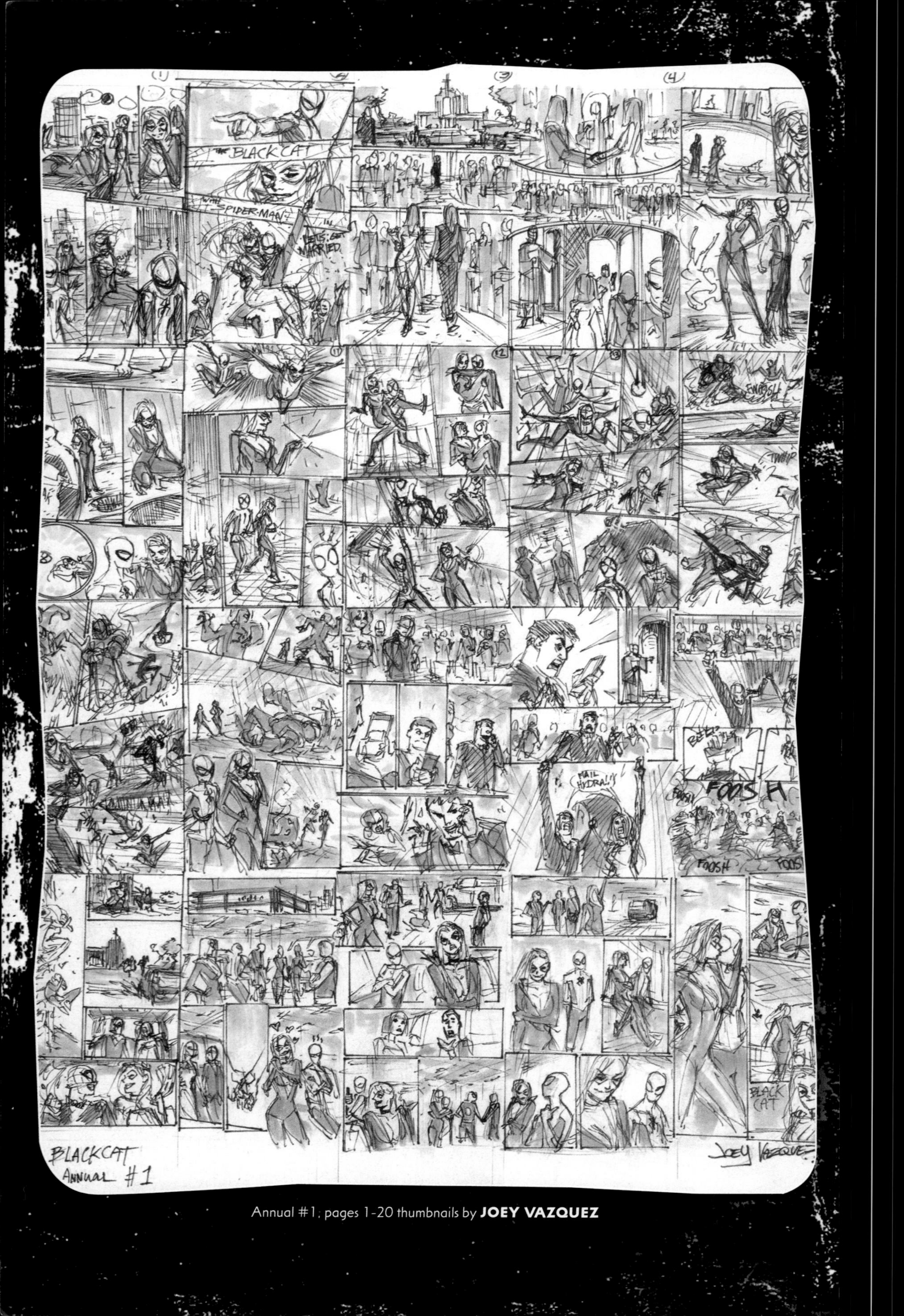

BLACK CAT
WITH SPIDER-MAN
FOOSH
THWIP
HAIL HYDRA!!
BLACKCAT Annual #1
JOEY VAZQUEZ

Annual #1, pages 1-20 thumbnails by **JOEY VAZQUEZ**

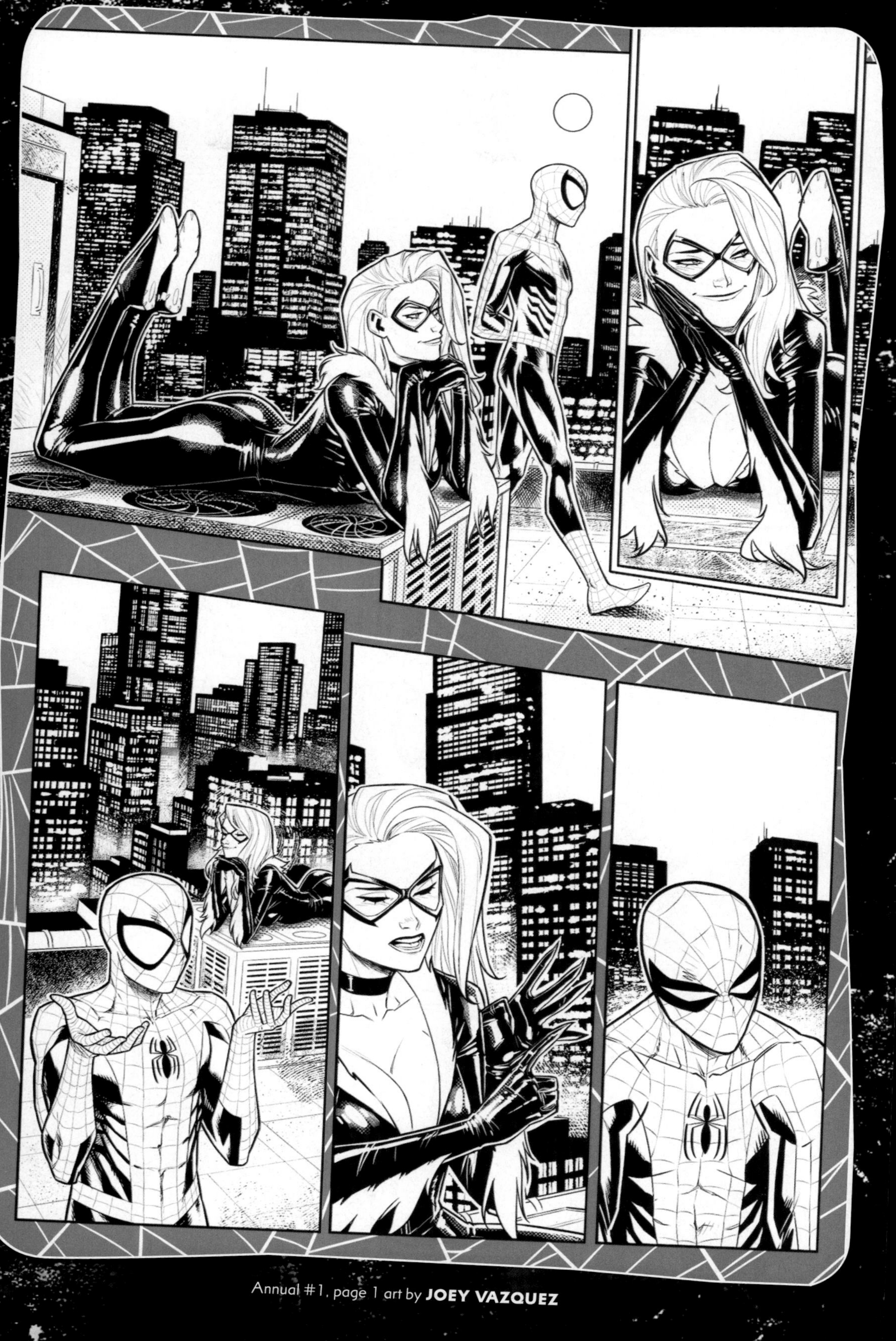

Annual #1, page 1 art by **JOEY VAZQUEZ**

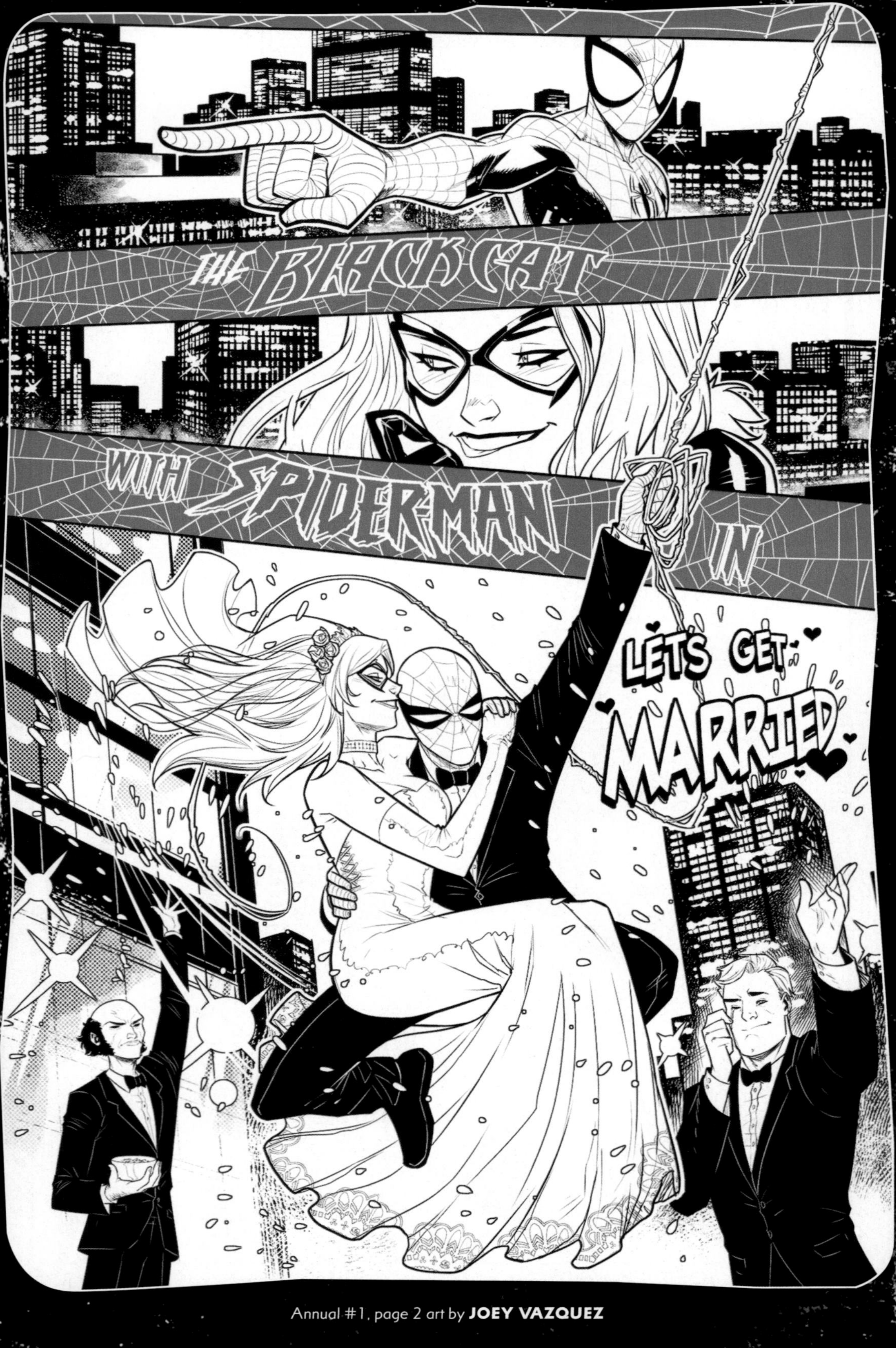
THE BLACK CAT
WITH SPIDER-MAN
IN
LET'S GET MARRIED

Annual #1, page 2 art by **JOEY VAZQUEZ**

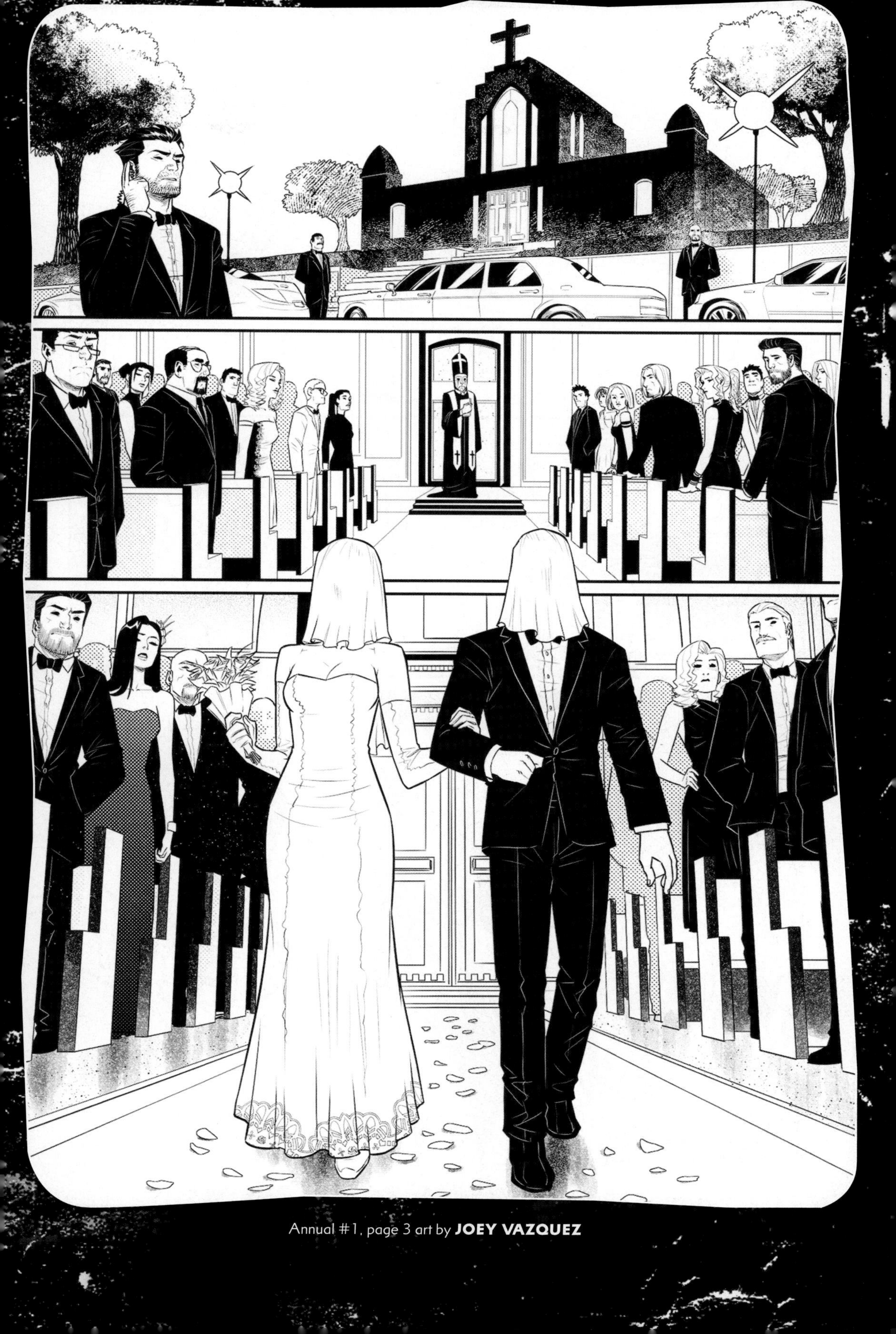

Annual #1, page 3 art by **JOEY VAZQUEZ**

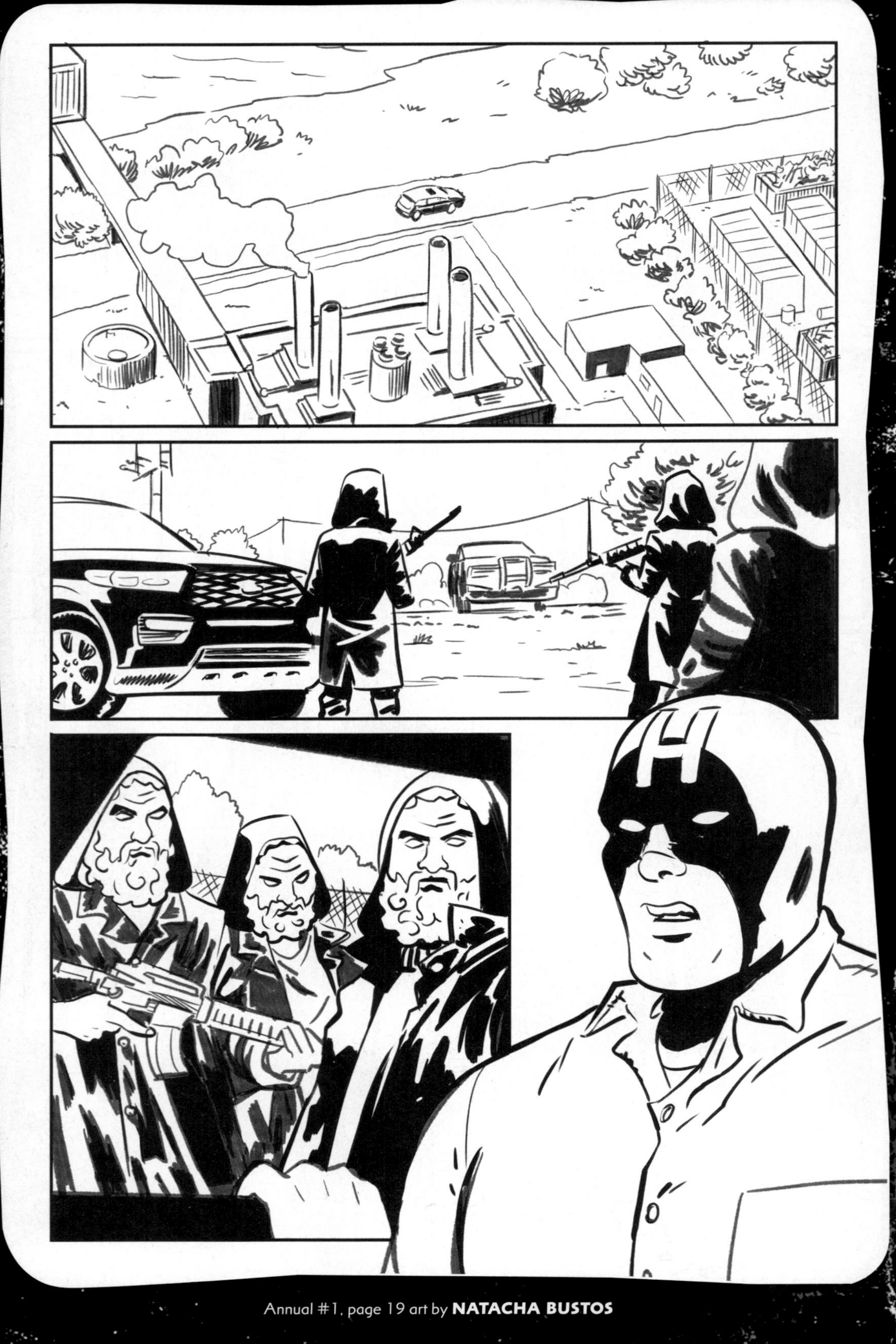

Annual #1, page 19 art by **NATACHA BUSTOS**

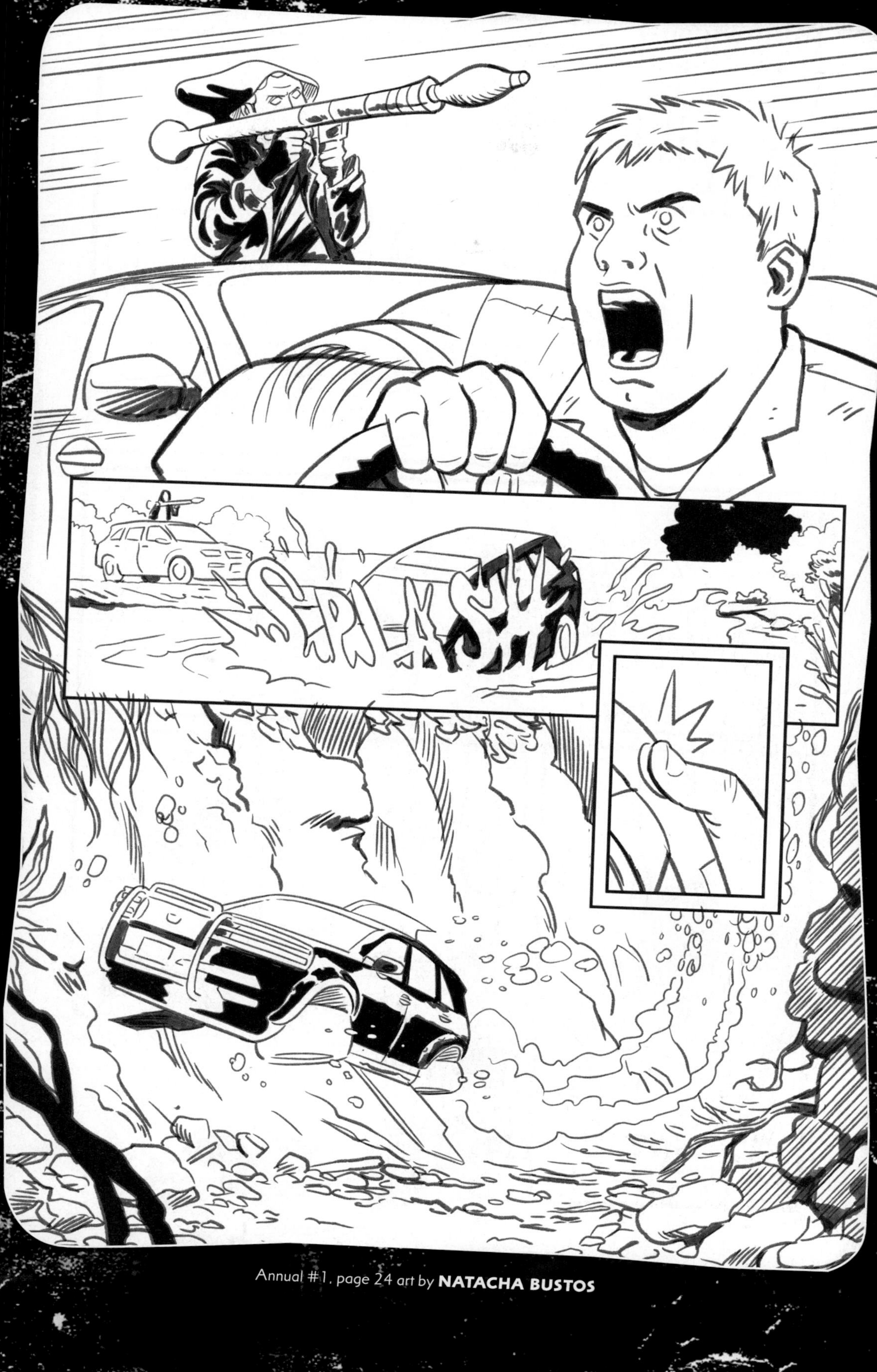
SPLASH

Annual #1, page 24 art by **NATACHA BUSTOS**

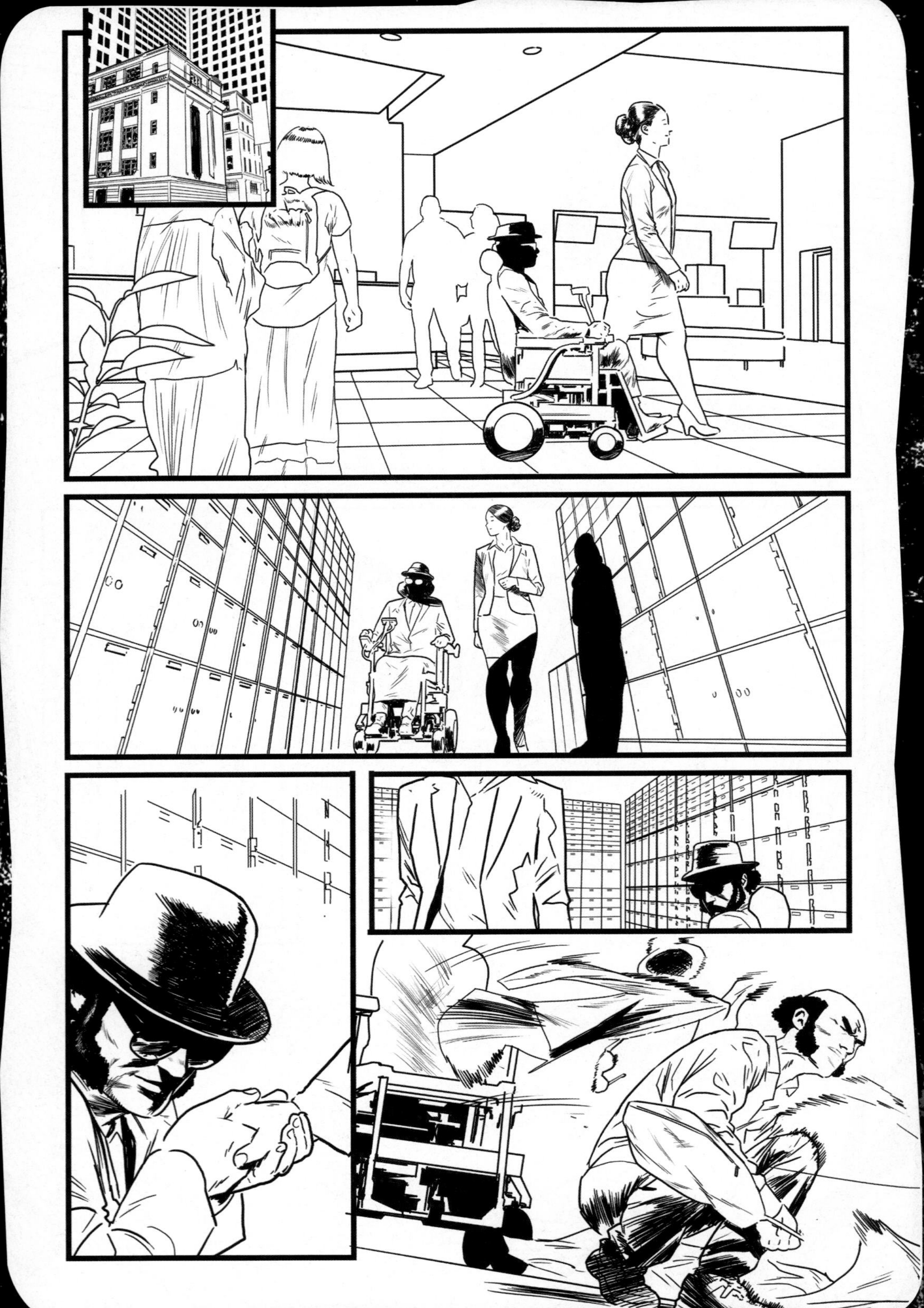

Annual #1, page 6 art by **JUAN GEDEON**

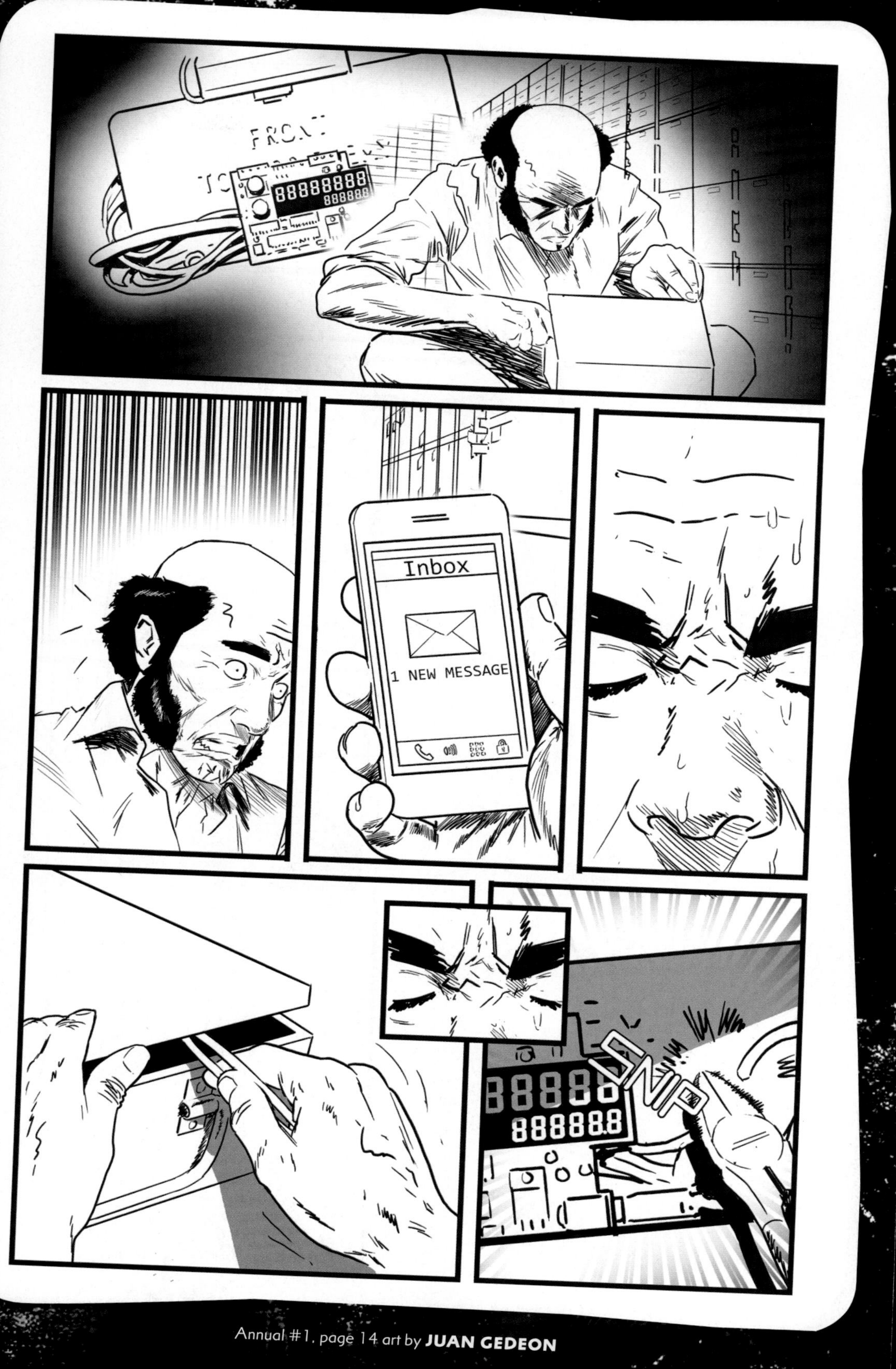
Inbox
1 NEW MESSAGE
SNIP

Annual #1, page 14 art by **JUAN GEDEON**

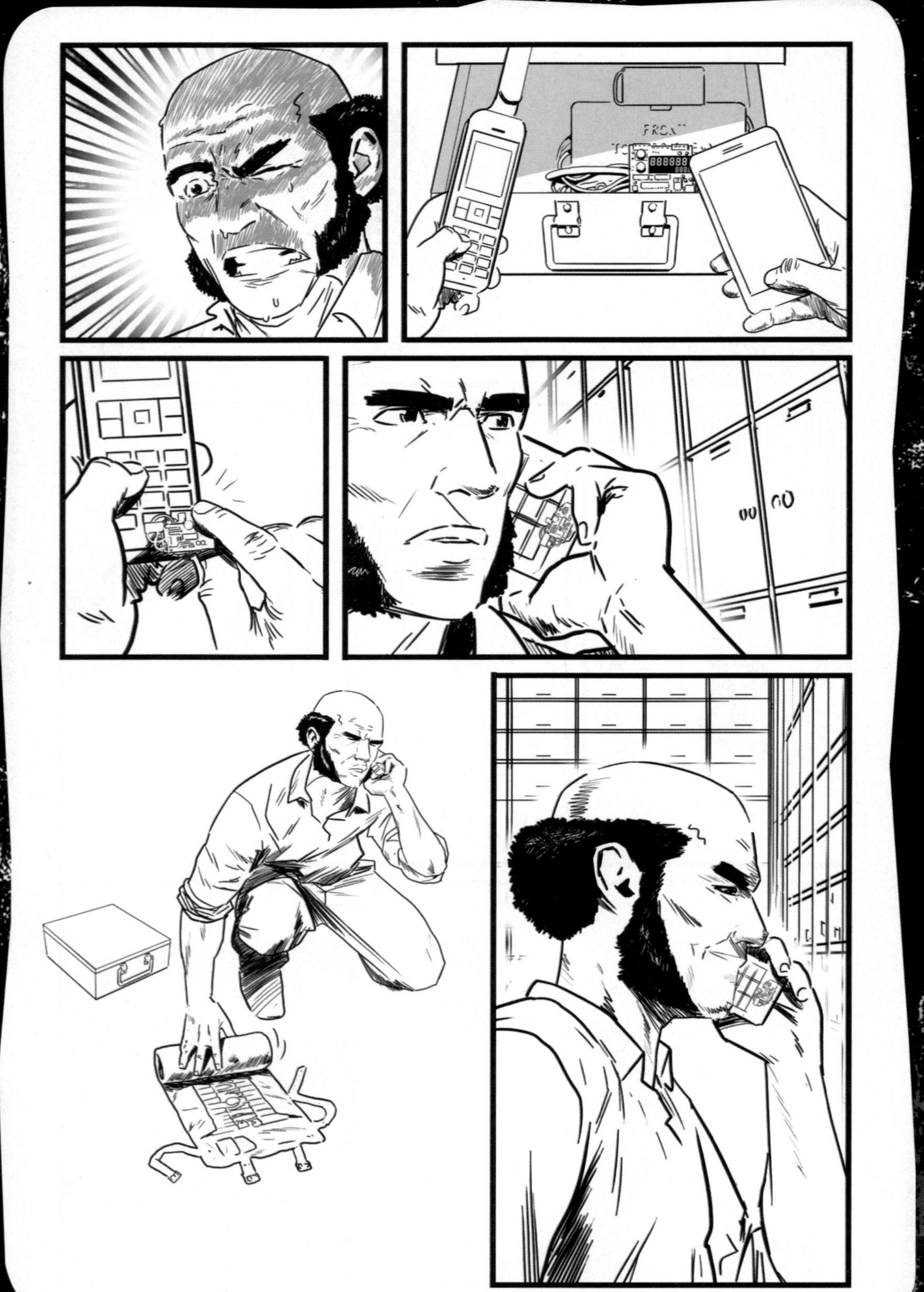
FRONT

Annual #1, page 15 art by **JUAN GEDEON**